Mark Deans

£10 99

AC

22/8

D1591124

ESTIMATING AND INTERPRETING
THE YIELD CURVE

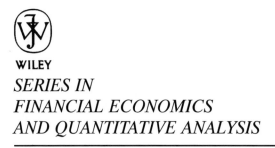

WILEY

SERIES IN
FINANCIAL ECONOMICS
AND QUANTITATIVE ANALYSIS

Series Editor: Stephen Hall, *London Business School, UK*

Editorial Board: Robert F. Engle, *University of California, USA*
John Flemming, *European Bank, UK*
Lawrence R. Klein, *University of Pennsylvania, USA*
Helmut Lütkepohl, *Humboldt University, Germany*

ESTIMATING AND INTERPRETING THE YIELD CURVE

Nicola Anderson
Francis Breedon
Mark Deacon
Andrew Derry
Gareth Murphy

JOHN WILEY & SONS

Chichester • New York • Brisbane • Toronto • Singapore

Published by John Wiley & Sons Ltd,
        Baffins Lane, Chichester,
        West Sussex PO19 1UD, England

        National   01243 779777
        International (+44) 1243 779777

Reprinted January 1997

Other Wiley Editorial Offices

John Wiley & Sons, Inc., 605 Third Avenue,
New York, NY 10158-0012, USA

Jacaranda Wiley Ltd, 33 Park Road, Milton,
Queensland 4064, Australia

John Wiley & Sons (Canada) Ltd, 22 Worcester Road,
Rexdale, Ontario M9W 1L1, Canada

John Wiley & Sons (Asia) Pte Ltd, 2 Clementi Loop #02-01
Jin Xing Distripark, Singapore 129809

Library of Congress Cataloging-in-Publication Data

Estimating and Interpreting the Yield Curve / Nicola Anderson . . . [et al.].
        p.   cm. – (Series in financial economics and quantitative analysis)
    Includes bibliographical references and index.
    ISBN 0-471-96207-4 (cloth : alk. paper)
    1. Bonds — Prices — Great Britain — Economics models.
    2. Investments — Great Britain — Econometric models.   3. Monetary
    policy — Great Britain — Econometric models. 1. Anderson, Nicola.
    II. Series.
    HG5441.Y54 1996
    332.63'23'0941 – dc20   95-43597
                                                                                         CIP

British Library Cataloguing in Publication Data

A catalogue record for this book is available from the British Library

ISBN 0-471-96207-4

Typeset in 10/12pt Times from author's disks by Laser Words, Madras
Printed and bound in Great Britain by Biddles Ltd, Guildford
This book is printed on acid-free paper responsibly manufactured from sustainable forestation,
for which at least two trees are planted for each one used for paper production.

Contents

Series preface

This series aims to publish books which give authoritative accounts of major new topics in financial economics and general quantitative analysis. The coverage of the series includes both macro- and microeconomics, and its aim is to be of interest to practitioners and policy makers as well as the wider academic community.

The development of new techniques and ideas in econometrics has been rapid in recent years and these developments are now being applied to a wide range of areas and markets. Our hope is that this series will provide a rapid and effective means of communicating these ideas to a wide international audience and that in turn this will contribute to the growth of knowledge, the exchange of scientific information and techniques and the development of cooperation in the field of economics.

Stephen Hall
London Business School, UK

Introduction

Following Sterling's dramatic exit from the European Exchange Rate Mechanism in September 1992, the UK authorities were confronted with the need to develop a new analytical framework on which to base monetary policy. Instead of relying on a single indicator to guide policy decisions — as had been the case during Sterling's membership of the ERM, and during the early 1980s when M3 had played this role — it was decided to consider a wider range of economic indicators. These would then be assessed at a monthly meeting between the Chancellor of the Exchequer and the Governor of the Bank of England. One such indicator that was mentioned explicitly at the inception of this new monetary framework was information derived from asset prices on market expectations of future inflation and interest rates.

The elevation of market expectations to the status of a primary indicator led the Bank of England to review its work on modelling the term structure of interest rates — especially comparisons of nominal and index-linked government debt prices that could be used extract information on market expectations of future movements in inflation. In turn this led to a review of the technique used by the Bank to estimate yield curves, which had until then been used only to price new issues of government debt and to value loans to public corporations and local authorities. This review — which necessarily grew to cover more than simply the best way to estimate the term structure of interest rates — was carried out primarily by the five authors of this book, all then members of the Bank's Quantitative Financial Economics group.

This book draws together information from many aspects of the review, ranging from a description and comparison of standard terminology and valuation techniques used across different bond markets, through technical mathematical and economic issues concerning the estimation and interpretation of term structure models, to the evaluation of how such models have performed in interpreting past data. It is designed to be useful both to market practitioners with an interest in using statistical and economic models to price debt instruments, and to academic and institutional economists requiring an understanding of how these techniques can be applied to macro-economic problems.

When starting out on the work that eventually appeared in this book, we found a range of sophisticated techniques pioneered both by academics and by market practitioners — mostly published in academic journals — and a lot of information detailing the more mundane but equally important issues surrounding market conventions and bond arithmetic. However, we could not find any publication that we felt successfully combined these, providing a guide to theoretical techniques for pricing securities and modelling interest rates, whilst never losing sight of their use in 'real-world' applications. Having completed the work at the Bank, we felt it would be useful to provide a book to bridge this gap — aimed at academics, policy makers and market practitioners with some background in finance and statistical methods who want to extend their understanding in this area.

The book is set out in such a way that it could be either read from cover to cover, or used for reference on a chapter by chapter basis. It is organised as follows:

Chapter 1 sets out the basic tools required for the economic analysis of bond markets, while Chapter 2 considers a number of the issues regarding the statistical estimation of the term structure of interest rates, including a thorough survey of the academic literature. Chapter 3 describes how to test these models using market data and details the results of such analysis carried out in the Bank. Chapter 4 moves away from the statistical methods for fitting yield curves to the more theoretical techniques for modelling the term structure provided by the academic literature. The second section of the book covers two chapters that provide some detail on market-specific factors that can have a significant impact on term structure estimation. Chapter 5 covers the effects of taxation, while Chapter 6 describes how the existence of bonds with embedded options can be incorporated into the estimation process. The final three chapters of the book deal with the economic interpretation of information contained in yield curves. Chapter 7 discusses index-linked bonds and how they can be used in conjunction with nominal bonds to measure market expectations of inflation. Chapter 8 details how the random nature of asset prices can impact inferences about expectations, through convexity (Jensen's inequality) and risk premia, and Chapter 9 reviews the empirical evidence on the success or otherwise of market expectations as predictors of future economic variables.

ACKNOWLEDGEMENTS

Whilst any views expressed in this book are those of the authors and not necessarily those of the Bank of England (or any other institutions we are associated with), this book would not have been possible without the help of numerous people at the Bank. We would especially like to thank Peter Andrews, David Barr, Kath Begley, Stephen Bland, Ian Bond, Martin Brookes, Neil Cooper, Jonathan Curtiss, Rosie Denney, Mandy Ferdy, Tony Grove, Anna Hitchen, Jim Lewin, Mandy Livermore, Stephen Loach, John Lumsden, Katerina Mastronikola, Lisa Milson, Howard Picton, David Sclater, Robert Scott, Toby Vennings,

Michelle Window. We would also like to thank Peter Breedon, Roger Brown, Les Clewlow, Savvas Ladonikolas, Stephen Schaefer, Nick Webber, who made many useful suggestions on the material in this book, although any remaining errors and views expressed are, of course, our responsibility. Finally, special thanks go to our families — particularly Jo Breedon and Clare Derry — without whose support and encouragement this book would never have been completed.

CHAPTER 1

The term structure of interest rates

1.1 INTRODUCTION

This book is primarily concerned with the relationship between market interest rates and the valuation of debt instruments. All such instruments are contracts by which an investor lends money to a borrower in return for a promise of future cashflows. For this reason, different forms of debt are distinguished primarily by the creditworthiness of the borrower. The governments of some developed countries — such as the USA, Japan, Germany, France and the UK — are deemed to be the borrowers least likely to default on their debt repayments, meaning that the cost of borrowing funds in one of these countries will never be lower than that faced by the government[1]. For this reason, the interest rates charged to such governments are of particular importance.

Large institutions — such as national governments and large companies — can borrow money on the world's capital markets, and do so primarily by issuing *fixed-income bonds*. An investor purchasing such an instrument is buying the right to receive fixed income payments over the life of the bond, along with the repayment of the principal amount at the bond's expiry date. An investor can purchase 'new' bonds directly from the issuer in the *primary* market, or older bonds from other investors in the *secondary* market. An investor purchasing a bond issued by a government with a high credit rating in either the primary or secondary market will view both the size and timing of the cashflows to be known with certainty, so the primary factor influencing the investor's valuation of the instrument will be its *guaranteed* rate of return (if held to maturity), compared to rates on other forms of investment which may have risky rates of return. It is for this reason that default-free government bonds, without the added complication of credit issues, provide a useful means of measuring market interest rates.

This chapter introduces some of the tools required to value default-free government bonds. In particular, it introduces the *term structure of interest rates* and details its important role in the valuation of debt instruments. The manner in which the term structure is represented and the associated bond arithmetic techniques form the basis of the analysis described through the rest of the book.

1.2 BOND PRICES AND INTEREST RATES

A fixed-income bond is simply the obligation on the bond's issuer to provide one or more future cashflows on pre-specified dates. Many bonds exist that are more complicated than this simple definition may suggest, having cashflows indexed to the rate of inflation, for example, or providing either the holder or the issuer with a choice on the timing of the cashflows[2]. However, the majority of bonds have fixed *nominal* interest payments and a fixed *redemption* or *maturity* date on which the issuer undertakes to repay the principal amount originally invested. The frequency at which interest payments are made varies from market to market, but generally they are made either annually or semi-annually (see Fage, 1986, and McClean, 1993, for details on individual markets). The interest payment on a bond is often referred to as a *coupon* payment since, historically, bonds were *bearer* instruments — meaning that interest payments would be made to whoever presented the bond on the payment date. The bonds typically had coupons attached: these would be removed from the bond and presented to the issuer in return for the corresponding interest payment. Many bonds are now *registered*, meaning that the issuer or his or her agent maintains a list of bond holders (and is notified of transfers) so that the physical presentation of a coupon is no longer required. However, the historical terminology has remained in use.

1.2.1 THE BOND PRICE EQUATION

How should an investor value a fixed-income debt instrument? The first stage is to consider the value today of a single guaranteed nominal payment due on a future date. For example, what is the value of an amount X due in n years time? Suppose the interest rate z over the period is known, then the present value PV of X is:

$$PV(X) = \frac{X}{(1+z)^m} \qquad (1.1)$$

The interest rate z is usually referred to as the *spot interest rate* for maturity m years, because it is the interest rate that is applicable today ('spot') on an m-year loan[3].

A bond is simply a stream of future cashflows — a series of coupon payments of size C payable at times $1, 2, \ldots, m$ and a redemption payment R payable on the maturity date in m years time. Government bonds from many developed countries are perceived to be free from the risk that the issuer will default on the payment of one or more cashflows. In such cases, the value of a bond to an investor is simply the present value of the stream of future cashflows it provides.

Supposing that the spot interest rates for every future period are known, then the present value of an m-period bond is:

$$PV(m\text{-period bond}) = \frac{C}{(1+z_1)} + \frac{C}{(1+z_2)^2} + \cdots + \frac{C+R}{(1+z_m)^m} \qquad (1.2)$$

Equation (1.2) is often referred to as the *bond price equation*, formalizing the relationship between spot interest rates and bond prices.

Market participants may not agree on the series of spot interest rates $z_j (j = 1, \ldots, m)$, meaning that they will value the bond differently. However, the investor who attaches the highest value to the bond will be willing to pay the most for it and so, assuming the seller is rational and sells to the highest bidder, this investor will set the market price of the bond. In other words:

$$\text{Bond price} = \text{present value of cashflows to marginal investor} \qquad (1.3)$$

1.2.2 ACCRUED INTEREST AND CONTINUOUS COMPOUNDING

Equation (1.2) is oversimplified since in practice there are a number of factors that complicate its formulation. Most obviously, the first coupon payment in (1.2) is assumed to be due in exactly one period's time[4]. In fact, while coupon payments on individual bonds are usually made only once or twice a year, bonds can be traded on any working day. Whenever a bond changes hands on a day that is not a coupon payment date, the valuation of the bond will reflect the proximity of the next coupon payment date. In most markets, this is effected by the payment of *accrued interest* to compensate the seller for the period since the last coupon payment during which the seller has held the bond but for which they will receive no coupon payment. The accrued interest is by market convention computed simply as the proportion of the coupon foregone by the seller:

$$\text{Accrued interest} = t_0 C \qquad (1.4)$$

where C is the (annual) coupon on the bond and t_0 is the proportion of a period passed since the last coupon payment was made[5]. The price the buyer pays for a bond can therefore be decomposed into two components: the accrued interest and the bond's *quoted* or *clean* price. The total amount payable when the bond is transacted is simply the sum of these two, and is usually referred to as the *total* or *dirty* price. If market conditions are stable, such that underlying factors affecting the valuation of the bond do not change, then the dirty price of the bond will still increase daily by the amount that the accrued interest payment increases. Since this change is exactly predictable and independent of any fundamental change in the bond's value, market practice is to quote the *clean* price.

The computation of t_0 in (1.4) depends on market convention and varies across countries: each market has a convention for the number of days in a month and the number of days in a year. For example, the convention in the USA is that each month has 30 days and each year has 360 days (called '30/360' convention), while in the UK the actual number of days in each month is used and the 'standard' year is assumed to have 365 days ('Actual/365 convention').

A similar adjustment needs to be made to the bond price equation (1.2) since, when a bond is traded on a day other than a coupon payment date, cashflows are no longer an exact number of coupon periods in the future. The time to the first coupon payment (t_1 say) is computed in a similar way to t_0, as the proportion of a coupon period represented by the time from the trade settlement date[6] to the next coupon payment date. Although the convention used to compute t_0 is often the same as that used to compute t_1, this need not be the case — in Japan, for example, interest accrues on an Actual/365 basis, while discounting (the computation of t_1) is done using Actual/360 convention. Although seemingly trivial, using a method other than the market convention can significantly alter the valuation of a bond (or any debt instrument) — again, McClean (1993) and Fage (1986) provide such details for individual markets.

The bond price equation (1.2) therefore generalizes[7] to:

$$p + ai = \frac{C/v}{(1 + z(t_1)/v)^{vt_1}} + \frac{C/v}{(1 + z(t_2)/v)^{vt_{12}}} + \cdots + \frac{C/v + R}{(1 + z(t_M)/v)^{vt_m}} \quad (1.5)$$

where:

p = *clean* price of bond
ai = accrued interest
C = annual coupon payment
R = redemption payment
t_M = maturity of bond (in years, using the appropriate day count convention)
$z(t_j)$ = spot rate applicable to payment j due at time t_j (time measured in years)
v = frequency of coupon payments (e.g. $v = 2$ for semi-annual coupons)

1.2.3 DISCOUNT FACTORS AND THE DISCOUNT FUNCTION

Consider an individual payment of size X due at time t. Its present value, using (1.1) is simply:

$$PV(X) = \left[\frac{1}{(1 + z(t))^t} \right] \cdot X \quad (1.6)$$

The factor by which X is multiplied to obtain its present value is called the *discount factor*. It is simply a transformation of the appropriate spot rate $z(t)$. Since time is continuous, a continuous discount *function* denoted $\delta(\cdot)$ can be defined that maps time t to a discount factor. Given such a function the present value of any future cashflow can be computed by multiplying the cashflow by

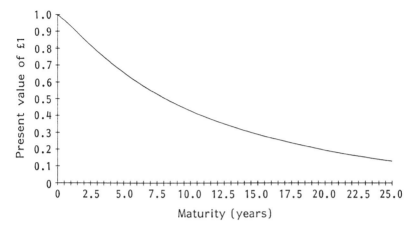

Figure 1.1   Discount function (UK gilt market — 10 March 1995)

the appropriate point on the discount function:

$$PV(X) = \delta(t) \cdot X \qquad (1.7)$$

A useful property of the discount function is that it describes the present value of one unit (e.g. £1, $1, etc.) payable at any time in the future and so, if an instrument exists that provides a single, unit cashflow t years into the future, its price should correspond to the value of the discount function at that point, $\delta(t)$ (Figure 1.1). Such an instrument would be a zero-coupon bond, a bond that pays no coupon payments and a unit redemption payment on the maturity date. For this reason, a discount factor is sometimes referred to as a *zero-coupon bond price* — the two are exactly equivalent.

It is straightforward to rewrite the bond price equation (1.5) in terms of the discount function rather than spot rates:

$$p + ai = \delta(t_1)C + \delta(t_2)C + \cdots + \delta(t_m)(C + R)$$

$$= C \sum_{i=1}^{m} \delta(t_i) + \delta(t_m)R \qquad (1.8)$$

1.2.4   CONTINUOUS COMPOUNDING

Although the accrued interest computations described earlier are conceptually straightforward, in practice they can be an awkward complication to both theoretical and empirical work. To avoid this, many authors in the academic literature (McCulloch, 1971, being an early example) approximate the bond price equation by assuming that coupon payments are made continuously rather than at discrete points in time, so that interest does not accrue. Under this assumption of *continuous compounding* (1.8) can be slightly simplified because the need to compute accrued interest is avoided:

$$p = C \int_0^m \delta(\mu)d\mu + R\delta(m) \tag{1.9}$$

where p is the *clean* price of the bond.

This approximation can significantly alter estimates of the discount function (and of derived yield curves), so this error should be weighed against the perceived benefit from simplifying the calculations. Although such an approximation may facilitate theoretical work, practical applications typically require greater precision[8].

1.2.5   MEASURING THE RETURN ON A BOND

A fixed-income government bond that is not subject to default risk has a stream of future cashflows that are guaranteed with regard both to their size and their timing. Observing the price of a bond in the market, it is therefore straightforward to measure the *ex ante* return associated with that price. Two measures are commonly used: the *flat yield* (sometimes referred to as the *current* or *running yield*) and the *redemption yield*.

The flat yield is analogous to the 'dividend yield' on a share, and is defined as:

$$\text{Flat yield} = \frac{\text{Coupon}}{\text{Clean price}} \tag{1.10}$$

The flat yield is normally used to represent the return from holding a bond for a short period — and is often thought of as the *income* generated by the bond. Common market practice is to compare the flat yield on a bond with a short-term interest rate — this difference is called the *carry* of the bond. Holding a bond with a flat yield below the short-term interest rate induces a negative carry because if the bond's price remains constant a cost is incurred (relative to putting funds on short-term deposit rather than purchasing the bond). For example, if a bond purchase is financed by overnight borrowing rolled over on a daily basis, a constant flat yield might be compared against rising short rates — indicating the cost of carrying the bond. Of course, this cost will be offset in the long run by increases in the bond's price towards par as the bond approaches maturity.

The *redemption yield* (or *yield to maturity*) is the bond's internal rate of return — it is the single interest rate at which the dirty price of a bond is equal to the present value of the stream of cashflows discounted at that rate. As such, it is derived from the bond price equation (1.5), constraining all cashflows to be discounted at a single rate:

$$p + ai = \frac{C/v}{(1+y/v)^{t_1}} + \frac{C/v}{(1+y/v)^{vt_2}} + \cdots + \frac{C/v+R}{(1+y/v)^{vt_m}} \tag{1.11}$$

where y is the (gross) redemption yield and p, ai, C, v and R are as defined above.

Given a price p, the only unknown in (1.11) is the yield y which can be computed using an iterative algorithm (e.g. the bisection or Newton–Raphson technique[9]).

Both measures can easily be augmented to provide measures of return net of tax. Suppose an investor faces an income tax rate τ payable on coupon income, but is exempt from tax on capital gains. The equations to generate the net yields are:

$$\text{Net flat yield} = \frac{(1 - \tau)\ \text{Coupon}}{\text{Clean price}} \qquad (1.12\text{a})$$

$$p + ai_N = \frac{(1 - \tau)C/v}{(1 + y_N/v)^{vt_1}} + \frac{(1 - \tau)C/v}{(1 + y_N/v)^{vt_2}} + \cdots + \frac{(1 - \tau)C/v + R}{(1 + y_N/v)^{vt_m}} \qquad (1.12\text{b})$$

where y_N is the net redemption yield and ai_N is the accrued interest net of tax.

The flat yield is obviously the simplest measure of return to compute, but makes no allowance for the fact that a bond's price will approach par as the bond approaches maturity — the *pull to par* effect. Although more complicated to compute, the redemption yield better represents the return on the bond — particularly if an investor intends to hold the bond to maturity. However, even the redemption yield has its drawbacks: some of the market-day count conventions can distort the computed yield from the 'true' yield (computed using 'Actual/Actual' convention). More importantly, assuming that all cashflows are discounted at the same rate implies that all future coupon payments can be reinvested in the same bond at this same rate of return. In general this is not the case since investors face *reinvestment risk* — the risk that they will not be able to reinvest future coupon payments at the redemption yield.

Despite its disadvantages, the redemption yield (either gross or net of tax) is the most widely used *ex-ante* measure of return, and when market participants use the term 'yield' they are usually referring to the redemption yield. This is the usage employed throughout the rest of this book.

1.3   INTEREST RATE RISK AND IMMUNIZATION

1.3.1   DURATION

The life of a bond is often described by its maturity, but this measure gives little indication of the timing or sizes of the cashflows other than the date by which the final one will be received. For example, consider two bonds with the same maturity date but very different coupons: the high-coupon bond provides a larger proportion of its return in the form of coupon income than the low-coupon bond. Since coupon payments are made before the redemption payment, the high-coupon bond essentially provides the same nominal return at a faster rate than the low-coupon bond.

A useful measure to capture the speed of payment is the average maturity of the stream of cashflows. For all bonds this average will be less than the time to maturity, since coupon payments are made before the redemption payment[10]. The weighted average time to cashflows is known as the bond's *duration* and is computed using the following formula[11]:

$$\text{Duration} = \frac{\displaystyle\sum_{i=1}^{m} \delta(t_i)C_i t_i + \delta(t_m)Rt_m}{\displaystyle\sum_{i=1}^{m} \delta(t_i)C_i + \delta(t_m)R} = \frac{1}{p+ai}\left\{\sum_{i=1}^{m} \delta(t_i)C_i t_i + \delta(t_m)Rt_m\right\}$$

(1.13)

where y, C, v, R, p and ai are as defined above, and $\delta(t_i) =$ discount factor applicable to the ith cashflow $= (1 + y/100v)^{vt_i}$

1.3.2 MODIFIED DURATION AND INTEREST RATE SENSITIVITY

Another measure commonly used by market practitioners is *modified duration*:

$$\text{Modified duration} = \frac{\text{Duration}}{(1 + y/100v)}$$

(1.14)

where y and v are as defined above. It can be shown (e.g. Fage, 1986) that:

$$\text{Modified duration} = \frac{100}{(p+ai)}\frac{\partial p}{\partial y}$$

(1.15)

Equation (1.15) shows that modified duration represents the (percentage) change in a bonds price corresponding to a small change in yield. Although in theory this relationship holds only for infinitesimally small changes in yield, in practice it can be useful for fairly large change in yields[12]. If the yield on a bond has changed by a small amount Δy, then the corresponding price change Δp is approximately given by:

$$\Delta p = -0.01(p+ai)\Delta y \cdot (\text{modified duration})$$

(1.16)

The primary use of (1.15) and (1.16) is to compute portfolio *hedge* ratios. Given the modified duration of two bonds, the hedge ratio describes the ratio in which the bonds should be bought and sold so that the overall exposure of the portfolio to changes in yield remains roughly constant. For example, suppose a long position in bond L (trading at price p_L with accrued interest ai_L and modified duration MD_L) is to be hedged by selling bond S (price p_S, accrued interest ai_S and modified duration MD_S). To be hedged against changes in yields, we require that $\Delta y_L = \Delta y_S$. The required hedge ratio HR is given by:

$$\Delta p_L = HR \cdot \Delta p_S \tag{1.17}$$

So, combining (1.16) and (1.17):

$$HR = \frac{\Delta p_L}{\Delta p_S} = \frac{(p_L + ai_L)}{(p_S + ai_S)} \cdot \frac{MD_L}{MD_S} \tag{1.18}$$

1.3.3   CONVEXITY

Although modified duration describes changes in bond prices corresponding to small changes in yield, this approximation can break down under larger changes in yield. This breakdown is due to the fact that the function defining a bond's price as a function of its yield (1.11) is not linear but is in general *convex*.

Figure 1.2 shows the price–yield relationships for two imaginary bonds. Around par, both functions are approximately linear and very similar — these two bonds therefore have the same modified duration. However, as yields move away from par the price of bond 1 is always higher than the price of bond 2 because the curvature or *convexity* of its price–yield function is greater. Bond 1 is clearly preferable to bond 2, because at all levels of yield its price is equal to or greater than the price of bond 2. Equivalently, a portfolio formed by buying one unit of bond 1 and selling one unit of bond 2 (a modified duration matched portfolio) will never lose money but could make money because as yields move away from par the price of bond 1 will move above that of bond 2. Since the market attaches a higher value to bonds with greater convexity precisely because of this property, the opportunity to construct this kind of portfolio in practice will occur only rarely.

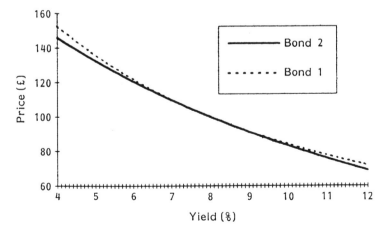

Figure 1.2   Price–yield curves

Formally, the convexity of a bond is defined by

$$\text{Convexity} = -\frac{10\,000}{(p+ai)} \cdot \frac{\partial^2 p}{\partial y^2} \tag{1.19}$$

The fact that coupon-paying bonds have positive convexity complicates the relationship between bond yields and market expectations of future interest rates — an issue discussed in detail in Chapter 8.

1.4 THE TERM STRUCTURE OF INTEREST RATES

The discount function introduced in the previous section describes the present value of future single cashflows. Given this, the present value of any future cashflow can be readily computed by simply multiplying its nominal value by the appropriate point on the discount function. Although useful computationally, the discount function does not immediately provide a measure of the return associated with purchasing future cashflows at their present value. For this reason, the discount function is often transformed to be presented as a *spot interest rate* curve, a *par yield* curve or an *implied forward rate* curve, all of which describe in different ways the return from purchasing a stream of future cashflows. Moreover, the transformation between any two of these curves is unique — given any one, the other three can be obtained[13].

This section describes the purpose of the three curves and outlines how each can be constructed from an observed discount function. However, as with all measures of return, it is important to be clear about the basis on which the rate is being computed. Mathematically, it is often useful to consider instantaneous rates of interest — the rate of return from lending money and receiving it with interest an instant later. Of course, in reality this is never the case, since money is lent for discrete periods of time. When these periods are short — for example, lent and repaid during the same day — the instantaneous rate of interest will be close to the true, discrete rate. However, the longer the investment period, the less useful instantaneous rates become and the more important it is to compute the discrete rates. For each of the curves, both the continuous and discrete versions are described below.

1.4.1 THE IMPLIED FORWARD RATE CURVE

The relationship between a spot rate and the corresponding discount factor was described in the previous section (1.6 and 1.7). The discount factor for a discrete period of time j (ending at time t_j), d_j, is given in terms of the corresponding spot rate z_j by:

$$d_j = \delta(t_j) = (1+z_j)^{-j} \tag{1.20}$$

The discount factor d_j is the discount factor applicable to a single payment end of period j, and so the spot rate z_j is the single rate of return applied over all discrete periods from today until the end of period j. It is usually defined as the average[14] of the individual one period rates applicable to periods $1, 2, \ldots, j$. Algebraically, if f_j represents the interest rate applicable from the end of period $j - 1$ to the end of period j, then:

$$1/d_1 = (1 + z_1) = (1 + f_1)$$

$$1/d_2 = (1 + z_2)^2 = (1 + f_1)(1 + f_2)$$

$$\vdots$$

$$1/d_j = (1 + z_j)^j = (1 + f_1)(1 + f_2) \ldots (1 + f_j) \qquad (1.21)$$

Suppose that the series of discrete discount factors $d_1, d_2, \ldots, d_j$ have been observed (using the techniques described in Chapter 2, for example), then any one period rate f_j can be isolated:

$$\frac{1/d_j}{1/d_{j-1}} = \frac{(1 + f_1)(1 + f_2) \ldots (1 + f_{j-1})(1 + f_j)}{(1 + f_1)(1 + f_2) \ldots (1 + f_{j-1})}$$

$$\therefore \quad \frac{d_{j-1}}{d_j} = (1 + f_j) \quad \Rightarrow \quad f_j = \frac{d_{j-1} - d_j}{d_j}$$

So:

$$f_j = -\Delta d_j / d_j \qquad (1.22)$$

where $\Delta d_j = d_j - d_{j-1}$.

The series of discount factors $d_1, d_2, \ldots, d_j$ therefore also describes the series of one-period interest rates between the end of period $j - 1$ and the end of period j[15]. These rates $f_1, f_2, \ldots, f_j$ implied by the discount factors are called *implied forward interest rates*, and a plot of these values against time produces an *implied forward interest rate curve*. Whereas the spot rate z_j describes an *average* rate of return over j periods, the implied forward rate f_j describes the *marginal* rate of return over period j — for example, the one-year rate in 20 years' time rather than today's 20-year interest rate. More formally, the implied forward rates $f_j\{j = 1, 2, \ldots\}$ represent the marginal return from substituting a j-period (zero-coupon) bond for a $(j - 1)$-period bond in a portfolio.

The discrete forward rate equation (1.22) can easily be amended to produce an *instantaneous* forward rate curve $\rho(t)$ from a continuous discount function $\delta(t)$ by considering periods j and $(j - 1)$ infinitesimally close together (Figure 1.3):

$$\rho(t) = \frac{-\delta'(t)}{\delta(t)} \qquad (1.23)$$

where $\delta'(t)$ is the derivative of the discount function $\delta(\cdot)$ evaluated at the point t. This instantaneous forward rate curve is a theoretical construct, providing the

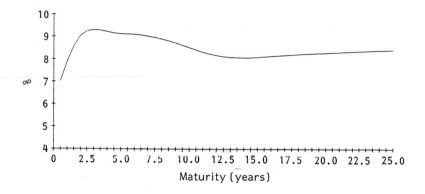

Figure 1.3   Implied forward rate curve (UK gilt market — 10 March 1995)

interest rate applicable to a future loan that will be repaid an instant later. A more useful measure (while still assuming that interest is compounded continuously) might be to average $\rho(t)$ over a particular time interval $[t_1, t_2]$. The resulting *mean forward rate* is given by:

$$f(t_1, t_2) = \frac{1}{t_2 - t_1} \int_{t_1}^{t_2} \rho(\mu) \, d\mu \tag{1.24}$$

The forward rate $f(t_{j-1}, t_j)$ in (1.24) represents the continuously compounded approximation to the true discrete forward rate f_j in (1.22).

1.4.2   THE SPOT (OR ZERO-COUPON) YIELD CURVE

The spot rate z_j is sometimes called the *zero-coupon yield* since it represents the yield to maturity on a (hypothetical) pure discount or zero coupon bond. Given an observed discount factor d_j, the zero-coupon yield can be easily derived using (1.20):

$$z_j = (1/d_j)^{1/j} - 1 \tag{1.25}$$

The set of spot rates z_j ($j = 1, \ldots m$, where m represents some arbitrary maturity date) is the *term structure of (spot) interest rates*, or the *zero-coupon yield curve* (Figure 1.4).

The approximation to the term structure of interest rates using continuous compounding, $\eta(t)$, can be derived from (1.24) since the spot rate for payment at time t in the future is the average instantaneous forward rate between now ($t_1 = 0$) and time $t(t_2 = t)$. So:

$$\eta(t) = f(0, t)$$

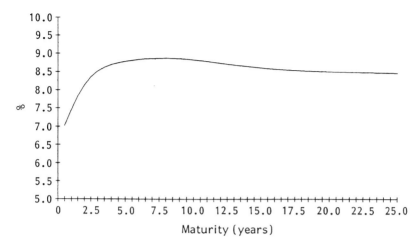

Figure 1.4   Zero-coupon yield curve (UK gilt market — 10 March 1995)

Hence, from (1.24):

$$\eta(t) = \frac{1}{t} \int_0^t \rho(\mu) d\mu$$

and using (1.23):

$$\eta(t) = \int_0^t \frac{-\delta'(\mu)}{\delta(\mu)} d\mu$$

Therefore, assuming $\delta(0) = 1$, the continuously compounded approximation to the term structure of interest rates is given by[16]

$$\eta(t) = \frac{-\ln[\delta(t)]}{t} \tag{1.26}$$

1.4.3   THE PAR YIELD CURVE

While the zero-coupon yield curve is the construct financial economists are usually referring to when talking about the term structure of interest rates, it is based on rates for of zero-coupon bonds. There are many bond markets in which there are no or only very few such instruments, and coupon-paying bonds still dominate. In such markets the zero-coupon yields as described above may be quite different from observed yields on coupon-paying bonds. For this reason, many practitioners like to look at the *par yield curve* (Figure 1.5).

A coupon-paying bond is said to be *priced at par* if its current market price is R, its face (or *par*) value. Using the equation for the redemption yield (1.11), it can be verified that:

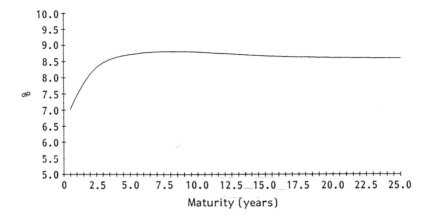

Figure 1.5   Par yield curve (UK gilt market — 10 March 1995)

$$R = \sum_{j=1}^{n} \frac{y}{(1+y)^j} + \frac{R}{(1+y)^n}$$

and so, for a bond to be trading at par, its redemption yield must equal its coupon. Using this fact, the *par yield* y_m can be derived from (1.8) for any period m (given the set of discount factors $d_1, \ldots, d_m$) by setting the coupon $C = y_m$ and the price $P = R$:

$$R = y_m \sum_{j=1}^{m} d_j + d_m R$$

$$\therefore \quad y_m = \frac{R(1 - d_m)}{\sum_{j=1}^{m} d_j} \tag{1.27}$$

Similarly, the continuous compounding approximation to the par yield curve $y(t_m)$ can be estimated using a rearranged version of (1.9), setting $C = y(t_m)$:

$$y(t_m) = \frac{R(1 - \delta(t_m))}{\int_0^{t_m} \delta(\mu)\,d\mu} \tag{1.28}$$

The par yield curve $y(t_m)$ describes the coupon required on a (hypothetical) coupon-paying bond with time to maturity t_m for that bond to trade at par. In fact, in the absence of default risk, the par yield curve is equivalent to a swap rate curve, since the coupon on a swap valued at par is calculated in the same way as a par yield using (1.27). For this reason, comparing a par yield curve derived from the prices of government bonds with a curve derived from

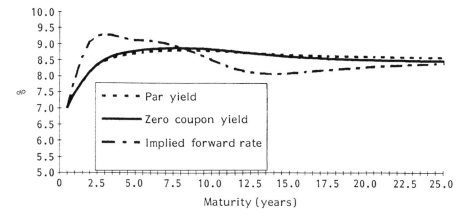

Figure 1.6   Yield curves (UK gilt market — 10 March 1995)

market swap rates gives an indication of the relative credit quality of government and non-government issues (since swaps are generally agreements between non-government organizations). Liquidity and anomalies in the bond market aside, the curves will differ only inasmuch as government bonds and swaps differ in terms of credit risk. In countries like the USA, the UK and Germany, for example, the risk of government default is perceived to be lower than that of institutions in the private sector. This is reflected by the swap curve being above the government par bond curve in those countries. The reverse is true in countries where the government is thought more likely to default than the major private sector institutions.

1.4.4   FORWARD YIELD CURVES

The implied forward rate curve describes (in the discrete case) the marginal one-period interest rates implied by the current term structure of spot interest rates. Market practitioners are often interested in what this implies about future term structures — for example, given a current term structure, what is its (implied) expected shape in one period's time? Having computed the set of implied forward rates $f_1, \ldots, f_m$ this is a straightforward exercise. If the current one-period spot rate is assumed to apply over the forthcoming period, then the one period-forward term structure can be derived from (1.21):

$$(1 + z_{11}) = (1 + f_2)$$

$$(1 + z_{21})^2 = (1 + f_2)(1 + f_3)$$

$$\vdots$$

$$(1 + z_{j1})^f = (1 + f_2)(1 + f_3) \ldots (1 + f_j)(1 + f_{j+1}) \qquad (1.29)$$

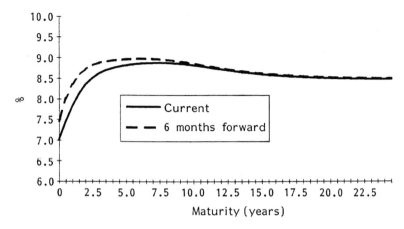

Figure 1.7   Zero-coupon yield curves (UK gilt market — 10 March 1995)

where z_{j1} represents the jth period spot rate one period forward. In the same manner as before, the one-period forward discount function and par yield curve can also be constructed. Such forward yield curves are often used to represent market expectations of future yield curves (Figure 1.7).

1.5   THE EXPECTATIONS THEORY OF THE YIELD CURVE[17]

Implicit in the construction of a forward yield curve is the idea that the current term structure of interest rates embodies a forecast of future short-term interest rates. The *expectations theory* of the yield curve formalizes this and, in its purest form[18], says that the implied forward interest rate profile represents the market's expectations of future short-term rates:

$$f_t^j = E_t(r_{t+j}) \tag{1.30}$$

where f_t^j represents the jth one-period forward rate observed at time t and $E_t(r_{t+j})$ is the short-term rate of interest expected by the market to apply j periods ahead.

The intuition behind this theory is that, in a deterministic world, expected rates of return on different investment strategies are equalized only when all forward rates equal expected short-term interest rates. Suppose, for example, that both the observed one- and two-month spot rates are 8%, implying a one-month interest rate one month forward of 8%. If an investor expects the one-month rate to be different from 8% in one month's time then, conditional on this expectation being realized, the investor can make a higher return than the market. Combined with the often-used *efficient markets hypothesis* — that has several forms, all of which suggesting that market participants use information efficiently — the pure expectations theory states that the observed market forward rate curve provides the best forecasts of future spot interest rates.

The expectations theory of the yield curve is therefore of fundamental importance to both market practitioners and to the authorities monitoring market interest rates. Profitable opportunities may arise for market participants whose expectations of future interest rates deviate greatly from those embodied in the market yield curve. For the authorities to infer expectations of future short-term interest rates from the current term structure, the expectations theory in some form must be used. However, the extent to which the expectations theory holds in practice is governed by two factors. First, the price of a coupon-paying bond will reflect the fact that it is a *convex* instrument, thus giving an investor some protection against upward moves in market interest rates. This means that risk-averse investors will pay a premium for a coupon-paying bond by accepting a yield lower than that implied by their expectations of future short-term interest rates. Second, risk-averse investors will demand premia on yields to compensate them for holding long-term and hence more volatile assets. These issues are discussed in detail in Chapters 8 and 9.

NOTES

1. Although specialist credit rating agencies (such as Moody's and Standard and Poor's) also give some corporate institutions their highest credit rating.
2. Such 'non-standard' bonds are discussed in more detail in subsequent chapters.
3. Note that z actually represents the interest rate divided by 100%, so that (for example) $z = 0.125$ corresponds to an interest rate of 12.5%.
4. One period being the length of time between two consecutive coupon payments.
5. Or since the issue date if this is the first-ever coupon payment.
6. A trade is usually settled — and the bond changes hands — a few days after the trade is agreed. Again, this settlement period is a convention of the particular market and the rules can be complicated — for example, French OATs (long-term Treasury bonds) currently settle 3 days after the trade date for domestic trade while BTANs (shorter-term Treasury bonds) settle next day.
7. Equation (1.5) does not allow for bonds issued on dates other than coupon payment dates (causing the size of the first coupon payment to differ from subsequent payments), or those issued 'partly paid' (some UK gilts have been issued this way), introducing negative cashflows into the right-hand side of the equation. The required algebraic alterations are reasonably straightforward but are not given here.
8. The concept of continuous compounding derives from the mathematical result that $(1 + z/v)^{nv} \to e^{zn}$ as $v \to \infty$, where z is the interest rate, v is

the compounding frequency and n is the number of years for which interest is to be compounded. Hull (1993, pages 45–47) discusses this result and its implications in some detail.

9. See, for example, Jeffrey (1985, pages 718–719).

10. Except in the case of zero-coupon bonds that have only one cashflow and so the average time to cashflows is the same as the time to the redemption payment.

11. The measure described by (1.13) is sometimes referred to as Macaulay duration — accredited to Macaulay (1938).

12. Fage (1986) suggests (1.15) can be useful for changes in yield of up to about 100 basis points (or 1%).

13. Most of the transformations come directly from equations presented later in this chapter. One that is not straightforward is the transformation from par yield to forward rate, zero coupon and discount function curves. This transformation (and its derivation) is presented in an appendix to Deacon and Derry (1994).

14. In fact, as can be seen from (1.21), $(1 + z_j)$ is the *geometric mean* of $(1 + f_1), (1 + f_2), \ldots, (1 + f_j)$ where z_j is the spot rate applicable to a single payment due at the end of period j and $f_1 \ldots f_j$ are the one-period rates applicable to individual periods $1, \ldots, j$.

15. This discussion is in terms of one-period rates. More generally, the forward rate over the period Δt is give by:

$$ f_j \Delta t = \frac{\delta(t_j + \Delta t) - \delta(t_j)}{\delta(t_j)} $$

16. The assumption that the discount function has a value of unity at time $t = 0$ is a sensible restriction, implying that an amount of money receivable now is not discounted. This, and other, restrictions on the shape of the discount function are discussed in more detail in Chapter 2.

17. See Blake (1990) or Hull (1993) for more discussion of the expectations theory of the yield curve.

18. Assuming no risk permia.

REFERENCES

Blake, D. (1990) *Financial Market Analysis*, McGraw-Hill, Maidenhead.

Deacon, M. and Derry, A. (1994) Estimating the term structure of interest rates, Bank of England Working Paper No. 24 (July).

Fage, P. (1986) *Yield Calculations*, CSFB Research, London.

Hull, J. (1993) *Options, Futures and Other Derivative Securities* (2nd edition), Prentice Hall, Englewood Cliffs, NJ.

Jeffrey, A. (1985) *Mathematics for Engineers and Scientists* (3rd edition), Van Nostrand Reinhold (UK), Wokingham.

Macaulay, F. (1938) *The Movement of Interest Rates, Bonds, Yields and Stock Prices in the United States since 1865*, Columbia University Press, New York.

McClean, J. (ed.) (1993) *The European Bond Markets* (5th edition), Probus, Cambridge.

McCulloch, J.H. (1971) Measuring the term structure of interest rates, *Journal of Business*, **XLIV** (January), 19–31.

CHAPTER 2

Estimating yield curves

2.1 INTRODUCTION

There are two distinct approaches to modelling the term structure of interest rates. The first is essentially to measure the term structure using statistical techniques — smoothing data obtained from asset prices to describe the current yield curve without taking a view on the factors driving it. Conversely, the second approach is based on models which make explicit assumptions about the evolution of state variables and asset pricing methods using either equilibrium or arbitrage arguments. This chapter considers only the former, the latter being discussed in detail in Chapters 4 and 8. This section briefly introduces some of the problems inherent in yield curve estimation — problems relating to tax are discussed in Chapter 5. Section 2.2 provides a historical perspective on the early use and development of yield curve estimation techniques, while Section 2.3 considers the relative merits of estimating the term structure from either the discount function or the par yield curve. Finally, Section 2.4 discusses in detail the choice of approximating function to be used in the estimation process.

The previous chapter detailed the relationships between variables and curves on the basis that either a set of discrete discount factors or a continuous discount function is known. Also, since the discount function, par yield curve, zero-coupon yield curve and implied forward rate curves are all algebraically related, knowing any one of these four means that the other three can be readily computed. In reality, however, none of the four curves is directly observable; they must instead be derived from asset prices. The most common assets for which yield curves are computed are interest rate swaps and government bonds. Estimation of swap curves is simpler than that of bond curves due to the fact that the observations occur at regular discrete intervals. However, while bond rates may be available for maturities of up to 25 or 30 years, swap rates are typically only available for maturities of up to 10 years. More importantly, swap rates and curves include an element reflecting credit risk — this credit risk premium is difficult to estimate.

There are two fundamental problems that need to be addressed by any model attempting to identify the term structure of interest rates implied by the prices of government bonds. The first is the problem of 'gaps' in the maturity spectrum — there is not always a suitable bond, or any bond at all, maturing at a date of interest. Second, the term structure is defined in terms of zero-coupon bonds — but in most markets, government bonds pay coupons, and so it is not possible *directly* to infer zero-coupon yields from the prices of these bonds.

These two problems lead to further practical estimation problems. First, there is the problem of filling the gaps — what shapes should the term structure be allowed to take? To answer this question, a decision on the appropriate trade-off between 'smoothness' (removing 'noise' from the data) and 'responsiveness' (flexibility to accommodate genuine 'bends' in the term structure) is required. Second, is it preferable to estimate the term structure via the discount function or via the par yield curve?

There are other practical hurdles to overcome: for example, at present in the UK many investors pay income tax on coupon payments whereas any capital gain is tax-free. This differential taxation of coupon payments and capital gains results in taxpayers preferring (and hence paying a premium for) low coupon bonds; so the size of the coupon on a bond will affect its yield. Such coupon effects, along with any other tax effects, need to be removed from any estimate of the term structure — methods for doing this are considered in Chapter 5. An additional topic worth just a brief mention is the treatment of outliers. In markets where all bonds are of roughly similar characteristics (e.g. coupon, liquidity, etc.) outliers are not really an issue. However, in most markets there will typically be a few issues which are either illiquid or have particularly high or low coupons. It may be prudent to exclude such bonds from the estimation process — though decisions concerning outliers are inevitably subjective.

2.2 EARLY USE AND DEVELOPMENT OF YIELD CURVES

Early work on fitting curves to data from bond markets consisted of constructing simple yield-to-maturity curves rather than attempting to identify the true term structure of interest rates. The empirical estimation of such curves dates back to at least 1929 and Harry Guthmann's dissertation 'The relation of the maturity factor to yield differences among investment securities'. The approach adopted by Durand (1942) — whose study covered a 40-year period — was much the same and involved using a French curve[1] to draw a curve under[2] the scatter of yield/maturity points in such a way that he believed reasonable. Subsequent researchers sought automatic methods for fitting yield curves but also adopted these conventions. Notable among these were Cohen, Kramer and Waugh (1966), and Fisher (1966), who investigated yield curve fitting using functional forms which could be estimated using ordinary least squares (OLS) regression techniques.

The idea of treating the yield on a long-term bond as an average of forward rates is generally attributed to Irving Fisher (1907, 1930). Meiselman (1962) used Durand's yield data to estimate forward rates treating them as if they were derived from zero-coupon bonds rather than coupon-paying bonds, as did Nelson (1972). The problem with Durand's graphical method and its offshoots is that they try to explain the yield on a bond solely in terms of its maturity, with no reference to coupon. This inevitably reduces the extent to which these derived estimates are useful — see Macaulay (1938) and Fisher (1959). It appears that Fisher and Weil (1971) were the first to take proper account of coupons in inferring forward rates from yield curves in a substantial empirical study. The publication of McCulloch's 1971 paper on term structure estimation marked a significant step forward, acting as a basis for much of the recent academic studies on the subject. Accordingly, it is dealt with in some detail in the following sections.

2.3   YIELD CURVE OR DISCOUNT FUNCTION?

Models used to estimate the term structure of interest rates fall into two distinct categories: those that fit the par yield curve and those that fit a discount function. Most academic studies are based on the latter, the approach that was pioneered by McCulloch (1971).

2.3.1   FITTING A CURVE THROUGH REDEMPTION YIELDS

One such model is described by Mastronikola (1991). This essentially fits a curve through redemption yields, derived directly from observed prices using (1.11). While simple to understand, this methodology has the theoretical drawback that it does not explicitly restrict payments due on the same date to be discounted at the same rate. To see why this is the case, consider two bonds; the first, bond A, maturing in one period's time and the second, bond B, in two periods:

$$\text{Price of bond A} = \frac{C_A + R_A}{(1 + y_A)}$$

$$\text{Price of bond B} = \frac{C_B}{(1 + y_B)} + \frac{C_B + R_B}{(1 + y_B)^2}$$

where C_A, C_B, R_B, y_A, and y_B are respectively, the coupons, redemption payments and redemption yields of the two bonds.

Estimating the yield curve by fitting a curve through the redemption yields on these two bonds does not restrict the first coupon payment on bond B to be discounted at the same rate as the redemption payment on bond A, even though both payments are due at exactly the same time. Instead, when estimating a yield curve in this manner the assumption must be made that the first coupon on bond B is discounted using the rate indicated by the yield on bond A, the yield on bond B reflecting the difference in rates between period 1 and period 2. In other words, bond A is assumed to provide all the information required for inferences about how the earlier coupon payment on bond B is discounted.

Given a specification of the functional form for the yield curve, the estimation procedure is simply to fit a curve of the given functional form to minimize the sum of squared differences between the observed and fitted redemption yields. The estimated curve is implicitly a par yield curve. Problems with redemption yields are discussed by Schaefer (1977).

2.3.2 FITTING A DISCOUNT FUNCTION

Most researchers follow McCulloch (1971) in explicitly constraining cashflows from different bonds due at the same time to be discounted at the same rate, and estimates a discount function from which the term structure can be derived. McCulloch uses a form of the bond price equation with a continuous discount function and makes the assumption of continuous compounding. Subsequent studies take account of the fact that coupon payments are made at discrete intervals. Using this convention the price on bond i $(i = 1, \ldots, s)$ can be written as:

$$p_i + ai_i = c_i \sum_{l=1}^{n} \delta(t_l) + R_i \delta(t_n) \tag{2.1}$$

where, for the ith bond:

ai_i = accrued interest
R_i = redemption payment
n = number of outstanding annual[3] coupon payments of size c_i
t_l = time to the lth coupon payment of the ith bond.

To estimate $\delta(m)$ — the discount function at some maturity m — it is defined to be a linear combination of a set of k (linearly independent) underlying *basis functions*:

$$\delta(m) = 1 + \sum_{j=1}^{k} a_j f_j(m) \tag{2.2}$$

where $f_j(m)$ is the jth basis function, and a_j is the corresponding coefficient ($j = 1, \ldots, k$). There are a number of functional forms that the basis functions $f_j(m)$ can take to produce a sensible discount function, and this choice is discussed in detail in the next section.

A system of s linear equations can be derived[4] (one for each bond) by combining (2.1) and (2.2), with the function weights a_j as the coefficients in each equation:

$$y_i = \sum_{j=1}^{k} a_j x_{ij} \tag{2.3}$$

where

$$y_i = p_i + ai_i - nc_i - R_i$$

$$x_{ij} = c_i \sum_{l=1}^{n} f_j(l) + R_i f_j(n)$$

The coefficients $a_j(j = 1, \ldots, k)$ can be estimated from (2.3) using OLS, and the estimated discount function can then be calculated using (2.2).

Having estimated the discount function, (1.24), (1.26) and (1.28) can be used to derive estimates of the implied forward rate, zero-coupon and par yield curves respectively.

2.4   ESTIMATING FUNCTIONS

The two alternative approaches to yield curve estimation discussed in the previous section both require a specification of one or more estimating function(s): when fitting through redemption yields, the functional form needs to be specified; whereas estimating a discount function using McCulloch's methodology requires the specification of basis functions ($f_j(m)$ in (2.2)). The choice of functions in both cases is crucial since it ultimately determines the trade-off between smoothness and flexibility discussed earlier, and therefore reflects prior beliefs about the shapes a yield curve should be able to take. This choice is unavoidably subjective but certain properties are essential; in particular, an estimated discount function should be both positive and monotonic non-increasing (to avoid negative forward rates) and should equal unity at time $t = 0$ (the present value of £1 receivable now is £1).

The simplest approach to fitting the discount function is that used by Carleton and Cooper (1976), who estimate the term structure of interest rates for US government coupon securities (i.e. notes and bonds). They utilize the fact that the semi-annual interest payments made by nearly all securities in this market are made on only four days of each year[5]. This even spacing of data points means that the discount factors can be estimated directly from (1.8) using OLS for maturities up to seven years[6], thus avoiding the need for approximating functions (and McCulloch's formulation) altogether. Although Carleton and Cooper did not apparently constrain their estimates of the discount function, in most cases these displayed attributes that might be expected — i.e. they were monotonic decreasing and non-negative. The main problem with this approach is the reliance on regularly spaced interest payment dates, and as such it is unsuitable for application to most markets (or even to the US market beyond seven years). Furthermore, this method imposes no smoothness on the discount function (since the discount factors are estimated independently from one another), leading to jagged implied forward rate curves.

2.4.1   POLYNOMIAL SPLINES

If data are not regularly spaced (as is the case in the UK and most other bond markets) the approach used by Carleton and Cooper is not feasible and instead an approach based on estimating or approximating functions is often used. The motivation behind this is Weierstrass' Approximation Theorem[7], which states that there is a class of functions that may be used to approximate any continuous function over an interval with an arbitrarily small degree of error. McCulloch's (1971, 1975) implementation is given in (2.2) in which the discount function $\delta(m)$ is described as a linear combination of k approximating functions $f_j(m)$ $(j = 1, \ldots, k)$ on which the coefficients $(a_j, j = 1, \ldots, k)$ are estimated. One of the simplest implementations — discussed by McCulloch (1971) — is to let $f_j(m) = m^j$ for $j = 1, \ldots, k$. The discount function generated by this set of approximating functions will then be a simple kth-degree polynomial. However, such a polynomial has uniform resolving power and so, unless observations are spaced equally through the maturity range, tends to fit well at the short end and badly at the long end or vice versa — depending on where the greatest concentration of observations occurs. To solve this problem it is possible to increase k, the order of the polynomial, but this can cause instability in the parameter estimates.

To solve these problems McCulloch suggested the use of piecewise polynomial functions or *splines* to approximate the discount function. According to Rice (1969) 'spline functions are the most successful approximating functions for practical application so far discovered'. Intuitively, a polynomial spline can be thought of as a number of separate polynomial functions, joined 'smoothly' at a number of so-called *join, break* or *knot* points. The word 'smooth' has a precise mathematical meaning, but in the context of a piecewise r-degree spline it is generally taken to mean that the $(r - 1)$th derivatives of the functions either side of each knot point are continuous[8]. Using this piecewise approach the polynomials can be of much lower order and generate a more stable curve. One of the main advantages of splines is their flexibility for modelling special curvature or shape in different regions of the term structure.

In his first paper McCulloch (1971) uses a quadratic spline to estimate the discount function. This has superior properties to that of the simple polynomial but also has several shortcomings. A major drawback is that use of a quadratic spline for the discount function can lead to what McCulloch terms 'knuckles' in the corresponding forward rate curve. This effect, illustrated in Figure 2.1, is caused by the fact that specifying the discount function by a piecewise quadratic function means that it has a discontinuous second derivative, resulting in a forward rate curve with a discontinuous first derivative[9].

The obvious way to avoid this effect is to increase the order of the estimating functions and use (for example) a *cubic spline*. The simplest implementation of a cubic spline is that presented by McCulloch (1975). In this formulation the basis functions $f_j(m)$ in (2.2) are specified as a family of cubics that are constrained to be smooth around each knot point[10]. This specification is certainly flexible enough to model any reasonably-shaped discount function (and, therefore, the corresponding yield curve). It can in fact be *too* flexible, as it does not constrain

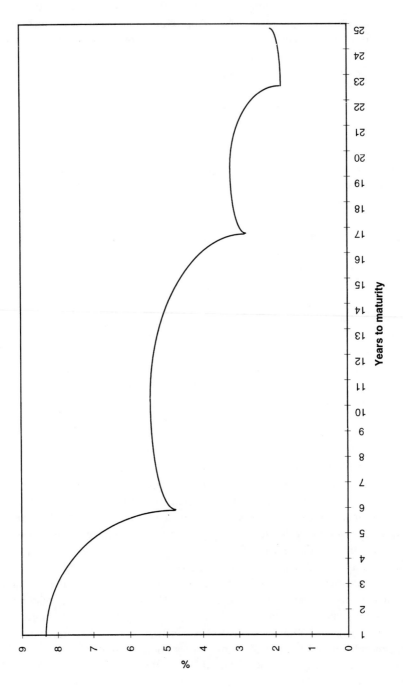

Figure 2.1   McCulloch's 'knuckle' effect on forward rates

the discount function to be non-increasing; so forward rates calculated using (1.24) may be negative.

An example of a more complex cubic spline is described by Mastronikola (1991)[11]. Unlike McCulloch's methodology, where cubic functions define basis functions along the length of the discount function which are weighted and then added together, this methodology uses a set of cubic functions each of which fits a sub-interval of the yield curve (i.e. each function fits the curve in the space between two consecutive knot points). The second derivatives of adjoining functions are constrained to be equal at the knot point, meaning that the entire estimated curve is 'smooth' in the sense described above. By constraining the two ends of the curve, each individual function is a cubic with two constraints and (for a set of fixed knot points) is therefore unique — it then follows that the entire fitted curve is also unique. Moreover, the short end of the yield curve is constrained to have constant slope (i.e. zero second derivative) and the long end is constrained to be flat (i.e. zero first and second derivatives). The number of knot points and their maturities are fixed, and the yields at each knot point are estimated such that the sum of squared residuals between observed and fitted yields is minimized.

2.4.2 BERNSTEIN POLYNOMIALS

Schaefer (1981) uses approximating functions to estimate the discount function in a similar manner to McCulloch — his equation defining the discount function being:

$$\delta(m) = \sum_{j=0}^{k} a_j \theta_j(m) \tag{2.4}$$

However, his approach imposes the restrictions that the discount function should be non-negative and monotonic non-increasing (in order to avoid negative forward rates[12]), by using approximating functions $\theta_j(m)$ (derived from Bernstein polynomials) given by[13]:

$$\theta_j(m) = \begin{cases} \text{sign } [\delta(0)] = 1 & j = 0 \\ \sum_{r=0}^{k-j} (-1)^{r+1} \binom{k-j}{r} \dfrac{m^{(j+r)}}{(j+r)} & j = 1, \dots, k \end{cases}$$

where m is measured without loss of generality on the interval [0,1], and $a_j \geq 0$, $j = 0, \dots, k$ in (2.4) in order to ensure that the discount function is monotonic non-increasing.

In addition, by imposing the constraint that $a_0 = 1$ Schaefer ensures that $\delta(0) = 1$. Equation (2.4) then reduces to the familiar McCulloch equation for the discount function, namely:

$$\delta(m) = 1 + \sum_{j=1}^{k} a_j \theta_j(m)$$

Finally, in order to ensure that the discount function is non-negative, Schaefer imposes the constraint that $\delta(1) \geq 0$, i.e. that $\sum_{j=1}^{k} a_j \theta_j(1) \geq -1$.

One advantage of these functions over conventional polynomial approximating functions is that they give considerably better approximations to the derivatives. This is important since the forward rate curve depends on the first derivative of the discount function[14].

2.4.3   EXPONENTIAL SPLINES

One of the main criticisms levelled at both cubic splines and Bernstein polynomial functions as a choice of approximating functions is that these can lead to forward rate curves which exhibit undesirable (and unrealistic) properties for long maturities. Figure 2.2 shows how such curves can rise (or fall) steeply at the long end — this particular example being from a McCulloch model.

Vasicek and Fong (1982) detail a method that can be used to produce asymptotically flat forward curves. Central to their approach is the characterization of the discount function as essentially exponential in shape. This accords with modern equilibrium theories of the term structure, which suggest that for many plausible stochastic processes, the discount function will have an exponential form. They argue that conventional splines, as piecewise *polynomials*, have a different curvature from exponentials and so will not provide a good local fit to the discount function[15]. In fact, Schumaker (1969) shows that to construct an accurate approximating spline for an exponential form requires either a very high order spline or a large number of knots. Vasicek and Fong claim that this poor local fit will result in the spline 'weaving' around the discount function, thus producing highly unstable forward rates. Also, polynomial splines of the type used by McCulloch cannot be forced to tail off in an exponential form as maturity increases.

Vasicek and Fong suggest applying a transform to the argument m of the discount function $\delta(m)$. This transform has the form:

$$m = -\left(\frac{1}{\alpha}\right) \ln(1 - x) \qquad \text{for } 0 \leq x < 1 \tag{2.5}$$

and has the effect of transforming the discount function from an approximately exponential function of m to an approximately linear function[16] of x. Polynomial splines can then be employed to estimate this transformed discount function. Using this transform, it is easy to impose additional constraints on the discount function[17]. The parameter α constitutes the limiting value of the forward rates, and can be fitted to the data as part of the estimation.

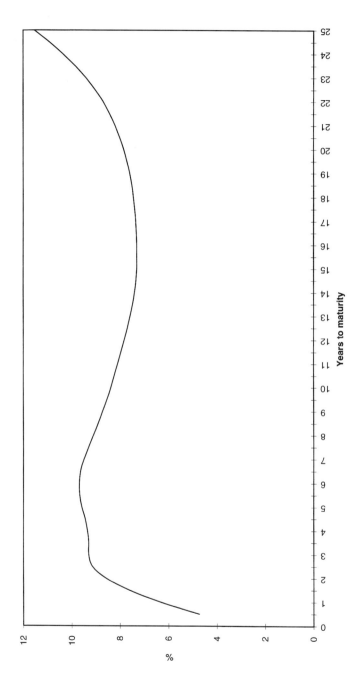

Figure 2.2 Implied forward interest rates for 7 June 1994

Vasicek and Fong use a cubic spline to estimate the transformed discount function. In terms of the original variable m, this is equivalent to estimating the discount function by a third-order exponential spline, i.e. between each pair of knot points $\delta(m)$ takes the form:

$$\delta(m) = b_0 + b_1 e^{-\alpha m} + b_2 e^{-2\alpha m} + b_3 e^{-3\alpha m}$$

Although Vasicek and Fong claim to have tested exponential splines successfully, they provide no evidence. Subsequently, Shea (1985) presented some empirical results and concluded that there is no evidence to support the claim that exponential splines produce more stable estimates of the term structure than polynomial splines — the discount function often deviating from the expected exponential decay. Shea found that the asymptotic property only constrained the forward curve to flatten at maturities beyond the longest observable bond and exhibited little influence over its shape or level at other maturities. An additional observation was that one of the factors driving the instability of the Vasicek and Fong model was the data-conditioning properties of the exponential transform, $x = 1 - e^{-\alpha m}$. Small values of $\hat{\alpha}$ cause the observed x to become bunched so that substantial portions of the estimation interval $[0,1]$ contain no data, leading to particularly unstable and unrealistic asymptotic forward rates. In such circumstances Shea had to coax the non-linear estimation program to converge to a solution. It is possible that this problem was caused by Shea's choice of knot points, which appears to be in line with McCulloch's convention of placing equal numbers of observations (if possible) between knots[18].

Langetieg and Smoot (1989) fit a cubic spline to the term structure of interest rates — equivalent to fitting an exponential function to the discount function. This they refer to as the 'exponential yields' model, the discount function being given by the equation:

$$\delta(m) = \exp\left[-m \sum_{j=1}^{k} a_j f_j(m)\right]$$

As with Vasicek and Fong, they reason that if the discount function is truly exponential then the exponential yields model should, *ceteris paribus*, provide a more accurate approximation of the discount function compared with a model that applies a cubic spline directly to it. Conversely, if the discount function is not exponential then imposing an exponential restriction will quite probably result in an inferior fit. Since their tests indicate a superior fit for the exponential yields model Langetieg and Smoot view this as vindication of equilibrium theories of the term structure which support an exponential discount function. They also found that their model gave better results than that of Vasicek and Fong. This, they argue, is to be expected, since the exponential transformation model can be viewed as an approximation of the exponential yields model.

Coleman, Fisher and Ibbotson (1992) treat the forward rate curve, rather than the discount function, as the fundamental variable — primarily for mathematical convenience. They approximate the instantaneous forward rate curve $f(m)$ by a piecewise constant function:

$$f(m) = f_j \qquad \text{for } m_{j-1} < m \le m_j$$

— the periods (m_{j-1}, m_j) over which the forward rate curve is a given constant, f_j, being arbitrarily chosen. It follows that this is equivalent to using exponential splines to estimate the discount function — for example, for $m_2 < m < m_3$, the discount function would be evaluated as:

$$\delta(m) = \exp\{-[f_1 m_1 + f_2(m_2 - m_1) + f_3(m - m_2)]\}$$

The authors argue that over a period in which the forward rate is actually constant, this approach is capable of providing an exact fit, while a quadratic or cubic spline is not. Although the discount function produced by this method will be continuous, its first derivative will be discontinuous. The authors suggested that economic theory only requires that the discount function be monotonic decreasing, and that further restrictions are not justified. However, other researchers such as Langetieg and Smoot (1989) reason that a smooth forward rate curve is consistent with the notion of market efficiency — any discontinuities, kinks and other irregularities tending to be quickly priced out by local or global arbitrageurs.

2.4.4   B-SPLINES

An important observation made by both Shea (1984) and Steeley (1991) concerns the choice of basis functions when defining a spline function. They find that some spline bases, such as that chosen by McCulloch (1971, 1975), can generate a regressor matrix with columns that are nearly perfectly collinear, resulting in possible inaccuracies arising from the subtraction of large numbers in estimates obtained using OLS. As a solution they advocate the use of a basis of 'B-splines'. These are functions which are identically zero over a large portion of the approximation space (unlike those used by McCulloch) and thus avoid loss of accuracy. By using a B-spline basis, it is also easier to impose constraints on the spline function.

Steeley (1991) defines a g-order B-spline function as:

$$B_p^g(m) = \sum_{l=p}^{p+g+1} \left[\prod_{h=p, h \ne l}^{p+g+1} \frac{1}{(m_h - m_l)} \right] (m - m_l)_+^g \qquad -\infty < m < \infty \quad (2.6)$$

Here $(m - m_l)_+ = \max[0, (m - m_l)]$, and the subscript p denotes that $B_p^g(m)$ is only non-zero if m is in the interval $[m_p, m_{p+g+1}]$. Figure 2.3 gives examples of

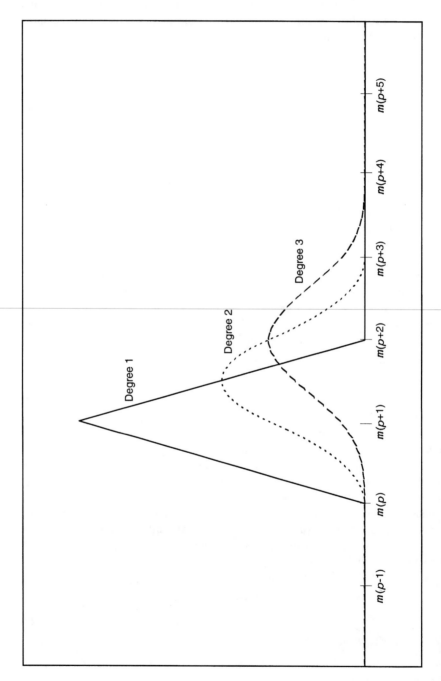

Figure 2.3 B-splines of degrees one, two and three

first-, second- and third-order B-splines. If the approximation space is divided into n sections, it will be spanned by $n + g$ basis functions.

For example, a linear B-spline function ($g = 1$) would be given by:

$$B_p^1(m) = \sum_{l=p}^{p+2} \left[\prod_{h=p, h \neq l}^{p+2} \frac{1}{(m_h - m_l)} \right] (m - m_l)_+^g \qquad -\infty < m < \infty$$

This is non-zero over the interval $[m_p, m_{p+2}]$ and takes the values:

$$B_p^1(m) = \begin{cases} 0 & m \leq m_p \\ (m - m_p)/(m_{p+1} - m_p)(m_{p+2} - m_p) & m_p < m \leq m_{p+1} \\ (m_{p+2} - m)/(m_{p+2} - m_p)(m_{p+2} - m_{p+1}) & m_{p+1} < m \leq m_{p+2} \\ 0 & m_{p+2} < m \end{cases}$$

Steeley (1991) demonstrates how to construct the necessary basis of $n + g$ B-splines. The first natural step is to include the $n - g$ functions $\{B_p^1 : p = 0, 1, \ldots, n - g - 1\}$ because they are linearly independent. For example, in the simple case where the approximation space has just two segments ($n = 2$ and, say, $p = 0$), first include the $B_0^1(m)$ which can be evaluated as above, and appears as the solid line in Figure 2.4. It is zero until m_0, at which point it has a positive linear slope m_1, whereupon it takes a negative linear slope until becoming zero once more m_2. Since a total of $n + g$ basis functions are required, another $2g$ basis functions are needed.

A convenient way of defining these extra functions so that they are also B-splines is to introduce some extra knots outside the interval $[a, b]$[19]. A total basis of B-splines can then be constructed as $\{B_p^g(m) : p = -g, -g + 1, \ldots, n - 1\}$. In the example, by adding the knots m_1 and m_3 the approximation interval can be spanned by the $n + g = 3$ functions $B_{-1}^1(m)$, $B_0^1(m)$ and $B_1^1(m)$ (Figure 2.3). For spline functions of higher degree the extra $2g$ functions have the effect of including the right-hand 'tails' of those functions which were first non-zero in regions to the left of m_0. In the linear example presented here, over the interval m_0 to m_1, the right-hand portion of $B_{-1}^1(m)$ is added to the existing left-hand portion of $B_0^1(m)$. Hence in general, each segment has present within it non-zero portions of $g + 1$ functions, two in the simple example above.

To obtain a smooth forward rate curve a spline function of at least order three must be used. Instead of deriving such spline functions from (2.6), Powell (1981) suggests that a more efficient solution is to employ the recurrence relation:

$$B_p^g(m) = \frac{(m - m_p)B_p^{g-1}(m) + (m_{p+g+1} - m)B_{p+1}^{g-1}(m)}{(m_{p+g+1} - m_p)}$$

which holds for all real values of m.

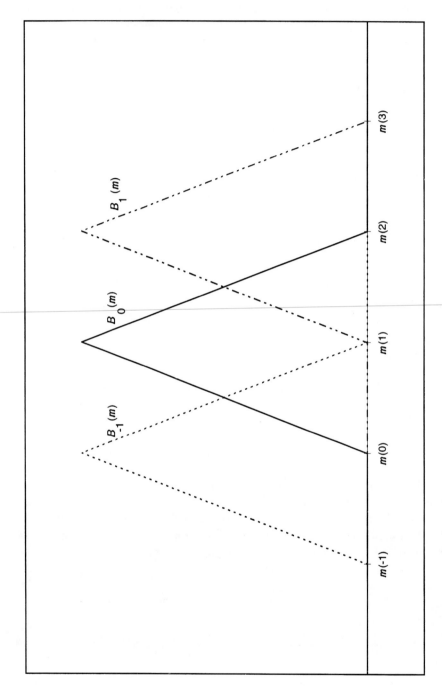

Figure 2.4   B-splines of degree one

Using B-splines, the region of the discount function between any two knots m_p and m_{p+1} is defined as:

$$\delta(m) = \sum_{j=p-g}^{p} a_j B_j^g(m) \qquad \text{where } m_p \leq m < m_{p+1}$$

For example, in the case of a *cubic* B-spline:

$$\delta(m) = \sum_{j=p-3}^{p} a_j B_j^3(m) \qquad \text{where } m_p \leq m < m_{p+1}$$

The only constraint imposed by Steeley is that the discount function should take a value of unity at time zero, that is, $\delta(0) = 1$. An important conclusion that he draws from his research is that by employing B-spline bases, splines can be viewed as a robust alternative to Bernstein polynomials. B-spline bases are also used by Langetieg and Smoot (1989) and Fisher, Nychka and Zervos (1995).

2.4.5   PROBLEMS USING SPLINES AS ESTIMATION FUNCTIONS

Shea (1984) considers some of the pitfalls encountered when using splines to model the term structure. First, he demonstrates that the constraints implicit in the McCulloch cubic spline do not in fact restrict the discount function to its desired negative slope, and can consequently produce an estimate for the discount function which starts to slope upward at the longest maturities. The forward rate curve generated by such a discount function will therefore be negative in sections. Without the imposition of constraints (discussed earlier), the use of Bernstein polynomials would induce similar characteristics. Shea argues that Schaefer's constraint on the slope of the discount function to be everywhere negative, though serving to prevent negative forward rates, does nothing for the general stability of the forward rate curve.

One alternative 'fix' suggested by Shea on such occasions is the use of *ad hoc* constraint specification. In its more obvious form this might consist of changing the number or location of the knot points. However, Shea goes on to suggest the use of localized constraints to deal with specific problem areas. One such constraint suggested is a simple restriction of fixed proportions between the first derivatives of the discount function at different maturities[20]. This is of particular use at the long end where it can be applied to ensure that the discount function remains negatively sloped. Although these manual adjustments to the term structure might be acceptable in a research and development context, they will clearly be of limited use for practitioners in an operational environment, where yield curve updates may be required on a real-time basis. Also, the introduction of such subjectivity may also cause problems interpreting the term structure — changes in the curve may be wrongly attributed to events in the market when in fact they are solely due to a change in the constraint specification.

Another decision that needs to be made when using spline functions is the number and location of the knot points. If the number of knots is too low then the model will not fit the data closely when the term structure takes on difficult shapes, while if it is too high the estimated curve may conform too readily to unrepresentative outliers. The approach adopted by McCulloch (1975) and several subsequent researchers is to set the number of knots to be equal to the nearest integer to the square root of the number of bonds in the estimation process. These knots are then spaced evenly among the number of observations (maturities). One advantage of McCulloch's suggestion is that the positioning of the knots will automatically change with a shift in the maturity structure of government debt. However, allowing the knots to move on a day-to-day basis may induce unrealistic movements in the term structure.

An alternative suggested by Litzenberger and Rolfo (1984) consists of placing the knots at 1-, 5- and 10-year maturities — this placement corresponding roughly to an economic interpretation as short-, medium- and long-term money. Langetieg and Smoot (1989) test the McCulloch knot placement scheme against that recommended by Litzenberger and Rolfo, and conclude that the latter typically performs better. Their tests also show that this can be enhanced by placing a further knot at six months' maturity, especially if Treasury bill data are being used in the estimation.

Figures 2.5 and 2.6 illustrate the kinds of effect that changing the number of the knots in the Bank of England's spline-based model can have on the forward rate curve[21]. In the case of 30 September 1992, reducing the number of knot points from six to four raises the forward curve by over 30 basis points at some maturities. This smoothing also removes the point of inflection at the 3-year horizon.

Aside from Steeley (1991) and Fisher, Nychka and Zervos (1995), there has been little coverage of sophisticated techniques for specifying the optimal number and location of knot points. That such techniques have existed for sometime (e.g. de Boor, 1978) makes this all the more surprising. Such methods are discussed in greater detail later in the chapter.

2.4.6   PARSIMONIOUS FUNCTIONAL FORMS

As reported earlier, McCulloch found that approximating the term structure using a simple polynomial can lead to substantive problems. Specifically, he concluded that a simple polynomial cannot adequately fit both ends of the term structure simultaneously. In contrast, using either splines or Bernstein polynomials permits different parts of the term structure to be approximated without severely affecting the others — they give a term structure estimate that fits reasonably well over the entire range.

An alternative proposal by Chambers, Carleton, and Waldman (1984) is to use an 'exponential polynomial' to model the discount function — equivalent to

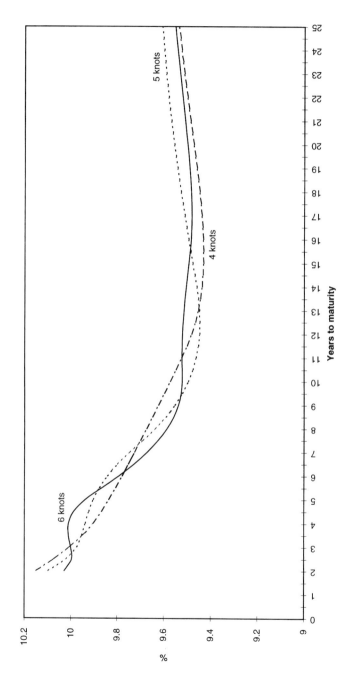

Figure 2.5   Implied forward interest rates for 30 March 1992 (for different numbers of knots)

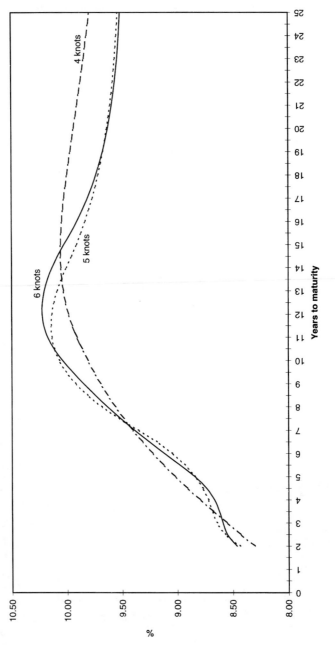

Figure 2.6 Implied forward interest rates for 30 September 1992 (for different numbers of knots)

modelling the term structure using a simple polynomial. Mathematically:

$$\delta(m) = \exp\left(-\sum_{j=1}^{k} a_j m^j\right)$$

The authors analyze the effects of varying the polynomial degree j from one to five, and conclude that a third- or fourth-degree polynomial is sufficient to approximate the term structure. They also confirm earlier studies that found that simple polynomials do not provide an acceptable fit to the term structure using least squares regression — the fit being worst at the short end. They observe that this may relate to the heteroscedasticity in the data (i.e. higher variance in short yields than longer ones) and find that maximum likelihood estimation allowing for this gave a better fit — though at the expense of computational complexity — sixth-degree polynomials performing best.

Nelson and Siegel (1987) cite Milton Friedman (1977) as providing motivation for the development of a parsimonious model of the yield curve — his view being that 'Students of statistical demand functions might find it more productive to examine how the whole term structure of yields can be described more compactly by a few parameters'. An important aspect of the approach to yield curve modelling adopted by Nelson and Siegel (1987) is that they explicitly attempt to model the implied forward rate curve (rather than the term structure of interest rates). They choose a functional form for the forward rate curve that allows it to take a number of shapes that the authors feel are 'sensible'. The functional form that they suggest is:

$$f(m) = \beta_0 + \beta_1 \exp\left(-\frac{m}{\tau_1}\right) + \beta_2\left[\left(\frac{m}{\tau_1}\right)\exp\left(-\frac{m}{\tau_1}\right)\right] \qquad (2.7)$$

where $f(m)$ is the forward rate at maturity m, and β_0, β_1, β_2 and τ_1 are the parameters to be estimated. The coefficients are estimated from the equation for the discount function[22]:

$$\delta(m) = \exp\left\{-m \cdot \left[\beta_0 + (\beta_1 + \beta_2) \cdot \left(1 - \exp\left(-\frac{m}{\tau_1}\right)\right) \cdot \frac{\tau_1}{m} - \beta_2 \exp\left(-\frac{m}{\tau_1}\right)\right]\right\}$$

By considering the three components that make up this function (see Figure 2.7) it is clear how, with appropriate choices of weights, it can be used to generate forward rate curves of a variety of shapes, including monotonic and 'humped'. An important property of this model is that β_0 specifies the long rate to which the forward rate curve horizontally asymptotes. Furthermore, this approach avoids the problem in spline-based models of choosing the 'best' knot point specification. The trade-off is that it represents a much less flexible functional form than spline-based models and so will typically fit the data less well (see Chapter 3). From the Nelson and Siegel forward rate equation it is possible to

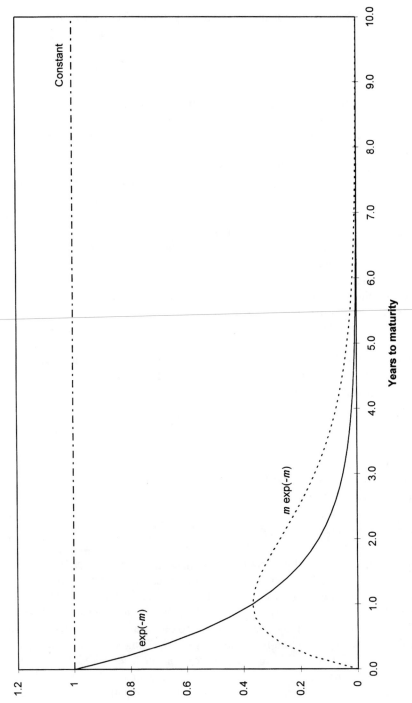

Figure 2.7 Components of the Nelson and Siegel implied forward rate curve

derive algebraic expressions for both the spot curve and the discount function, though not for the par yield curve[23].

Svensson (1994a) estimates spot and forward rate curves from *coupon bond data* using McCulloch's (1971, 1975) approach of fitting a discount function, but uses the Nelson and Siegel functional form instead of a spline function — arguing that for *monetary policy applications*, a simplistic functional form of this nature is perfectly acceptable. In Svensson (1994b), he increases the flexibility of the original Nelson and Siegel model[24] by adding a fourth term to (2.7). The revised forward rate equation has the form:

$$f(m) = \beta_0 + \beta_1 \exp\left(-\frac{m}{\tau_1}\right) + \beta_2 \left[\left(\frac{m}{\tau_1}\right) \exp\left(-\frac{m}{\tau_1}\right)\right] + \beta_3 \left[\left(\frac{m}{\tau_2}\right) \exp\left(-\frac{m}{\tau_2}\right)\right]$$

This has two extra parameters compared to the original Nelson and Siegel model, and allows for a second 'hump' in the forward rate curve. Comparative tests of the original and extended Nelson and Siegel models are discussed in Chapter 3.

A final parsimonious yield curve model worth discussing is the Exponential Model used by J. P. Morgan and described by Wiseman (1994). Again, the structure of interest is the forward rate curve, which is specified as:

$$f(m) = \sum_{j=0}^{n} a_j e^{-k_j m}$$

where the a_j's and k_j's are the parameters to be estimated — with $k_j > 0$ $\forall j \geq 1$ — and n is a fixed integer chosen in advance of the estimation. As a matter of convention $k_j > k_{j+1} \forall j$.

Wiseman (1994) reports that this model is very adept at capturing the macro shape of the yield curve while not fitting to the peculiarities of individual issues. As such, he advocates its use in cheap/dear analysis — essentially a comparison of how cheap or expensive each stock is trading relative to its intrinsic value, as measured by the yield curve. Other practitioners have mixed views on what constitutes a good model for cheap/dear analysis, some employing similar models to that used by J. P. Morgan while others prefer a more flexible approach.

2.4.7   NON-PARAMETRIC TECHNIQUES

In contrast to the other studies considered earlier, Fisher, Nychka and Zervos (1995) fit *smoothing splines* instead of regression splines. Smoothing splines have a penalty for excess 'roughness' and a single parameter controls the size of this penalty — an increase in the penalty being interpreted as a reduction in the effective number of parameters in the estimation. Hence the entire parameterization of the spline is controlled by a single value. By fitting smoothing splines and using generalized cross-validation to choose adaptively the roughness penalty

and hence the number of parameters, this method circumvents the need to exogenously supply the number and location of the knots. A similar approach is used
by Gourieroux and Scaillet (1994).

An alternative use of non-parametric techniques is presented by Tanggaard
(1992), who proposes using non-parametric kernel smoothing methods to estimate the *yield curve* — leading to what he terms a non-linear non-parametric
regression model. Here, the yield curve is estimated using locally weighted least
squares, with the weights being derived from *a kernel function* — a symmetric,
continuously bounded real function that integrates to unity — to give more weight
in the regression to bonds of maturities close to the maturity of interest. One of
Tanggaard's motivations for using such an approach is that it does not assume
a particular shape of the yield curve from the outset, thereby avoiding a specification bias — though, as he rightly points out, it is possible that a bias may
be introduced at a later stage. Tanggaard tests his non-parametric approach using
actual bond data as well as simulated data from a Nelson and Siegel model,
and finds it produces a good fit. Again, Gourieroux and Scaillet (1994) also
consider such an approach. Hardle (1990) provides an introduction to and survey
of non-parametric regression analysis.

2.5   SUMMARY

This chapter has provided an account of some of the better-known approaches
to yield curve estimation. Of these, it is impossible to identify one method as
being definitively superior to all others, though the authors have attempted to
draw out the strengths and weaknesses of each. A major factor affecting the
choice of which model to use is the purpose to which it is to be put. Thus,
for macroeconomic analysis, a parsimonious model such as Nelson and Siegel
(1987) may be deemed appropriate, while at the other end of the spectrum the
highly flexible non-parametric approaches may be better suited to pricing (though
some practitioners also use parsimonious models for pricing). For those seeking a
reasonable compromise between 'smoothness' and 'flexibility', a cubic B-spline
or a Bernstein polynomial approach with appropriate 'economic' constraints is
probably best.

APPENDIX A: DERIVING THE McCULLOCH EQUATIONS

To estimate the discount function $\delta(m)$ from the observed prices of s bonds, the
discount function is written as a linear combination of basis functions:

$$\delta(m) = 1 + \sum_{j=1}^{k} a_j f_j(m) \tag{A2.1}$$

where $f_j(m)$ is the jth basis function, and a_j is the corresponding coefficient $(j = 1, \ldots, k)$.

The price of the ith bond is given by:

$$p_i + ai_i = c_i \sum_{l=1}^{n} \delta(l) + R_i \delta(n) \qquad \text{(A2.2)}$$

where p_i, ai_i, R_i and n are the *clean* price, accrued interest, redemption payment and number of outstanding annual coupon payments (of size c_i) of the ith bond.

Substituting the expression for the discount function (A2.1) into the ith price equation gives:

$$p_i + ai_i = c_i \sum_{l=1}^{n} \left[1 + \sum_{j=1}^{k} a_j f_j(l) \right] + R_i \left[1 + \sum_{j=1}^{k} a_j f_j(n) \right]$$

$$\Rightarrow p_i + ai_i = nc_i + c_i \sum_{l=1}^{n} \sum_{j=1}^{k} a_j f_j(l) + R_i + R_i \sum_{j=1}^{k} a_j f_j(n)$$

$$\Rightarrow p_i + ai_i - nc_i - R_i = \sum_{j=1}^{k} a_j \left[c_i \sum_{l=1}^{n} f_j(l) + R_i f_j(n) \right]$$

So the regression equation for the McCulloch yield curve is defined by

$$y_i = \sum_{j=1}^{k} a_j x_{ij} \qquad \text{(A2.3)}$$

where

$$y_i = p_i + ai_i - nc_i - R_i$$

$$x_{ij} = c_i \sum_{l=1}^{n} f_j(l) + R_i f_j(n)$$

Equation (A2.3) can then be used to obtain least-squares estimates $\hat{a}_j$, and the estimate of the discount function $\delta(m)$ is then given by:

$$\hat{\delta}(m) = 1 + \sum_{j=1}^{k} \hat{a}_j f_j(m)$$

APPENDIX B: McCULLOCH'S CUBIC SPLINE SPECIFICATION

Assume k knots $\kappa_1, \ldots, \kappa_k$ where $\kappa_1 = 0$ and κ_k = maturity of the longest existing bond, the other knots being positioned so that there is approximately the same number of bonds between each pair of knots.

The functions used when $j < k$ are:
For $m < \kappa_{j-1}$
$$f_j(m) = 0$$

For $\kappa_{j-1} \leq m < \kappa_j$
$$f_j(m) = \frac{(m - \kappa_{j-1})^3}{6(\kappa_j - \kappa_{j-1})}$$

For $\kappa_j \leq m < \kappa_{j+1}$
$$f_j(m) = \frac{c^2}{6} + \frac{ce}{2} + \frac{e^2}{2} - \frac{e^3}{6(\kappa_{j+1} - \kappa_j)}$$

where
$$c = \kappa_j - \kappa_{j-1}$$
$$e = m - \kappa_j$$

For $\kappa_{j+1} \leq m$
$$f_j(m) = (\kappa_{j+1} - \kappa_{j-1}) \left[\frac{2\kappa_{j+1} - \kappa_j - \kappa_{j-1}}{6} + \frac{m - \kappa_{j+1}}{2} \right]$$

When $j = k$:
$$f_k(m) = m \qquad \forall m$$

NOTES

1. A graphical method for hand-fitting a curve to the data.
2. As Durand's data were for corporate bonds he (subjectively) drew his yield curves to pass under the bulk of the plotted points in order to obtain rates for absolutely risk-free loans.
3. For markets where coupon payments are made either quarterly or semi-annually c_i should be scaled accordingly — i.e. divided by 4 or 2 respectively.
4. See Appendix A for the full derivation.
5. Namely, 15 February, 15 May, 15 August and 15 November.
6. Data beyond seven years could not be used due to the sparsity of observations in that maturity range.
7. See, for example, Phillips and Taylor (1973).
8. One consequence of this definition is that the rth derivative of the spline is a step function.
9. Since, if $\delta(m)$ is the discount function and $\rho(m)$ is the forward rate curve it can be shown that $\rho'(m) = (\delta'(m)/\delta(m))^2 - (\delta''(m)/\delta(m))$. In other words,

the first derivative of the implied forward rate curve depends on the second derivative of the discount function.

10. The actual forms specified by McCulloch are reproduced in Appendix B, but in practice any set of cubic equations that are constrained to be smooth around the knot points could be used. Note also that the basis functions are in fact defined for the entire length of the estimation space (i.e. from zero to the maturity of the longest bond) and combined using (2.2) (and the weights estimated by (2.3)) to obtain the estimated discount function.

11. Here, the cubic spline is fitted through redemption yields rather than to the discount function.

12. If $\rho(m)$ is the forward rate curve and $\delta(m)$ the discount function it can be shown that $\rho(m) = -\delta'(m)/\delta(m)$ (1.23). Clearly, $\rho(m)$ will be negative if either $\delta'(m)$ is positive or $\delta(m)$ is negative.

13. Schaefer (1979) shows that non-negative combinations of the functions $\theta_j(m)$ will approximate any monotonic non-increasing function with arbitrary accuracy.

14. For a more detailed account of the use of Bernstein functions in this context see Schaefer (1982).

15. This is refuted by Shea (1985), who insists that a *piecewise* polynomial function should be able to mimic well a *piecewise* exponential function.

16. Here, x measures transformed time.

17. One such condition that they impose is the non-negative condition.

18. This was certainly the rule used in Shea (1984). The selection and positioning of knot points is discussed later.

19. Specifically, let $\{m_j : j = -g, -g+1, \ldots, -1\}$ and $\{m_j : j = n+1, n+2, \ldots, n+g\}$ and be any points on the real line that satisfy the conditions

$$m_{-g} < m_{-g+1} < \ldots < m_{-1} < m_0 = a$$
$$b = m_n < m_{n+1} < m_{n+2} < \ldots < m_{n+g}$$

20. One such example discussed by Shea consists of constraining the slope of the discount function at the last knot point to be half the slope of the discount function at the preceding knot point.

21. Such effects also occur when considering a par or zero-coupon yield curve, but are less significant.

22. Nelson and Siegel fit US Treasury bill data (because Treasury bills are zero-coupon instruments).

23. To obtain a par yield curve numerical methods must be applied.

24. In fact, Nelson and Siegel (1987) make their own suggestion for how their model could be extended. This stems from the observation that (2.6) can be viewed as a constant plus a *Laguerre function* — the product of a polynomial and an exponential decay term. Thus the model could be generalized by using a higher-order polynomial. More details on Laguerre functions can be found in Courant and Hilbert (1953).

REFERENCES

Carleton, W.T. and Cooper, I.A. (1976) Estimation and uses of the term structure of interest rates, *Journal of Finance*, **XXXI**, No. 4 (September), 1067–83.

Chambers, D.R., Carleton, W.T. and Waldman, D.W. (1984) A new approach to estimation of the term structure of interest rates, *Journal of Financial and Quantitative Analysis*, **19**, No. 3 (September), 233–52.

Cohen, K.J., Kramer, R.L. and Waugh, W.H. (1966) Regression yield curves for US government securities, *Management Science*, **13**, No. 14 (December), B168–75.

Coleman, T.S., Fisher, L. and Ibbotson, R.G. (1992) Estimating the term structure of interest rates from data that include the prices of coupon bonds, *The Journal of Fixed Income*, September, 85–116.

Courant, E. and Hilberts, D. (1953) *Methods of Mathematical Physics*, Wiley, New York, Chapter 1, 93–7.

de Boor (1978) *A Practical Guide to Splines* Springer-Verlag, New York.

Durand (1942) Basic Yields of Corporate Bonds, 1900–1942, New York National Bureau of Economic Research.

Fisher, D. (1966) Expectations, the term structure of interest rates, and recent British experience, *Economica*, **13** (August) 319–29.

Fisher, I. (1907) *The Rate of Interest*.

Fisher, I. (1930) *The Theory of Interest as Determined by Impatience to Spend Income and the Opportunity to Invest It*, Macmillan, New York.

Fisher, L. (1959) Determinants of risk premiums on corporate bonds, *Journal of Political Economy*, **67** (June), 217–37.

Fisher, L. and Weil (1971) Coping with the risk of interest-rate fluctuations: returns to bondholders from naive and optimal strategies, *Journal of Business*, **44** (October), 408–31.

Fisher, M.E., Nychka, D. and Zervos, D. (1995) Fitting the term structure of interest rates with smoothing splines, Federal Reserve Bank Finance and Economics Discussion Paper 95-1, January.

Friedman, M. (1977) Time perspective in demand for money, University of Chicago, unpublished paper.

Gourieroux, C. and Scalliet, O. (1994) Estimation of the term structure from bond data, *Crest*, No. 9415, May.

Guthmann, H.G. (1929) *The Relation of the Maturity Factor to Yield Differences Among Investment Securities*, PhD dissertation, University of Chicago.

Hardle, W. (1990) *Applied Non-Parametric Regression*, Cambridge University Press, New York.

Langetieg, T.C. and Smoot, J.S. (1989) Estimation of the term structure of interest rates, *Research in Financial Services*, **1**, 181–222.

Litzenberger, R.H. and Rolfo, R. (1984) An international study of tax effects on government bonds, *Journal of Finance*, March 1–22.

Macaulay, F.R. (1938) *Some Theoretical Problems Suggested by the Movements of Interest Rates, Bond Yields, and Stock Prices in the United States Since 1856*, National Bureau of Economic Research, New York.

Mastronikola, K. (1991) Yield curves for gilt-edged stocks: a new model, Bank of England Discussion Paper (Technical Series), No. 49, December.

McCulloch, J.H. (1971) Measuring the term structure of interest rates, *Journal of Business*, **XLIV** (January), 19–31.

McCulloch, J.H. (1975) The tax-adjusted yield curve, *Journal of Finance*, **XXX**, No. 3 (June), 811–30.

Meiselman, D.I. (1962) *The Term Structure of Interest Rates* (Ford Foundation Dissertation Series), Prentice Hall, Englewood Cliffs NJ.

Nelson, C.R. (1972) Estimation of term premiums from average yield differentials in the term structure of interest rates, *Econometrica*, **40**, No. 2 (March), 277–87.

Nelson, C.R. and Siegel, A.F. (1987) Parsimonious modeling of yield curves, *Journal of Business*, **60**, No. 4, 473–89.

Phillips, G.M. and Taylor, P.J. (1973) *Theory and Applications of Numerical Analysis*, Academic Press, London.

Powell, M.J.D. (1981) *Approximation Theory and Methods*, Cambridge University Press, Cambridge.

Rice, J.R. (1969) *The Approximation of Functions*, Addison-Wesley, Reading, MA, **2**.

Schaefer, S.M. (1977) Problem with redemption yields, *Financial Analysts Journal*.

Schaefer, S.M. (1979) *Consistent Bond Prices*, unpublished PhD thesis, University of London.

Schaefer, S.M. (1981) Measuring a tax-specific term structure of interest rates in the market for British government securities, *The Economic Journal*, **91**, 415–38.

Schaefer, S.M. (1982) Tax-induced clientele effects in the market for British government securities, *Journal of Financial Economics* **10**, 121–59.

Schumaker, L.L. (1969) *Some Algorithms for the Computation of Interpolating and Approximating Spline Functions*, in *Theory and Applications of Spline Functions*, edited by Greville, Academic Press, New York.

Shea, G.S. (1984) Pitfalls in smoothing interest rate term structure data: equilibrium models and spline approximation, *Journal of Financial and Quantitative Analysis*, **19**, 253–69.

Shea, G.S. (1985) Interest rate term structure estimation with exponential splines: a note, *Journal of Finance*, **XL**, No. 1 (March), 319–25.

Steeley, J.M. (1991) Estimating the gilt-edged term structure: basis splines and confidence intervals, *Journal of Business, Finance and Accounting* **18** (4) (June), 512–29.

Svensson, L. (1994a) *Monetary policy with flexible exchange rates and forward interest rates as indicators*, Institute for International Economic Studies, Stockholm University.

Svensson, L. (1994b) *Estimating and interpreting forward interest rates: Sweden 1992–94*, International Monetary Fund Working Paper No. 114, September.

Tanggaard, C. (1992) *Kernel smoothing of discount functions*, The Aarhus School of Business, Denmark, 21 December.

Vasicek, O.A. and Fong, H.G. (1982) Term structure modeling using exponential splines, *Journal of Finance*, **XXXVII**, No. 2 (May), 339–56.

Wiseman, J. (1994) *European Fixed Income Research: Second Edition Technical Specification — The Exponential Yield Curve Model, JP Morgan*, 16 December.

CHAPTER 3

Comparing yield curve models

3.1 INTRODUCTION

The previous chapter outlined a number of estimation methods for measuring the term structure of interest rates. The purpose of this chapter is to offer a more comparative approach to assessing the performance of these methods, both in theory and in practice.

As was noted in the previous chapter, there is a trade-off between smoothness and the goodness-of-fit of yield curve estimates. This is because there are a number of factors other than the underlying term structure that might influence the market price of a bond, including taxation rules, the existence of derivative markets, embedded optionality and the classification of certain bonds as 'benchmarks'. These idiosyncrasies affect the relative pricing of bonds and thereby transform the relationship between the estimated yield curve and the underlying term structure. If they are not explicitly accounted for by the estimation procedure, they can distort the resulting term structure estimate. It is important therefore to consider all the possible complications — and perhaps augment the methods described in Chapter 2 — before estimating the yield curve.

These factors also need to be taken into account when choosing a method of yield curve estimation for a particular market. However, as has already been discussed, it is important to strike a balance between those models which are too flexible, overfitting the data and treating outliers as the norm, and those which are too parsimonious. In the latter case, it is conceivable that a smooth yield curve may be too inflexible to capture the underlying market behaviour. It is useful therefore to test whether the restrictions imposed by a particular model, chosen *a priori*, are upheld by the data. Thus although the choice between alternative yield curve models is essentially subjective, it is also important to be aware of their limitations with respect to market behaviour.

3.2   BOND MARKET CHARACTERISTICS

There is a wide range of features of different government bond markets that can affect the relative valuation of the bonds. These range from idiosyncrasies of individual bonds to factors that effectively 'segment' the market into distinct groups of securities. It is often not possible to model all such effects when attempting to isolate the underlying term structure of interest rates, but it is useful to know the factors other than the term structure itself that can influence bond prices, to understand the effects that these can have and to have an idea of their relative significance.

3.2.1   OPTIONALITY

A 'conventional' fixed-income bond entitles the holder to a number of future cashflows whose timing and nominal size are known *with certainty* when the bond is purchased. However, in many markets, bonds exist with embedded optionality, giving either the issuer or the holder some discretion to redeem early or to convert to another security. For example, many UK and US government bonds are *callable*[1], giving the Treasury (the issuer) the option to redeem the bond at face value at any time between two dates specified at the time of issue[2]. All bonds issued by the Japanese government have embedded call options, though, to date, none have been exercised. Another example occurs in Italy, where the government has issued *puttable* bonds (CTO). The holder of a puttable bond has the option (again on pre-specified dates) to sell the bond back to the Italian Treasury at face value. A further example, from the UK but also common in many corporate bond markets, is the *convertible* bond that gives the holder the option (on one or more pre-specified dates) to convert a bond (at a pre-specified ratio) into another (pre-specified) bond.

   The embedded optionality will affect the valuation of such bonds relative to other bonds in the market. The extent to which the option will impact on a bond's price depends on the perceived market value of the option. For example, if a bond with a call option is thought unlikely to ever be called, then it is likely that it will be valued similarly to a conventional bond with the same (final) maturity date. Such bonds could reasonably be included in the term structure estimation process as conventional bonds. However, in the (more likely) case that the option is perceived to have some value, this optionality needs to be accounted for if the bonds are to be used. These issues are discussed in more detail in Chapter 6.

3.2.2   DURATION

When the yield curve is estimated directly from redemption yields, differences in the duration of two apparently similar bonds can distort the resulting estimate. As described in Chapter 1, other things being equal, a high coupon bond will be preferred to a low coupon bond because it provides the same nominal return at a faster rate. The result of this 'duration effect' is that the yield on the high coupon bond is driven below that of the low coupon bond. Techniques that explicitly model the size and timing of cashflows such as those due to McCulloch (1971, 1975) implicitly account for such effects, but more care needs to be taken when a curve of yields against maturity is fitted.

3.2.3   BENCHMARK AND ILLIQUID BONDS

An investor wanting to own government bonds as part of a wider portfolio may not be interested in the fine details of bond markets, requiring simply an asset that has the desired maturity and a reasonably large issue size so that it can easily be traded if required. Many issuers recognize this fact and issue bonds at standard maturities (such as 5 and 10 years) and maintain the size of such issues. These issues are generally referred to as *benchmark* or *on-the-run* bonds and often have a larger amount outstanding — are more *liquid* — than the *off-the-run* bonds. In some markets, such as the US government bond market, the issuer actively and explicitly maintains benchmark bonds while in others, such as the UK, they can be observed to be maintained even though the Bank of England does not itself describe the issues as benchmarks.

The existence of relatively liquid bonds at convenient points along the yield curve attracts investors to those particular bonds, often at the expense of similar issues that are less liquid. Liquidity itself is often reflected by the bid–ask spread on a bond — the difference between the prices at which a trader is willing to buy and sell the bond. An illiquid bond will usually have a wider bid–ask, reflecting the difficulty of matching the other side of the transaction. However, the greater demand for liquid bonds (such as the benchmarks) can also drive their prices up relative to similar but illiquid issues. For example, a plot of the yields on UK government bonds against maturity immediately identifies the benchmark bonds, their yields lying below the others and below the estimated par yield curve (Figure 3.1).

Opinion differs as to the treatment of benchmark bonds when estimating the term structure. Fitting through the benchmarks would produce a curve significantly below one drawn through the remaining, less liquid issues — but which represents the underlying term structure? It is often argued that the benchmarks represent the true curve since, as a result of their liquidity, they are less prone to the idiosyncrasies that can distort the prices of other bonds. Common market practice is to define the 10-year yield (for example) as the yield on the 10-year benchmark bond, thus implicitly defining the term structure in terms of bench-mark bond yields. However, a curve based simply on benchmarks will be difficult to estimate since there are typically very few benchmarks in a market (usually five or six). Conversely, a curve fitted to prices of bonds that are so illiquid that they rarely trade runs the risk of being uninformative. It can also be difficult to

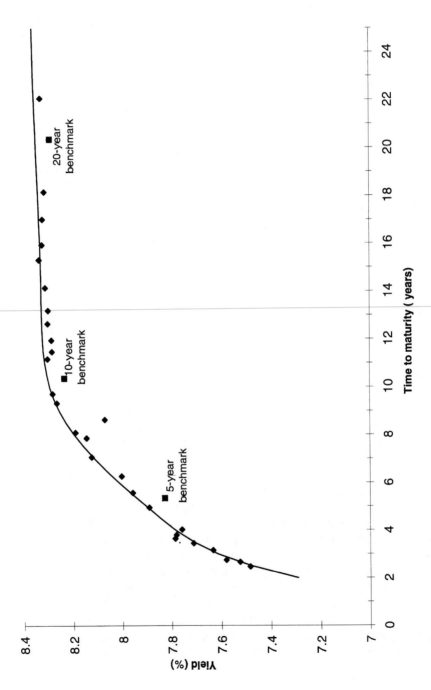

Figure 3.1   Benchmark bonds versus par yield curve and other bonds — 28 July 1995

get good prices for rarely traded securities, and so very illiquid bonds are often dropped from the estimation process. For example, a simple proxy that can be used to build an automatic liquidity criterion into the estimation procedure is to exclude all stocks of size below a given amount outstanding.

3.2.4   DERIVATIVE MARKETS

All the major government bond markets support at least one bond futures contract — futures contracts on US, UK, Italian, German and Spanish government bonds are traded on the London International Financial Futures and Options Exchange (LIFFE). The terms of bond futures contracts typically require the delivery of a bond from a pre-specified list of eligible bonds — the *basket of deliverable bonds* — on a future delivery date at a price specified when the trade is agreed. If a bond appears in the basket for a futures contract, this clearly distinguishes it from other bonds of similar maturity that cannot be delivered into the futures contract.

It is not clear how the existence of futures contracts affects the underlying cash market — if at all. It may be related to the 'benchmark' effect described above, since bond futures contracts are typically on bonds of around benchmark maturities. The existence of a futures contract on a bond[3] in effect makes it more liquid, since an investor can buy or sell a futures contract in addition to the bond itself. This increase in liquidity might drive the yield of the instrument down, since demand for it is effectively increased. However, futures markets are popularly believed to be more volatile than the underlying cash markets, although economic theory has little to say on this matter and the empirical evidence is divided. If this volatility is perceived to feed through to the underlying cash market, investors might demand an increased yield to offset the volatility.

3.2.5   EX-DIVIDEND EFFECTS

As noted in Chapter 1, the price at which a bond is traded generally reflects an adjustment for accrued interest, which compensates the seller of the bond for the opportunity foregone of receiving the next dividend payment due on the bond. But during the ex-dividend period this coupon is no longer transferable — it will be paid to whoever held the bond at the start of the period. The price at which the bond is traded during this period will therefore lie below the market, thereby distorting the estimated yield curve. In the UK, for example, the ex-dividend period commences 37 days before the next dividend payment is due (though this period will be shortened to 7 days in 1996).

3.2.6   MARKET SEGMENTATION — 'PREFERRED HABITATS'

Another feature of bond markets that can complicate the estimation of the term structure is the possible existence of 'preferred habitats' that effectively segment the market. For example, banks are active in demanding short maturity bonds, while pension funds require long-dated securities. These influential classes of investor may drive up the prices of securities in which they are investing, since they simultaneously increase the demand for these bonds and reduce their effective liquidity. Since they presumably act upon the entire segment of the yield curve in which they are interested, the existence of such segmentation is difficult to remove from any estimation technique — although it is arguable whether such effects should be removed at all, since the dominant group of investors can be argued to be effectively determining, rather than distorting, the term structure. Moreover, agents indifferent between the segments should be able to arbitrage away any inconsistencies, particularly any discontinuities. Therefore, if the yield curve appears to reflect the existence of segmentation, it can reasonably be assumed that this segmentation is also reflected in the underlying term structure — the classes of investor that cause segmentation are also the marginal investors and hence are determining the rates at which other agents can borrow or lend.

3.2.7 TAX

By far the most important external factor acting on bond markets is the existence of tax regulations. The different regimes in place around the world have different impacts on the markets in which they operate, and in many cases significantly distort relative bond prices. This distortion can arise for two reasons: the first is due to the existence of tax rules that cause investors facing different tax treatments to view the same instrument differently. Although they see the same gross cashflows, the cashflows net of tax can be very different. Indeed, tax rules alone can cause, or at least amplify, some of the segmentation effects described above. Also, in some markets, tax rules exist that cause the same investor to discriminate between two apparently similar bonds (offering similar gross returns) since the returns net of tax can be significantly different. This issue is discussed in further detail in Chapter 5.

3.3   A SUBJECTIVE APPROACH

Since the true underlying term structure is unobservable, any decision concerning the treatment of these 'outliers' must necessarily be subjective. Similarly, when assessing the relative performance of competing methods, there is no obvious point of reference. Thus our choice of yield curve model is inevitably based upon personal preconceptions about the shape of the term structure and the underlying behaviour of the market.

3.3.1   THE SHAPE OF THE YIELD CURVE

Figure 3.2 illustrates the zero-coupon yield curve for the UK market derived from four alternative methods of estimation on 11 October 1994[4]. Each has been augmented to handle tax effects in the manner described by Mastronikola (1991)[5].

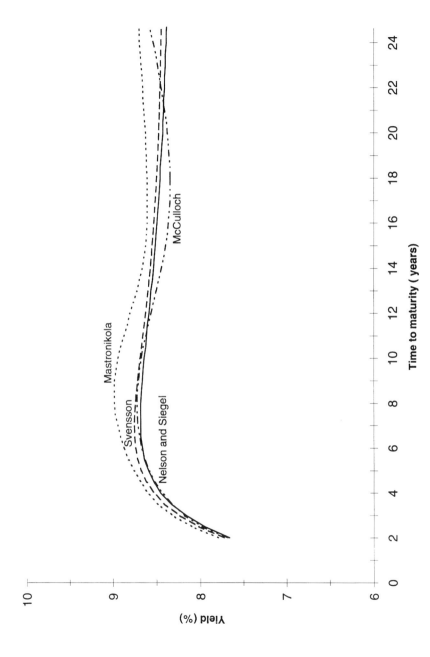

Figure 3.2 Zero-coupon yield curves — 11 October 1994

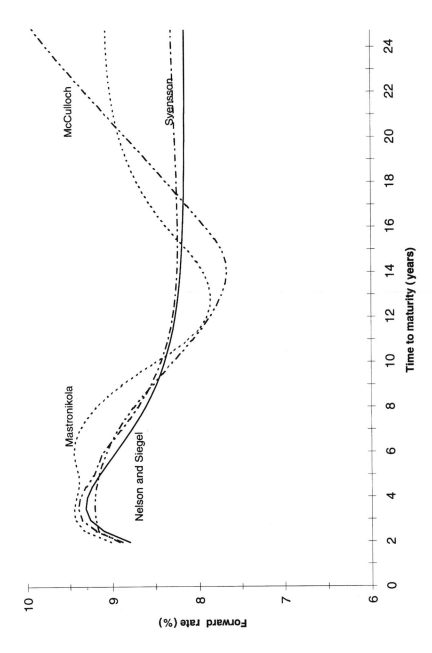

Figure 3.3   Forward rate curves — 11 October 1994

Observationally, in terms of the shape of the estimated yield curve, there would appear to be very little to choose between the four methods. Each gives an R^2 in the region of 0.95 to 0.99 and, despite differences in the level at which the yield curve is estimated, the four curves appear very similar in shape as a function of maturity. But for the forward rate curves implied by each model, shown in Figure 3.3, the differences between them are more striking.

Both the Svensson (1994) model and the Nelson and Siegel (1987) (N & S) model imply that forward rates smoothly gravitate towards a flattened long end whereas the McCulloch (1971, 1975) yield curve allows forward rates to fluctuate with maturity and rise steeply as the term to maturity lengthens beyond around 15 years. Combining characteristics of both, the forward rate curve implied by the Mastronikola (1991) model then flattens at the long end but exhibits greater curvature than either the Nelson and Siegel or Svensson yield curve models.

But what if the forward rates reflect expected future short rates? Then the McCulloch yield curve is clearly unsuitable at the long end since, even allowing for forward premia, it implies that these expectations tend towards infinity, the further they look into the future. The remaining three curves, on the other hand, reflect the common assumption that expectations of future interest rates are indistinguishable at the long end of the yield curve. In other words, as noted by Svensson (1994), investors are not expected to be any more informed about the future rate of interest in 25 years' time, say, than they are about the interest rate in 20 years' time.

3.3.2   THE CHOICE OF CURVE AND FUNCTIONAL FORM

Following Chapter 2, these four methodologies may be characterized in terms of their functional form and whether they fit a par yield curve or the discount function. These properties are listed in Table 3.1.

In reality, the Nelson and Siegel and Svensson models are simply the McCulloch model constrained to prevent the *forward curve* from taking undesirable shapes. In a sense, therefore, comparing the McCulloch model against the Svensson model (or the Nelson and Siegel model) can be viewed as a test of this restriction. Against the Mastronikola model, on the other hand, each of the other three models are evaluated with respect to the restriction imposed by the discount function, which constrains all coupon payments at a particular time in the future to be discounted at the same rate.

Table 3.1

	Curve	Functional form
Mastronikola	Par yield curve	Natural cubic spline
McCulloch	Discount function	Cubic spline
Nelson and Siegel	Discount function	Restricted functional form
Svensson	Discount function	More flexible version of N & S

Table 3.2

	Mastronikola	McCulloch	N & S	Svensson
Knot points	6	$\sqrt{n}^*$	–	–
Forward rate parameters	–	–	3	4
Maturity parameters	–	–	1	2
Tax effect parameters	4	4	4	4
XD, FOTRA[†]	2	–	–	–

[*]n is the number of bonds used to estimate the yield curve.

[†]XD refers to stocks which, at the time of estimation, are in their ex-dividend period. FOTRA refers to particular gilts which are designated Free Of Tax to Residents Abroad.

3.3.3   SMOOTHNESS VERSUS FLEXIBILITY

Each of the four yield curve models may be expressed as a non-linear regression of the general form[6]

$$y_i = f_i(\phi_i, X_i) + u_i \qquad u_i \sim N(0, \sigma^2) \tag{3.1}$$

where y_i is defined as the gross redemption yield on stock i. In each case, X_i is a vector of exogenous variables, typically consisting of bond i's coupon rate, c_i, maturity date, m_i, and accrued interest, AI_i. The vector, ϕ_i, represents the set of parameters characterizing each model and these are summarized by Table 3.2.

Notice that, of the four yield curve models, the Mastronikola yield curve is the only one to include dummy variables for ex-dividend and FOTRA effects, and is therefore better equipped to fit to individual stocks[7]. Furthermore, both the Mastronikola and McCulloch models estimate a spline function through a number of knot points, allowing the curves a fairly high degree of *flexibility*.

The drawback with highly flexible models is that they tend to overfit the data, giving a distorted view of the underlying situation. Similarly, if there are idiosyncrasies in the market which are not accounted for during the estimation process, the more flexible models are prone to treat these outliers as the norm. Conversely, the Nelson and Siegel and Svensson models, by constraining the implied forward rate curve, are implicitly promoting a more *stable* yield curve with reference to how the 'true' term structure is expected to behave. The interesting question is at what cost in terms of the accuracy of the fit is this stability achieved.

3.4   STATISTICAL METHODS

There are a number of empirical tests of the yield curve though many tend to concentrate on an isolated method of estimation. Fisher, Nychka and Zervos (1995), for example, apply a test of generalized cross-validation to their estimation procedure in order to control for the degree of flexibility of the curve and to avoid overfitting the data. Nelson and Siegel (1987), meanwhile, assess the validity of their model by testing whether it can predict yields or prices beyond the maturity range of the estimated sample. Dahlquist and Svensson (1994) take a more comparative approach, testing restricted and unrestricted versions of the Nelson and Siegel model against an application of the Longstaff and Schwartz (1993) model of the term structure (see Chapter 4).

3.4.1 DESCRIPTIVE STATISTICS

Two simple summary statistics which can be calculated for the estimated yield curve on any particular day are the mean average error and the root mean squared error. Denoted as the MAE, the first of these calculates the average difference between observed yields, y, and the set of fitted values, $\hat{y}$, derived for each stock i. It is calculated as:

$$\text{MAE} = \frac{\sum_{i=1}^{n} |y_{it} - \hat{y}_{it}| * 100}{n} \tag{3.2}$$

where n is the number of observations through which the curve is estimated. By scaling each statistic by 100, this measure is expressed in basis points where yields, y, are given in percentage points. Similarly, the root mean squared error or RMSE is calculated as:

$$\text{RMSE} = \left[\sum_{i=1}^{n} (y_{it} - \hat{y}_{it})^2 / n \right] * 100 \tag{3.3}$$

where by squaring each error term, this measure places greater weight upon larger errors and it therefore gives a greater indication as to how well the model fits the data at each particular observation.

Both sets of statistics measure errors as a general problem and do not distinguish between bias (consistent errors of one sign) and goodness-of-fit. The mean and standard deviation of each are measured over a number of days to demonstrate the trade-off between flexibility and reliability exhibited by each of the models. In other words, a low value for the mean of each measure is assumed to indicate that the model is flexible and, on average, is able to fit the yield curve fairly accurately. The standard deviation of each measure, on the other hand, indicates how reliable this fit is across the sample of trading days.

3.4.2 FORMAL TESTS

Each of the four yield curve models are not only non-linear but for each pairwise test they are also non-nested (i.e. one model is not simply a restricted version of the other). This is true even when testing the Svensson curve against the Nelson and Siegel model where, although the former is just a simple extension of the latter, the parameters defining each model can be thought as being positioned along a fixed portion of the curve. In order to maintain a balanced distribution of parameters over the maturity range, therefore, the inclusion of an additional parameter will cause those already in existence to shift along the curve, resulting in an extended but non-encompassing version of the original model.

Two formal tests which are available and are designed to cope with the fact that competing models are non-nested are the P test (see MacKinnon, White and Davidson, 1983) and the double-length regression test (see Davidson and MacKinnon, 1984) (DL test). The first of these is the easier to implement while the second has been shown by Pesaran and Pesaran (1994) to be the more powerful[8]. Each examines whether an alternative yield curve has any explanatory power over the set of error terms generated by the preferred model, defined as the null hypothesis. In general, the null and alternative hypotheses for each separate test may be written as:

$$H_0 : y_i = f_{0i}(\phi_{0i}, X_{0i}) + u_{0i} \tag{3.4}$$

$$H_1 : y_i = f_{1i}(\phi_{1i}, X_{1i}) + u_{1i} \tag{3.5}$$

where the set of fitted values in each case are denoted by a ' $\hat{}$ ' over the functions f_{0i} and f_{1i}. For a complete comparison of any two yield curve models, two sets of tests are performed, assuming a different null hypothesis in each case.

For the P test F_{0i} is defined as the vector of derivatives of f_{0i} with respect to the set of parameters, ϕ_{0i}, and the following regression is estimated:

$$y_i - \hat{f}_{0i} = \alpha(\hat{f}_{1i} - \hat{f}_{0i}) + \hat{F}_{0i} + v_{0i} \tag{3.6}$$

Under the null hypothesis, the estimated value of the parameter, α, is asymptotically distributed as $N(0,1)$, and a significant value suggests that the yield curve model which is held under the null should be rejected.

For the DL test each variable is defined in terms of a column vector so that u_0, for example, is an n-vector of error terms, u_{0i}. If y^* represents the vector, $\partial h_1(y)/\partial h_0(y)$, the DL test is based upon the regression:

$$\begin{bmatrix} u_0/\hat{\sigma}_0 \\ \tau \end{bmatrix} = \begin{bmatrix} -\hat{F}_0 \\ 0 \end{bmatrix} b + \begin{bmatrix} u_0/\hat{\sigma}_0 \\ -\tau \end{bmatrix} c + \begin{bmatrix} -u_1 \\ \hat{\sigma}_0 y^* \end{bmatrix} d + v_0 \tag{3.7}$$

Here, σ_0 is defined as the standard error of the residuals from the null hypothesis while τ represents a vector of ones of length n where n is the number of observations. Under the null hypothesis, defining SSR as the sum of squared residuals the statistic, $2n$-SSR, will be asymptotically distributed as χ^2 with one degree of freedom.

3.5   EMPIRICAL EVIDENCE

As an example the four yield curve models described above are compared. The data for each test are drawn from the UK gilts market over a period of 100 days in

1992. This is divided into two sample periods, 22 June to 28 August and 1 October to 9 December. September is excluded from the sample due to the atypical volatility exhibited by the market around Black Wednesday (16 September 1992). The first interval covers a period where the yield curve is downward sloping while observations for the latter imply an upward-sloping term structure. The number of stocks used to estimate the yield curve each day varies between 49 and 51. A detailed set of results is given in the Appendix. Tables A3.1 and A3.2 give the P test and DL test results respectively while summary statistics calculated over the two separate sample periods are given in Table A3.3.

3.5.1   RESULTS

On the whole, the P test fails to discriminate significantly between the competing yield curves. The Mastronikola yield curve does appear to behave slightly better than the rest, however, with Nelson and Siegel looking to be the weakest of the four models. Although the McCulloch model performs better than the Svensson curve when compared against the Mastronikola curve, a direct comparison of the two models appears to favour the Svensson yield curve. It is further interesting to note that each model appears to fit the data better in the first period, when the yield curve is downward sloping, than during the second period, when there is an upward-sloping term structure[9].

The DL test results serve to magnify both disparities between the various models and between results for the two separate sample periods. Table 3.3 summarizes the ratio of acceptances for curve 1 compared with curve 2, implied by the two types of test. Based on the double-length regression results, the Mastronikola model stands as a clear favourite, with Nelson and Siegel producing the worst performance. This time McCulloch's yield curve not only compares more favourably with the Mastronikola model than does the Svensson model but it also rejects the latter by a ratio of 2.11.

Looking at the summary statistics, the Mastronikola model is favoured by the two sets of tests. Not only does it consistently produce the lowest mean values of the MAE and RMSE, it also appears, on average, to be the most reliable of the four curves. Nelson and Siegel's yield curve appears to be the least flexible model across the sample period and produces the highest standard deviation figures for the MAE and the RMSE in the second period. In the first period, the parameters estimated by McCulloch's yield curve appear to be marginally less stable. The Svensson and McCulloch curves behave quite similarly, with the former holding a slight advantage in terms of reliability and the latter appearing to be marginally more flexible.

3.5.2   INTERPRETING THE RESULTS

When performing both the P test and the DL test, a number of assumptions are implicitly made. For example, the error terms, u_{0i} and u_{1i}, are typically

Table 3.3   Number of times curve 1 is accepted for every time curve 2 is accepted*

Curve 1 test	Curve 2	Period	P test	DL
Mastronikola model	Svensson model	Whole	1.95	∞
		1st	1.81	∞
		2nd	2.18	∞
Mastronikola model	McCulloch model	Whole	1.78	4.16
		1st	1.71	7.33
		2nd	1.86	2.69
Mastronikola model	Nelson and Siegel model	Whole	3.15	∞
		1st	3.45	∞
		2nd	2.85	∞
Svensson model	McCulloch model	Whole	1.11	0.47
		1st	0.96	0.60
		2nd	1.34	0.07
Svensson model	Nelson and Siegel model	Whole	0.98	1.50
		1st	1.16	1.50
		2nd	0.82	0
McCulloch model	Nelson and Siegel model	Whole	1.58	4.50
		1st	1.34	3.42
		2nd	2.13	∞

*A '∞' indicates that curve 2 was accepted 0 times.

assumed to be normally distributed with constant variance σ^2. The results should be qualified therefore by the possibility that there may be a loss in power of the tests if such assumptions are violated. It is perhaps worth noting, however, that Godfrey, McAleer and McKenzie (1988) suggest that, when errors are non-normally distributed, the P test is fairly robust[10].

Formal tests of alternative yield curves tend to favour the Mastronikola model. Summary statistics, calculated over the entire length of the curve, support this choice as it not only produces the lowest errors on average but it also appears to be the most reliable of the four models. But notice that each of these tests fail to make any adjustment for the number of parameters included in the estimation procedure. Thus the 'success' of the Mastronikola yield curve may simply be a function of its excess number of parameters over the competing models.

Nelson and Siegel's yield curve is favoured the least while the choice between the Svensson and McCulloch yield curves is less certain given that the former is generally more reliable while the latter allows for a greater degree of flexibility. But with regard to flexibility it is worth noting that the stocks used to estimate the four yield curves include callable bonds which are invariably difficult to model.

One reason why the Mastronikola and McCulloch yield curves tend to compare favourably with the other two in terms of average errors might be that they are flexible enough to fit through observations on callables, even though the inclusion of such stocks may, in fact, be distortionary.

3.6   CONCLUSION

When comparing alternative methods of yield curve estimation, there are various factors to consider: for example, the particular characteristics of the bond market and one's personal preferences regarding the behaviour of the yield curve. But it is also important to test how much the restrictions imposed by a particular model affect its fit. The trade-off between smoothness and flexibility is then largely subjective given the difference in fit, relative to a more flexible functional form, and given one's preferences regarding the shape of the implied forward rate curve.

APPENDIX: SET OF RESULTS

Table A3.1   P-test results for pairwise tests of competing models

Curve 1	Curve 2	Period	Accept 1 (%)	Accept 2 (%)
Mastronikola model	Svensson model	Whole	86	44
		1st	98	54
		2nd	74	34
Mastronikola model	McCulloch model	Whole	89	50
		1st	96	56
		2nd	82	44
Mastronikola model	Nelson and Siegel model	Whole	84.5	26.8
		1st	95.7	27.7
		2nd	74	26
Svensson model	McCulloch model	Whole	91	82
		1st	96	100
		2nd	86	64
Svensson model	Nelson and Siegel model	Whole	82.5	84.5
		1st	91.5	76.7
		2nd	74	90
McCulloch model	Nelson and Siegel model	Whole	81.5	51.6
		1st	100	74.5
		2nd	64	30

Table A3.2 Double-length regression results for pairwise tests of competing models

Curve 1	Curve 2	Period	Accept 1 (%)	Accept 2 (%)
Mastronikola model	Svensson model	Whole	78	0
		1st	88	0
		2nd	68	0
Mastronikola model	McCulloch model	Whole	79	19
		1st	88	12
		2nd	70	26
Mastronikola model	Nelson and Siegel model	Whole	80.4	0
		1st	93.6	0
		2nd	68	0
Svensson model	McCulloch model	Whole	27	57
		1st	52	86
		2nd	2	28
Svensson model	Nelson and Siegel model	Whole	21.6	14.4
		1st	44.7	29.8
		2nd	0	0
McCulloch model	Nelson and Siegel model	Whole	55.7	12.4
		1st	87.2	25.5
		2nd	26	0

Table A3.3 Summary statistics

Curve	MAE mean	MAE Std dev.	RMSE Mean	RMSE Std dev.
1st period				
Mastronikola model	4.32	0.19	5.8	0.28
Svensson model	4.58	0.23	6.16	0.28
McCulloch model	4.62	0.35	6.13	0.36
Nelson and Siegel model	4.86	0.28	6.54	0.35
2nd Period				
Mastronikola model	5.65	0.43	7.36	0.73
Svensson model	6.87	0.52	8.58	0.65
McCulloch model	6.76	0.61	8.58	0.73
Nelson and Siegel model	8.57	1.13	10.75	1.66

NOTES

1. Callable gilts with a final redemption date are often referred to by market practitioners as *double-dated* gilts.
2. In fact, in the UK, according to the terms attached to callable gilts, HM Treasury is required to give three months notice of its intention to 'call' a bond. It can, however, make the announcement three months prior to the first date, thus allowing the call to be made at the earliest opportunity.

3. A futures contract effectively exists on a specific bond if it is in the basket of deliverable stocks and is likely to be the 'cheapest to deliver' bond — or very close to it — at the delivery date.
4. This date is chosen purely arbitrarily.
5. This avoids the need to apply a 'filter' to select a subset of useable bonds, as advocated by Schaefer (1981). See Chapter 5 for further details.
6. In practice, the yield curve can be estimated by minimizing price errors *or* yield errors where each method is likely to produce a slightly different set of results. The implicit assumption here is that bond yields are the main focus of the exercise, for example for the purpose of assessing monetary conditions (see Svensson (1994)). For asset pricing purposes, it may well be preferable to focus on a yield curve model estimated by minimizing price errors.
7. In principle, the other three models may be modified to incorporate these parameters, in which case one might expect their performance to be enhanced.
8. Specifically, their results relate to a comparison of linear and log linear regression models.
9. This does not necessarily imply, however, that each model fits a downward-sloping yield curve better than an upward-sloping one. There are likely to be other differences between the two sample periods. For example, during the first, the exchange rate is constrained within a target zone regime while the second occurs after the UK's departure from the ERM. The second may therefore be subject to more uncertainty, in which case a greater margin of error in fitting the curve would be expected.
10. This result is based upon a test of linear against log-linear regression models.

REFERENCES

Dahlquist, M. and Svensson, L. E. O. (1994) Estimating the term structure of interest rates with simple and complex functional forms: Nelson & Siegel vs. Longstaff & Schwartz, University of Stockholm Seminar Paper No. 565.

Davidson, R. and MacKinnon, J. G. (1984) Model specification test based on artificial linear regressions, *International Economic Review*, **25**, 485–501.

Fisher, M., Nychka, D. and Zervos, D. (1995) Fitting the term structure of interest rates with smoothing splines, Federal Reserve Bank Finance and Economics Discussion Paper 95, 1 January.

Godfrey, L. G., McAleer, M. and McKenzie, C. R. (1988) Variable addition and Lagrange multiplier tests for linear and logarithmic regression models, *Review of Economic Statistics*, **70**, 492–503.

Longstaff, F. and Schwartz, E. (1993) Implementation of the Longstaff–Schwartz interest rate model, *Journal of Fixed Income*.

MacKinnon, J. G., White, H. and Davidson, R. (1983) Tests for model specification in the presence of alternative hypotheses: some further results, *Journal of Econometrica*, **21**, 53–70.

Mastronikola, K. (1991) Yield curves for gilt-edged stocks: a new model, Bank of England Discussion Paper (Technical Series), 49.

McCulloch, J. H. (1971) Measuring the term structure of interest rates, *Journal of Business*, **XLIV** (January), 19–31.

McCulloch, J. H. (1975) The tax-adjusted yield curve, *Journal of Finance*, **30**, 811–830.

Nelson, C. R. and Siegel, A. F. (1987) Parsimonious modeling of yield curves, *Journal of Business*, **60**, 473–89.

Pesaran, M. H. and Pesaran, B. (1994) A non-nested test of level-differenced versus log-differenced stationary models, *Econometric Reviews*, forthcoming.

Schaefer, S. M. (1981) Measuring a tax-specific term structure of interest rates in the market for British government securities, *Economic Journal*, **91**, 121–59.

Svensson, L. E. O. (1994) Estimating and interpreting forward interest rates: Sweden 1992–94, International Monetary Fund Working Paper No. 114, September.

CHAPTER 4

Equilibrium term structure models

4.1 INTRODUCTION

This chapter brings together some of the main ideas from theoretical finance which permeate the literature on term structure models. For more complete reading in this area, the reader is directed towards Ingersoll (1987), Merton (1990), Duffie (1992) and Strickland (1994) to name just a few. While avoiding much of the detail of what is a very technical area, it is hoped that in illustrating the tools of term structure modelling, this chapter gives insights into a framework which allows for the pricing of all term structure securities, not just bonds. It shows that the task of fitting the term structure is part of an overall problem of constructing a dynamic model of the term structure.

Security pricing starts with the concept of 'no-arbitrage equilibrium'. In essence, an arbitrage opportunity exists when two assets (or equivalent portfolios) are mispriced relative to one another. The mispricing allows an investor to make a riskless (certain) profit by selling the dearer asset and using part of the proceeds of this sale to buy the cheaper asset so that a (positive) remainder of cash is left over as profit. This is a relative price equilibrium in the sense that the absence of arbitrage imposes a relationship between the asset prices. This is not the most restrictive form of equilibrium that one can impose on a securities markets — Cox, Ingersoll and Ross (1985a) and Bick (1990) discuss asset prices in an equilibrium determined as a consequence of the actions of utility-maximizing agents — but it is the most important. Asset-pricing models that admit of exploitable arbitrage opportunities will be unstable. That said, in the reality of modern financial markets, a no-arbitrage equilibrium is in fact a paradox in the sense that it is the very existence of arbitragers who capitalize on arbitrage opportunities as they arise which means that markets can be regarded as functioning *as if* in a no-arbitrage equilibrium.

In the next section the relationship between no-arbitrage and risk-neutral pricing is discussed. The role of risk-neutral pricing — due to Cox and Ross (1976) and Harrison and Kreps (1979) — in finance is probably the next most important result after the advances in option pricing due to Black and Scholes (1973). It has much intuitive and computational appeal and can often simplify security pricing problems. It is not a panacea, however. Some security pricing problems are often best tackled using classical techniques of solving partial differential equations, as in the seminal paper of Black and Scholes.

In these models, prices are driven by random processes which by their uncertain nature are risky. This is formalized by defining state variables characterizing the state of the economy (relevant to the determination of the term structure) which are driven by these random processes and are related in some way to the prices of bonds. In no-arbitrage equilibrium models, particular attention is focused on the market prices of the sources of risk (randomness) in the economy. Examples are given of these models in Section 4.3. However, the risk-neutral pricing approach leads to an alternative 'evolutionary' modelling approach where market prices of risk need not be identified, and this is discussed in Section 4.4.

Section 4.5 provides an assessment of the models and modelling strategies. There are no set criteria for appraising models, certainly the practitioner is likely to have a different set of priorities compared to the theoretician. In some ways, these differences hark back to the ideas of Friedman (1958) when he contrasted the testing of models on the basis of the validity of their assumptions with the testing of models on the basis of their predictions. On the other hand, the differences often reduce to matters of implementation within a trading context.

4.2   A MODEL OF THE TERM STRUCTURE

In Chapter 8 we discuss the expectations hypothesis of the yield curve drawing on Cox, Ingersoll and Ross (1981) (henceforth referred to as CIR). In that paper, a general framework for pricing term securities in a continuous-time economy is presented. In this section, the general pricing equation for term structure securities given in that paper will be used to highlight the main elements of models of the term structure. This is not the most general framework for pricing interest rate securities but it will suffice in achieving one of the aims of this section, namely to introduce the *principal building blocks* in term structure models.

In constructing models of the term structure we make assumptions about:

(1)   How the economy is characterized: which features of the economy are sufficient to describe the investment and consumption opportunities for agents?

(2)   How agents behave in this economy. Do they maximize expected utility of consumption where decisions must be made about how much wealth to consume and how much to invest for the future?

(3)   How do markets function? Are there any institutional features which inhibit free trade e.g. taxes, transactions costs, quantity constraints, short sales restrictions? No-arbitrage models of the term structure assume that agents'

behaviour is consistent with the elimination of arbitrage opportunities in the market for tradable assets.

In the following model of the term structure, we assume that the prices of such bonds are determined by the underlying economy, the state of which is denoted by S_t — which may be a vector of variables. Considerable structure can be added to the model by creating a model for the determination of the state variable, S_t. For example, S_t might be a two-dimensional vector with elements corresponding to current inflation and real interest rates, which determine the current level of nominal interest rates. The dynamics of S_t might be described by underlying macroeconomic variables, for example money supply, the level of real GDP and some measure of external prices. To our knowledge, few models add such economic structure to the description of the state variable which underlies the term structure. Cox, Ingersoll and Ross (1985a) do present an intertemporal general equilibrium asset-pricing model from which their famous model (1985b) is constructed. However, to the extent that economists (conventionally) think of interest rates as being determined, for example in their role as an instrument in a counter-inflationary policy within an economic/political cycle, it is unclear how this could be incorporated into a general equilibrium model. Thus the macroeconomist and the financial economist are likely to speak in two different languages when exchanging ideas on the interest rate term structure.

The following paragraphs set out a no-arbitrage model of the term structure. Many of the technical details giving regularity conditions for the equations to be well-defined are glossed over — the interested reader is referred to Heath, Jarrow and Morton (1992).

Let $P(S_t, t, T)$ denote the current (time t) price of a zero-coupon bond which promises (without risk of default) to pay £1 at time T, i.e. $T - t$ periods from now. Suppose that the price of the zero-coupon bond evolves over time according to the following stochastic differential equation[1] which describes the changes in the asset price over short periods of time:

$$\frac{dP}{P} = \mu(S_t, t, T)\, dt + \sum_{j=1}^{s} \sigma_j(S_t, t, T)\, dB_{j,t} \qquad (4.1)$$

where μ is the drift of the bond price and σ_j is volatility[2] which scales the shocks of the jth Brownian motion $\{B_{j,t}, t \geq 0\}$. The Brownian motions also drive the state variables S_t (see equation (8.9)) and are assumed to be independent. Brownian motion is the most popular tool for introducing randomness (and hence risk) in the model[3]. The first term $\mu(S_t, t, T)$ determines the local drift (or instantaneous mean) of the process over time, the $\sigma_j(S_t, t, T)$ functions determine the local volatility (or instantaneous standard deviation) about this mean.

Consider a portfolio of $s + 1$ zero-coupon bonds of value V with[4] proportionate investment x_i (so that $\Sigma_i x_i = 1$) in each zero-coupon bond which is identified by its maturity T_i. Then

$$V = \sum_{i=1}^{s+1} x_i P(S_t, t, T_i) \tag{4.2}$$

and the proportionate change in the value of the portfolio over a short interval may be written as

$$\frac{dV}{V} = \sum_{i=1}^{s+1} x_i \frac{dP(S, t, T_i)}{P(S, t, T_i)} \tag{4.3}$$

We may choose x_i so that[5]

$$\sum_{i=1}^{s+1} x_i \sigma_j(S, t, T_i) = 0 \qquad j = 1, 2, \ldots, s \tag{4.4}$$

The portfolio composition of each asset is adjusted continuously so that (4.4) holds, in effect each x_i is a function of time t. Thus the portfolio is riskless, in the sense that at each point in time, the change in its value (over a short interval of time) is known. In a bond market where arbitrage opportunities are precluded, this portfolio must earn the same (instantaneous) return as the short rate at time t (denoted by r_t) where this rate corresponds to the return on a default-free zero-coupon bond of (infinitesimally) short maturity. Thus

$$\sum_{i=1}^{s+1} x_i(\mu_i(S, t, T_i) - r_t) = 0 \tag{4.5}$$

since $\Sigma_i x_i = 1$. Combining (4.4) and (4.5), we obtain $s + 1$ equations in $s + 1$ unknowns (namely the portfolio weights $\{x_1, \ldots, x_{s+1}\}$) which holds locally. This is the equilibrium condition which must hold if arbitrage opportunities are to be precluded in the market for zero-coupon bonds.

4.2.1 RISK PREMIA

Since $\{x_1, \ldots, x_{s+1}\}$ are not all necessarily zero, it follows that the $(s + 1) \times (s + 1)$ matrix M, which is given by

$$M = \begin{bmatrix} \sigma_1(S_t, t, T_1) & \sigma_1(S_t, t, T_2) & \cdots & \sigma_1(S_t, t, T_{s+1}) \\ \vdots & \vdots & \ddots & \vdots \\ \sigma_s(S_t, t, T_1) & \sigma_s(S_t, t, T_2) & \cdots & \sigma_s(S_t, t, T_{s+1}) \\ \mu_1(S_t, t, T_1) - r_t & \mu_2(S_t, t, T_2) - r_t & \cdots & \mu_{SH}(S_t, t, T_{s+1}) - r_t \end{bmatrix}$$

must have a rank which is strictly less than $s + 1$. Hence, there exist $\Lambda = (\lambda_1, \ldots, \lambda_{s+1})^T$ such that $\Lambda^T M = 0$. This follows since a square matrix with less than full column rank must have less than full row rank. We can rewrite this as

$$(-\lambda_{s+1})(\mu_j(S, t, T_j) - r_t) = \sum_{i=1}^{s} \lambda_i \sigma_i(S, t, T_j) \qquad j = 1, 2, \ldots, s+1 \quad (4.6)$$

Observe that since $\{\lambda_1, \ldots, \lambda_{s+1}\}$ implies a linear relationship between the rows of M, the selection of zero-coupon bond maturities is arbitrary and hence $\{\lambda_1, \ldots, \lambda_{s+1}\}$ is independent of the maturity of the bonds. Heath, Jarrow and Morton (1992) call this the *standard finance condition*, since it is equivalent to the absence of arbitrage and applies across markets for all assets not just term structure contingent claims (see also Duffie, 1992; Varian, 1987). Furthermore, we may choose a set of discount bonds such that $\lambda_{s+1} \neq 0$. (Since if $\lambda_{s+1} = 0$ then the right-hand-side of (4.6) equals zero so that we can write (at least) one of the volatility functions in terms of the others. As a consequence the system (4.1) could be defined in terms of (at most) $s - 1$ independent Brownian motions with no loss in information, which is a contradiction.) Normalize $\{\lambda_1, \ldots, \lambda_{s+1}\}$ by setting $\lambda_{s+1} = -1$. This gives

$$\mu(S, t, T) - r_t = \sum_{i=1}^{s} \lambda_i \sigma_i(S, t, T) \qquad j = 1, 2, \ldots, s+1, \quad \forall T \geq t \quad (4.7)$$

which is a fundamental equation in no-arbitrage pricing theory. This is often reinterpreted to mean that the drift of an asset price equals the risk-free rate plus a premium which depends on the sources of risk in the underlying economy. The parameters $\{\lambda_1, \ldots, \lambda_{s+1}\}$ are called market prices of risk corresponding to these individual sources of risk. Equation (4.7) shows that the market prices of risk determine the risk premium over the riskless rate which investors require to compensate for taking on the risks. Therefore, the required rate of return for holding a risky asset is the sum of the riskless return and the risk premium (above) where the σ-functions correspond to the asset in question, as in (4.1). Chapter 9 discusses empirical tests of the expectations hypothesis of the term structure and (4.7) shows that theoretical models of the term structure imply the existence of risk premia in general and that zero risk premia are a special case. The only restriction placed on the market prices of risk which determine the risk premia is that arbitrage opportunities are excluded. Heath, Jarrow and Morton (1992) give the technical details on this matter.

4.2.2   TERM STRUCTURE SECURITIES VALUATION

Given a set of s bonds such that

$$\Delta = \begin{bmatrix} \sigma_1(S_t, t, T_1) & \cdots & \sigma_1(S_t, t, T_s) \\ \vdots & \ddots & \vdots \\ \sigma_s(S_t, t, T_1) & \cdots & \sigma_s(S_t, t, T_s) \end{bmatrix}$$

is invertible, we may solve for $(\lambda_1, \ldots, \lambda_s)^T = (\Delta^T)^{-1} \cdot (\mu_1 - R_t, \ldots, \mu_s - R_t)^T$. Substituting for $(\lambda_1, \ldots, \lambda_s)^T$ in (4.7) above, we would have a pricing equation for zero-coupon bonds if we knew the relationship between $\mu(S_t, t, T_i)$ (local drift) and $\sigma_j(S_t, t, T_i)$ (local diffusion) with the price of the zero-coupon bond. Using Itô's formula, we write equation (4.1) in terms of the state variables as follows:

$$dP = \left[\sum_{i=1}^{s} \left(\alpha_i(S_t, t, T) \frac{dP}{dS_i} + \frac{1}{2} \sum_{j=1}^{s} \beta_{i,j}(S_t, t, T) \frac{d^2 P}{dS_i dS_j} \right) + \frac{dP}{dt} \right] dt$$

$$+ \sum_{j=1}^{s} \sum_{i=1}^{s} \beta_{i,j}(S_t, t, T) \frac{dP}{dS_i} dB_{j,t} \tag{4.8}$$

where the state of the economy at time t is given by the s state variables $S_t = \{S_{1,t}, \ldots, S_{s,t}\}$ which are assumed to evolve according to

$$dS_{i,t} = \alpha_i(S_t, t, T) \, dt + \sum_{j=1}^{s} \beta_{i,j}(S_t, t, T) \, dB_{j,t} \qquad i = 1, 2, \ldots, s \tag{4.9}$$

whence

$$\mu(S_t, t, T)P = \sum_{i=1}^{s} \left(\alpha_i(S_t, t, T) \frac{dP}{dS_i} + \frac{1}{2} \sum_{j=1}^{s} \beta_{i,j}(S_t, t, T) \frac{d^2 P}{dS_i dS_j} \right) + \frac{dP}{dt} \tag{4.10a}$$

and

$$\sigma_j(S_t, t, T)P = \sum_{i=1}^{s} \beta_{i,j}(S_t, t, T) \frac{dP}{dS_i} \qquad j = 1, 2, \ldots, s \tag{4.10b}$$

Note that the functions $\sigma_j(S_t, t, T)$ may not be constant functions in T, therefore in the case of zero-coupon bonds, they give rise to a theoretical *volatility term structure* which may be compared to the actual volatility term structure which is implied from prices of options on zero-coupon bonds.

Using (4.10a,b), we may write (4.7) as

$$\sum_{i=1}^{s} \left(\left(\alpha_i(S_t, t, T) - \sum_{j=1}^{s} \beta_{i,j}(S_t, t, T)\lambda_i \right) \frac{dP_t}{ds_i} + \frac{1}{2} \sum_{j=1}^{s} \beta_{i,j}(S_t, t, T) \frac{d^2 P_t}{ds_i ds_j} \right)$$

$$+ \frac{dP_t}{dt} - r_t P_t = 0 \tag{4.11}$$

where the adjusted drift terms are given by

$$\delta_i(S_t, t, T) = \alpha_i(S_t, t, T) - \sum_{j=1}^{s} \beta_{i,j}(S_t, t, T)\lambda_i \qquad i = 1, 2, \ldots, s$$

This is the fundamental valuation equation for the price of zero-coupon bonds, with the boundary condition $P(S, t, T) = 1$[6]. In fact, with appropriate boundary conditions, this equation can be used to value all term structure contingent claims.

4.2.3   RISK-NEUTRAL PRICING

One interesting consequence of the above result is given by the Feynman–Kac formula[7]. Given the above terminal condition for the value of the zero-coupon bond, it follows that

$$P(S_t, t, T) = E\left(\exp\left\{-\int_t^T r_s \, ds\right\} \Big| S_t\right) \qquad (4.12)$$

where the above expectation is taken with respect to the probability distribution for the state variables when they evolve according to the *risk-adjusted* stochastic differential equations

$$dS_{i,t} = \left(\alpha_i(S_t, t, T) - \sum_{j=1}^s \beta_{i,j}(S_t, t, T)\lambda_j\right) dt + \sum_{j=1}^s \beta_{i,j}(S_t, t, T) \, dB_{j,t}$$

$$i = 1, 2, \ldots, s \qquad (4.13)$$

In effect, the price of a zero-coupon bond is the expected discounted value of £1 at time T where the expectation is taken with respect to a *risk-adjusted process* for the state variables. Many other contingent claims can be valued in this way, though care must be taken to incorporate the boundary conditions when taking the expectation[8].

We noted in reference to (4.7) that risk premia existed, in general, thus complicating a formulation of the expectations hypothesis of the term structure. However, (4.12) presents the expectations hypothesis in a different light — prices are expectations of future pay-offs and (4.12) can be reworked for the purposes of empirical investigation to test the proposition that forward rates are efficient expectations of future interest rates but only in the world of a risk-adjusted state variable process which we do not observe. This means that in constructing equations to test a version of the expectations hypothesis which is consistent with the above model, we should allow for the presence of risk premia, in general.

To the extent that the form of the state variables has been left unspecified, this equation is really an 'empty mathematical shell'. Where the relationship between the state variables and the zero-coupon bond prices is unclear, the expressions we might obtain after solving for the market prices of risk may not identify the market prices if risk is in terms of the state variables. Additional structure must be added to equations (4.10a,b) to provide equations which are amenable to analytical or numerical solution. Heath, Jarrow and Morton (1992) show that a judicious choice of state variables makes the framework outlined above workable. They demonstrate that by considering the forward curve as the state variable — which has a simple relationship with zero-coupon bond prices — the market prices of risk may be readily obtained. They establish the regularity conditions on the process generating the forward curve under which a no-arbitrage equilibrium exists.

4.2.4 SUMMARY

The literature in this area draws heavily on some mathematical tools which to a large extent have been avoided in this section. The main result is that a no-arbitrage model of the term structure allows us to price bonds *as if* in a risk-neutral world, that is, by taking expected values of discounted payoffs. As Cox, Ingersoll and Ross (1981) are careful to point out, this does not imply the existence of a general equilibrium economy under which risk-neutral behaviour by economic agents is necessarily rational, rather it affords us with a powerful tool for pricing contingent claims in general. Duffie (1992) includes a useful overview of these ideas and he also highlights the role of Arrow–Debreu state-price theory in this context.

In arriving at (4.11), we have encountered some of the main building blocks of term structure models:

- A set of state variables $\{S_{i,t}, i = 1, 2, \ldots, s, t \geq 0\}$ which describe the relevant economy underpinning the term structure — in a general equilibrium economy the evolution of these variables is endogenous to the structure of the economy and actions of economic agents

- The 'dimension' of the term structure is given by the number of state variables, s, which are in turn generated by s independent Brownian motion processes

- A (default-free) interest rate process $\{r_t, t \geq 0\}$, corresponding to the return on a zero-coupon bond of (infinitesimally) short maturity

- Market prices of risk $\{\lambda_1, \ldots, \lambda_s\}$ due to different sources of randomness in the economy

- Equilibrium in the market for term structure securities arising from the requirement that arbitrage opportunities are precluded.

We see that these components are interrelated through the constraint of a no-arbitrage equilibrium. As Heath, Jarrow and Morton (1992, pp. 88–9) note: 'The dynamics for the bond price process, the spot rate process, and the market prices of risk cannot be chosen independently. Independently specifying these processes will in general lead to inconsistent models.'

The key results of note state that a no-arbitrage equilibrium imposes technical conditions on a model. First, we have the standard finance condition which says that no-arbitrage equilibrium is equivalent to the existence of market prices for the different sources of risk in the economy. Second, we have that a no-arbitrage equilibrium corresponds to the existence of a risk-adjusted state variable process under which securities may be priced as discounted expectations of future payoffs, as if in a risk-neutral world. Third, the expectations hypothesis of the term structure can be reformulated in a world where prices are driven by a risk-adjusted state variable process which is a convenient theoretical result but presents complications for empirical tests.

4.3   EQUILIBRIUM MODELS

This section provides some popular examples of models of the term structure which have been constructed for a given choice of state price processes where some notion of equilibrium in the economy is explicitly captured in the construction of the model. In addition, some of the models could be also be viewed as providing functional forms for discount functions, as in Chapter 2. Certainly, when thinking of the applicability of these models, it is helpful to bear in mind the comments of Chapters 2 and 3.

This and the following section mention three approaches to modelling the term structure:

(1)   Construct a general equilibrium model of the term structure in an economy with a representative agent where the market prices are endogenous to the structure of the economy and the optimal behaviour of the representative economic agent.

(2)   Follow the no-arbitrage approach of the previous section to determine the market prices of risk.

(3)   Apply the no-arbitrage result mentioned at the end of the previous section to obtain the risk-neutral process for the state variable which subsumes (but does not identify) the market price of risk.

However, to the extent that no-arbitrage equilibrium is a condition which we require of all term structure models, (1) and (2) must be equivalent in the sense that if we strip the general equilibrium model down to its bare essentials, namely, a state variable process, we should be able to apply the no-arbitrage methodology of Section 4.2 to arrive at the same model (unless there are multiple market prices of risk). Heath, Jarrow and Morton (1992) show that this is indeed the case and in particular, apply their methodology in the case of the (single-factor) general equilibrium model of Cox, Ingersoll and Ross (1985b).

4.3.1   VASICEK'S MODEL

Vasicek (1977) provides a model which is a single state variable application of the framework described in Section 4.2. Despite the relative simplicity of the model, the paper is notable for the fact that it uses many of the tools of modern bond pricing theory before they were popularized in the late 1980s. The single-state variable is conveniently chosen to be the short rate. This is assumed to evolve as

$$dr_t = \kappa(\varphi - r_t) + \sigma \, dB_t \qquad (4.14)$$

where φ is the asymptotic mean of the short rate, κ is the rate of mean reversion and σ determines the local volatility of the process for a given value of r_t. In (4.14), the short rate reverts towards its asymptotic mean of φ. However, it may be negative with positive probability — a feature which is often described as unrealistic of models which assume this process. The counter-argument often offered is that for appropriate values of κ, φ and σ, the probability of negative short rates is very small. There is a single constant market price of risk, $\lambda(r) = \theta$. The Vasicek version of (4.11) is

$$\frac{1}{2}\sigma^2 \frac{d^2 P_t}{dr^2} + (\kappa(\varphi - r) - \sigma\theta)\frac{dP_t}{dr} - rP_t + \frac{dP_t}{dt} = 0 \qquad (4.15)$$

with the appropriate boundary conditions. The price of a zero-coupon bond is given as

$$P(r, t, T) = \exp\left(\frac{1}{\alpha}(1 - e^{-\kappa(T-t)})(R_\infty - r) - (T - t)R_\infty\right.$$

$$\left. - \frac{\sigma^2}{4\kappa}(1 - e^{-\kappa(T-t)})\right) \qquad t \le T \qquad (4.16)$$

where $R_\infty = \varphi + \sigma\lambda/\kappa + \lambda^2/(2\sigma^2)$ — the yield on a consol. The discount function depends on the four parameters κ, φ, σ and θ and the level of the short rate at time t.

4.3.2   THE MODEL OF COX, INGERSOLL AND ROSS

The most comprehensive treatment of models in a general equilibrium framework is given in Cox, Ingersoll and Ross (1985a). They develop an intertemporal general equilibrium model of asset prices. In CIR (1985b) they apply this framework to construct one- and two-factor models of the term structure. In the case of the one-factor model, the structure of the general equilibrium effectively reduces to a state variable in the form of the short rate which evolves according to

$$dr_t = \kappa(\varphi - r_t) + \sigma\sqrt{r_t} \, dB_t \qquad (4.17)$$

and a market price of risk which emerges after solving for the representative agent's optimal consumption path.

Despite their differing equilibrium assumptions, the principal difference between this model and that of Vasicek is the square-root term in the local volatility. This precludes interest rates from being negative and when $2\kappa\varphi \geq \sigma^2$, the short rate is strictly positive. Later we shall see that there is only modest empirical support for this model of the short rate process. However, it should be noted at this juncture that in a modelling exercise such as this, the form of the stochastic differential equation is often the consequence of a judicious choice of state variable processes motivated by the need to have an analytically tractable model. It is worth noting that the only economic insights which guide the description of the short rate are (1) non-negative nominal interest rates and (2) the boundedness of interest rates, which is formalized through mean reverting drift.

CIR show that the assumption of constant relative risk aversion preferences for the representative investor implies that the risk premium on the short rate is proportional to the level of the state variable which for convenience is chosen to be the short rate. In the notation of Section 4.2, this means that the market price of risk is given by $\lambda(r) = \theta\sqrt{r}/\sigma$. Therefore, the general pricing equation simplifies to

$$\frac{1}{2}\sigma^2 r\frac{d^2 P_t}{dr^2} + (\kappa(\varphi - r) - \theta r)\frac{dP_t}{dr} - rP_t + \frac{dP_t}{dt} = 0 \qquad (4.18)$$

with the appropriate boundary condition depending on the asset being priced.

To summarize, these two single-factor models show that given the process for the short rate and a market price of risk, a pricing equation for any contingent claim can be given according to (4.11) with the appropriate boundary conditions. Despite the fact that the CIR model is developed from a general equilibrium framework we see that with appropriately defined state variables and market prices of risk, general equilibrium models can be readily viewed in the context of the no-arbitrage framework of Section 4.2. The Vasicek model establishes no-arbitrage equilibrium in exactly the same way as in the derivation of (4.11). Many other models follow this latter approach, but problems may arise if market price of risk is mis-specified. CIR (1985b) give an example where arbitrary specification of the market price of risk leads to a model which admits of arbitrage opportunities.

4.3.3   FITTING THE MODELS

In practice, when these models are fitted to bond data, the market price of risk parameters are subsumed into the mean reversion parameters so that they need not be explicitly identified. This corresponds to the term structure being driven by the risk-adjusted processes:

$$dr_t = \kappa(\varphi + \theta - r_t) + \sigma\sqrt{r_t}\,dB_t$$

in the case of the Vasicek model and

$$dr_t = (\kappa + \theta)\left(\frac{\kappa\varphi}{\kappa + \theta} - r_t\right) + \sigma\sqrt{r_t}\,dB_t$$

in the case of the CIR model. Of course, this means that only the risk-adjusted short rate process is identified, as opposed to the true process. Section 4.2 showed that securities are priced *as if* in a world where agents are risk-neutral but this does not mean that the economy can be viewed as being driven by the actions of agents who are in fact risk-neutral. This leads to difficulties of interpretation insofar as one would wish to relate the estimated parameters with one's priors concerning the term structure. For example, the asymptotic mean for the short rate is no longer φ, but $\varphi + \theta$ for the Vasicek model and $\kappa\varphi/(\kappa + \theta)$ for the CIR model. This can make the task of explaining the fitted model parameters to macroeconomists quite tricky. (Section 4.4 goes further, by considering models which start with the risk-adjusted state variable process, thereby ignoring altogether market prices of risk and the true process for the state variables.)

If we ignore equilibrium considerations, these models can be viewed as providing analytical functional forms for discount functions, as in Chapter 2. The advantage of these models lies in the fact that the structure for the short rate process constrains the zero-coupon term structures (1) at the short end to be equal to the short rate and (2) at the long end to be equal to some function of the asymptotic mean of the short rate, φ. In addition, unlike some curve-fitting approaches, e.g. cubic splines, the forward curves implied by the fitted discount functions are less 'volatile' since there is less freedom to overfit the data. Other models of this kind, (e.g. Longstaff and Schwartz, 1992) possess similar properties and have the additional advantage that their functional forms are more flexible so that they can be fit more accurately to different initial term structures.

In practice, these single factor models overly restrict the dynamics of the term structure and fit the term structure quite poorly. To rectify this two approaches are often followed. First, the models of the short rate process are made more flexible in a manner to be described in the next section. Alternatively, a second approach is to increase the number of random factors (state variables) driving the term structure. This leads to increased flexibility of the functional form of the discount bond pricing equation at the expense of complicating the pricing equation (4.11).

4.4 'EVOLUTIONARY' MODELS

This section describes how practitioners place additional demands on the models they use. We start by discussing some criteria for model selection and then move on to consider the shift by practitioners from general equilibrium models to 'evolutionary' models. Practitioners seek a model which, among other things,

- They readily understand what changes in its underlying parameters mean
- Assumes that the building blocks of the models (e.g. the dynamic equation for the short rate) are consistent with observed data

- Reasonably prices all the relevant states of the world — if only in the sense that relevant states are assigned positive probability. For example, if simple models of the term structure cannot be 'fitted' to the currently observed term structure then these models cannot assign positive probability to states of the world which might generate such a term structure
- Can be implemented within reasonable computer time.

In practice, the demands of the first and last of these points have meant that the model of Black and Scholes (1973), or variants thereof, have been used for pricing simple short-dated interest rate instruments. However, when pricing instruments with maturities in excess of one year — where contingent claims prices are more sensitive to the shape of the term structure — the variety of models in existence can lead to a multiplicity of prices which are not in agreement with one another.

But first, consider the third point, which encapsulates two ideas. To illustrate these ideas, we will refer to the model of CIR (1985b) mentioned earlier. However, the comments made in this section apply equally to the models of Schaefer and Schwartz (1987), Brennan and Schwartz (1979), Nielsen and Saá-Requejo (1992) and Longstaff and Schwartz (1992).

The CIR model provides a functional form for the zero-coupon curve which depends on the existing level of the short rate (the state variable) and the values of the parameters κ, φ, σ and θ which in a CIR world are exogenous to the system in the sense that they are part of the structure of the economy:

$$P(r, t, T) = A(T - t)\exp(-rB(T - t))$$

where

$$A(T - t) = \left[\frac{2\gamma e^{(\kappa+\gamma+\theta)(T-t)/2}}{(\kappa + \gamma + \theta)(e^{\gamma(T-t)} - 1) + 2\gamma}\right]^{2\kappa\varphi/\sigma^2}$$

$$B(T - t) = \left[\frac{2(e^{\gamma(T-t)} - 1)}{(\kappa + \gamma + \theta)(e^{\gamma(T-t)} - 1) + 2\gamma}\right]$$

$$\gamma = \sqrt{(\kappa + \theta)^2 + 2\sigma^2}$$

The volatility term structure for this one-factor model is simply given as $(\sigma\sqrt{r})\,d\log P/dr$ which is $-(\sigma\sqrt{r})B(T - t)$.

The functional form for the discount function (and the corresponding zero-curve) is reasonably flexible. Both upward- and downward-sloping zero-curves can be fitted. The conditions for this are $r < 2\kappa\varphi/(\gamma + \kappa + \theta)$ and $r > \kappa\varphi/(\kappa + \theta)$ respectively. When $\kappa\varphi/(\kappa + \theta) > r > 2\kappa\varphi/(\gamma + \kappa + \theta)$, the term structure is humped.

Strictly speaking, we would require that, in the absence of structural change in the economy which might impinge on the term structure, these parameters be constant. Thus the discount function is a function of one factor. However, for most countries, the interest rate term structure is too complicated for changes in it to be adequately explained by changes in a single state variable like the short rate — this does not even address the issue of jointly fitting the interest rate and volatility term structures. One approach to make the term structure work — which in the first instance means that it should be able to price discount bonds — is to treat the model as a five-parameter functional form, with the short rate given by the short end of the zero-coupon curve and the other four parameters fitted by some least-squares procedure. In effect, this approach seeks weak exogeneity of the structural parameters in the sense that they are not fixed for all time, rather, they vary independently of the state variables. In practice, this takes the form of 'daily recalibration' of the CIR model where the structural parameters are re-estimated each day so that the theoretical curve is consistent with the observed market curve[9]. This practical approach is tantamount to assuming a theoretical model which is radically different from what was originally intended, at least insofar as it assumes that there are risks in the market, proxied by the variability of the four parameters, which cannot be traded.

While the CIR term structure admits of humps, the functional form is insufficiently flexible to fit the hump which is often observed in the UK term structure — like that which prevailed for most of 1994. In this sense, there are ('humped') states of the world which are not captured by the model. If the model cannot incorporate such states, then it certainly cannot price such states since zero probability is being assigned to those states of the world. Experience in the UK, where there is often a pronounced hump which peaks around the ten-year maturity, has shown that even if both the state variables and the structural parameters are fitted to the current yield curve on a daily basis, the overall fit is quite poor. For example, the two-factor Longstaff and Schwartz model can be fit to within 4–5 basis points, on average over a 15-year maturity range, yet this can cause large variations when this yield differential translates into a bond price. Sometimes this can be in the order of full points, i.e. £s, depending on the maturity and the coupon of the bond.

So there are two limitations of concern in these parametric model: (1) the models frequently prescribe prices for a zero-coupon bond which are away from the market despite the fact that the model was fitted to the current term structure and (2) there are states of the world which are often unpriced leading to mispricing of interest rate contingent claims. The upshot of these limitations of 'fixed parameter' equilibrium models is the development of 'time-varying parameter' models or what Carverhill (1991) calls 'evolutionary' models[10]. In these models, the evolution of the term structure is determined mostly by the fit of the model to the initial observed term structure by incorporating the interest rate (and possibly the volatility) term structure wholly into the dynamic equation for the short rate.

4.4.1 THE MODEL OF HO AND LEE

Ho and Lee (1986) first introduced the methodology for fitting 'evolutionary' models in which assets are priced in a no-arbitrage market and the initial yield curve is calibrated to be entirely consistent with the observed yield curve. Their model is the simplest example of the 'evolutionary' approach of which others are due to Black, Derman and Toy (1988) and Hull and White (1990). These latter two models allow for the volatility of the term structure to vary along its maturity range. In fitting the models information from both the interest rate and volatility term structures is incorporated.

It is worth noting that evolution of the discount function takes place in discrete time. This changes the computational task of computing bond and option prices as security prices are computed from numerical algorithms rather than analytical formulae. Such models employ a whole technology of 'tree engineering' in the choice of algorithm as the discount function is allowed to evolve along recombining binary (in the Ho and Lee case) and trinary (in the case of Hull and White) trees. The design of the trees is motivated by a compromise between numerical accuracy and computer speed/memory. The following outline of the Ho and Lee model is intended to illustrate some of this construction. In addition, the role of the no-arbitrage equilibrium in adding structure to the model is highlighted. It should be noted that the framework of Heath, Jarrow and Morton (1992) encompasses these models in the sense that HJM models can be perfectly fit to the current term structure.

In the Ho and Lee model, the current term structure (at time 0) is taken as the starting point from which it evolves randomly over time. Thus bonds priced using this model (at time 0) will have the same value as those priced off the current term structure. Ho and Lee focus on the discount bond version of the term structure and assume that each discount bond of a given maturity evolves along a binomial tree, i.e.

$$P_i^{(n)}(T+1) \begin{cases} P_{i+1}^{(n+1)}(T) & \text{up-state} \\ \\ P_i^{(n+1)}(T) & \text{down-state} \end{cases} \qquad T = 0, 1, 2, \ldots \qquad (4.19)$$

where $P_i^{(n)}(t)$ denotes the price of a discount bond with t periods to maturity, at time n and in the ith state. In a world of certainty, the realized future yields on discount bonds would be equal to the forward rates implied by the current term structure, i.e.

$$P_i^{(n+1)}(T) = P_{i+1}^{(n+1)}(T) = \frac{P_i^{(n)}(T+1)}{P_i^{(n)}(1)} \qquad T = 0, 1, 2, \ldots \qquad (4.20)$$

Since the future prices of bonds are not certain, Ho and Lee model the future prices as binomial perturbations about the forward discount function, that is, in the up-state

$$P_{i+1}^{(n+1)}(T) = \frac{P_i^{(n)}(T+1)}{P_i^{(n)}(1)} q(T) \qquad T = 0, 1, 2, \ldots \qquad (4.21)$$

and in the down-state

$$P_i^{(n+1)}(T) = \frac{P_i^{(n)}(T+1)}{P_i^{(n)}(1)} d(T) \qquad T = 0, 1, 2, \ldots \qquad (4.22)$$

where d and q are the perturbation functions. In this model, the perturbation function depends solely on the maturity of the discount bond. Since discount bonds always have positive value less than or equal to par value, it follows that d and q will be positive functions with $d(0) = q(0) = 1$, from (4.21) and (4.22) above.

We have seen that in the absence of arbitrage, bonds can be priced as in a risk-neutral world where payoff prices are given as expected discounted values of future payoffs. Thus we require

$$\pi q(T) + (1 - \pi)d(T) = 1 \qquad (4.23)$$

for all $n > 0$ and $i > 0$ where π denotes the probability of jumping reaching the up-state and $1 - \pi$ is the probability of reaching the down-state. This implies that the price of a discount bond in state i at time n with maturity T is given by

$$P_i^{(n)}(T) = \left(\pi P_{i+1}^{(n+1)}(T-1) + (1-\pi)P_i^{(n+1)}(T-1) \right) P_i^{(n)}(1) \qquad T = 1, 2, \ldots$$

Thus far the recombining structure of the binomial lattice has not been imposed on the model. However, on a recombining binomial lattice, the price of a bond after an upward move and then a downward move should equal that of the bond after a downward move and then an upward move, i.e.

$$P_i^{(n+2)}(T) = \frac{P_i^{(n)}(T+2)}{P_i^{(n)}(2)} \frac{q(T+1)}{q(1)} d(T)$$

$$= \frac{P_i^{(n)}(T+2)}{P_i^{(n)}(2)} \frac{d(T+1)}{d(1)} q(T) \qquad T = 0, 1, 2, \ldots \qquad (4.24)$$

This implies that $d(1)d(T)q(T+1) = q(1)q(T)d(T+1)$ for $T = 0, 1, 2, \ldots$ Using equation (4.23) to eliminate d we can obtain a first-order linear difference equation in q from which we obtain

$$q(T) = \frac{1}{\pi + (1-\pi)\delta^T} \qquad d(T) = \frac{\delta^T}{\pi + (1-\pi)\delta^T} \qquad (4.25)$$

for $T = 1, 2, \ldots$ and δ is a constant which along with the risk-neutral probability determines the perturbation function.

In sum, the Ho and Lee model is a discrete-time model which takes the current term structure as its initial state and evolves therefrom. In a discrete-time world, the discount function (corresponding to the prices of zero-coupon bonds) is allowed to 'jump' either up or down according to a binomial process. However, by considering the discount function in each state (up or down), the no-arbitrage condition is imposed by requiring that the expected discount function (i.e. the up- and down-state discount functions weighted by the jump probabilities) equals the forward discount function implied by the current term structure. Thus for a given jump size and jump probabilities, a binomial tree is constructed in which existing zero-coupon bonds may be priced consistently with the currently observed market prices. Moreover, claims contingent on bonds may also be priced.

The inputs to this model are (1) the jump sizes (which vary according to the maturity of the discount rate) and (2) the jump probabilities which are constant for all discount maturities. These can be reduced to the two parameters δ and π. Since the discount bond term structure is given, these latter two parameters may be estimated using contingent claims on the bond options so that they capture information regarding the market's perception of term structure volatility.

Jamshidian (1987) shows that the Ho and Lee model corresponds to a continuous-time model in which the evolution of the short rate is given by

$$dr_t = \varphi(t)\,dt + \sigma\,dB_t \tag{4.26}$$

where the functional form of φ is determined by the current term structure. In the context of the previous reference to the CIR model, the evolutionary generalization of this model due to Hull and White (1990) leads to a stochastic differential equation for the short rate of the form

$$dr_t = \kappa(t)(\varphi(t) - r_t)\,dt + \sigma(t)\sqrt{r_t}\,dB_t \tag{4.27}$$

so that the 'degrees of freedom' of the corresponding zero-coupon curve are now determined by the functional form of the time-dependent 'parameters', $\kappa(t)$, $\varphi(t)$ and $\sigma(t)$. Since there are three functions to be determined, Hull and White use both the current interest rate term structure and the term structure of volatilities corresponding to discount rate of different maturities to determine these functions[11].

Black, Derman and Toy (1990) consider a model of the short rate which has a continuous time limit of the form

$$d\log(r_t) = (\theta(t) - \varphi(t)\log(r_t))\,dt + \sigma(t)\,dB_t \tag{4.28}$$

They describe a discrete-time algorithm calibrating their model by constructing a binomial tree which jointly incorporates information from the interest rate and volatility term structures.

These models differ substantially from those described in Section 4.3. First, they are primarily one-factor models of the term structure where the short rate is the state variable. By specifying time-varying drift and volatilities they allow for current interest rate and volatility information to be incorporated into the model. The techniques for incorporating this information invariably use binomial and trinomial trees and work in a manner similar to the description to the Ho and Lee model outlined earlier though with increasing complexity when two term structures must be fit. Being freely parameterized in this way and by working directly from (4.12) which says that all we need is the risk-adjusted short rate process to price interest rate securities, they avoid the issue of trying to think about actual processes driving the term structure which would require some specification of the market prices of risk.

4.5   ASSESSING THE MODELS

In Section 4.2 the no-arbitrage equilibrium framework for pricing interest rate contingent claims was outlined. This highlighted some of the main building blocks, tools and concepts related to the pricing interest rate contingent claims. These ideas were illustrated in Sections 4.3 and 4.4, where examples were given of the application of two broad methodologies for pricing interest rate contingent claims. This section presents an assessment of these modelling strategies in the light of the empirical evidence. Three approaches are pursued:

- How realistic are the building blocks of the different term structure models?
- What are the theoretical implications of the models, and how do these square with empirical evidence?
- What is the predictive power of models in pricing contingent claims?

The appraisal of term structure models presented in this section does not purport to be complete. We will give merely a flavour for some of the outstanding puzzles and problems in the construction and application of term structure models.

4.5.1   HOW REALISTIC ARE THE BUILDING BLOCKS?

We noted in the previous section that many practitioners seek models which have initial conditions which are consistent with the current state of the interest rate and volatility term structures. Two modelling approaches may be pursued to achieve this: first, a parametric approach in which the term structure is driven by an s-factor Brownian motion and with the drift and volatility functions given analytically; second, an 'evolutionary' framework — which draws on the result cited in Section 4.2 where no-arbitrage implies that it is valid to price securities *as if* in a risk-neutral world — where a single Brownian motion drives a state variable which has time-varying drift and volatility which must be estimated numerically using current interest rate and volatility term structure data. Sections 4.3 and 4.4 highlighted the fact that parametric models cannot be fitted perfectly to the initial term structure whereas evolutionary models can. This is often cited as an advantage of these models (e.g. Duffie and Kan, 1992, p. 3) since parametric models have a more transparent structure which is more conducive to economic interpretation than evolutionary models.

Whatever the framework for constructing term structure models, the first question in constructing such a model is: 'How many independent random factors should be included?' This results in an exercise to estimate the 'dimension' of the term structure: to the extent that it comprises 25–100 yields which are realized randomly over time, statistical techniques — mainly principal components analysis — are employed to identify the number of truly random factors that are driving the term structure. Applications of principal components analysis in this context are to be found in Steeley (1990) for UK data. He reports that the UK term structure is most adequately described by three random factors. Carverhill (1991) and Cohen and Heath (1992) mention the use of the factor weightings computed from principal components in the determination of σ-functions in the stochastic differential equations which drive the state processes underlying the term structure. Of course, if the factors impact on the term structure through some more complicated process (e.g. stochastic volatility or stochastic mean reversion level) then these techniques will not identify them correctly.

Once the number of factors has been estimated, a continuous-time model of the term structure can, in principle, be constructed. Reasonable, analytical models of the term structure will have parametric functional forms which can be fit closely to observed term structures and where random variation in the term structure is reflected mostly in changes in the 2–3 random factors as opposed to changes in the underlying structural parameters.

Interest rates of a given maturity are serially correlated. Fama (1976, 1984) notes that simple autoregressive models often have greater predictive power than models using forward rate predictions implied from the current yield curve. This has serious consequences for most models of the term structure which, by specifying a Markov[13] process for the state variables, effectively assume that all information relevant to a description of future movements in the term structure is impounded in the current values of those state variables. While Heath, Jarrow and Morton (1992) assume a model for the forward curve which admits of the non-Markov case, little by way of published literature, treats of this possibility.

There is a trade-off in choosing between Markov and non-Markov models of the term structure. First, the literature has evolved using Markov models because they are reasonably tractable and, in continuous time, can lead to neat analytical formulae which are easy to program and compute. On the other hand, these basic processes which underly these models have very low predictive power.

Chan *et al.* (1992) estimate the general non-linear short rate process, $\{r_t, t \geq 0\}$, which is given by

$$\mathrm{d}r_t = \kappa(\theta - r_t)\,\mathrm{d}t + \sigma r_t^{\gamma}\,\mathrm{d}B_t \qquad (4.29)$$

where process $\{B_t, t \geq 0\}$ is a Brownian motion. This model nests most of the short-rate processes assumed in the literature[13], so that tests of the restrictions can be simply constructed. They note that the mean reversion parameters κ and θ are poorly identified and that they obtain an estimate for the γ parameter of 1.36 which is at variance to that which appears in the most popular interest rate term structure models, such as those of Vasicek ($\gamma = 0$) and CIR ($\gamma = 0.5$). Their principal conclusion is that γ is the most important feature of these models of the short rate. Similar work by Murphy (1995), using daily UK interest rate data, confirms the observation that mean reversion parameters are poorly identified. The estimate for γ is 0.36 which, statistically, is indistinguishable from the CIR case of $\gamma = 0.5$. However, the estimated models are put to two further tests. Further, a weighted least squares regression of the realized change in the short rate on the predicted change (given by the estimated model) has an R^2 of 0.009, indicating very low predictive power.

Second, diagnostic tests on the residuals of the estimated model rejects the null hypothesis in independent increments which arises due to the fact that Brownian motion drives the short-rate process. Both of these facts suggest that there is considerable dynamic structure in the short-rate process (and, indeed in the term structure itself) which is lost by assuming that simple factor Markov processes drive the term structure. At the very least, predictions of future (realized) values of interest rate contingent claims are likely to be very inefficient, and perhaps biased.

Lastly, the observed significance of γ in the two studies cited above suggests that the appearance of the short rate in its local volatility is really just picking up the effect of other term structure factors which have not been identified in the simple short-rate model.

4.5.2   THEORETICAL IMPLICATIONS OF THE MODELS

Initial efforts to accommodate some of the empirical properties of term structure data employ econometric methods and construct models in discrete time. Backus and Zin (1994) give a useful illustration of such an approach. Moreover, their findings raise some questions about the implications of theoretical models. For example, representative agent general equilibrium models are shown to imply variations in asset prices which are considerably lower than those observed in practice. Also, they compute prices of risk which depend on the maturities of the bonds. This runs contrary to the implications of (4.7) in Section 4.2.

Carverhill (1991) contrasts the no-arbitrage and evolutionary methodologies for pricing interest rate contingent claims. He notes that a given specification of an equilibrium model can always be nested in an evolutionary model since the effective functional form of the evolutionary model has greater flexibility than that of equilibrium models[14].

In the case of both models, Carverhill notes that if the models are to be numerically stable (in the sense that the drift of the zero-coupon yields is finite), the volatility of a given zero-coupon yield should tend to zero: 'The volatility term structure attenuates to zero.' However, empirically observed volatility term structures tend to flatten out above zero (see Strickland and Kin, 1994).

4.5.3   PREDICTIVE POWER OF THE MODELS

Cohen and Heath (1992) present an alternative method for testing models of the HJM type. Their approach underlines the difference between, on the one hand, using term structure models in a purely descriptive role of fitting to all bond prices and, on the other, applying the models in a normative role where we ask 'what should the prices be?' They consider a number of term structure models which have been constructed in the HJM framework. These models are distinguished by the number of random factors driving the forward curve and the volatility functions which scale these random factors. To the extent that each term structure model can be used to price interest rate contingent claims, each model can be viewed as providing a prediction of the change in the future price of the contingent claim. They devise a maximum-likelihood based approach to testing the models. Using 14 months of price data, Heath and Cohen apply their method of testing interest rate models over weekly prediction intervals. To that extent, this method offers a limited assessment of their term structure models since the adequacy of the models in pricing long-dated instruments which are held or hedged to maturity is not considered. Tests of equilibrium-type models are often devised to match the trading strategies of the user. Thus if the user has a short investment horizon, the predictive power of the model over such periods will be of most interest. Some practitioners devise models where the underlying parameters are determined by prior beliefs about the economy — as opposed to fitting the parameters to current market prices — and which are revised infrequently. These models should be tested for predictive power over longer investment horizons.

4.6   CONCLUSIONS

This chapter has dealt with interest rate securities in continuous time, presents some of the main ideas in securities pricing and showing the building blocks that make up the models. The role of *no-arbitrage equilibrium* was seen to be central to the development of term structure models. It establishes the validity of risk-neutral pricing methods which often leads to particularly tractable methods of pricing interest rate contingent claims. Some examples of equilibrium models, in which the market prices of risk are explicitly incorporated into the model were given in Section 4.3. The evolutionary modelling approach, in which we start from the risk-adjusted process for zero-coupon bond prices was discussed in Section 4.4. These capture the main building blocks of term structure models.

Some of the outstanding issues in pricing interest rate contingent claims were mentioned in Section 4.5. Duffie (1992, p. xiv) describes the developments in securities pricing after the great advances of the 1970s as a mopping-up exercise. We have seen that this process is not yet complete. While satisfactory term structure models can be employed to price short-dated interest rate contingent claims, the pricing of longer-dated instruments is still problematic. Attention must, inevitably, focus on the oversimplifying assumptions concerning the specification and dynamics of the state variables driving the models.

The problems take two forms. First, in many cases equilibrium models cannot be adequately calibrated to current interest rate and volatility term structures, therefore prices for zero-coupon bonds will be significantly 'away from the market'. The development, and subsequent justification, of evolutionary models circumvents this problem. However, the underlying economic structure of evolutionary models is unclear. They are often rationalized as models which describe how the term structure will evolve over time (hence the name 'evolutionary'). In a risk-neutral setting we cannot assess whether this evolution is realistic since in fitting the model we only observe the dynamics of the term structure in a risk-neutral world. This does not readily accord with insights from conventional macroeconomics.

Second, puzzles remain concerning the theoretical implications of both the parametric and evolutionary models. Why do volatility term structures flatten out at positive volatility levels, when theory implies that they should attenuate to zero? The resolution of these problems may lie in the Markovian structure of the dynamic processes which underly these models.

As such, no-arbitrage equilibrium is the only economic idea of substance in these models. One is led to question whether future advances in these models will draw more heavily on economic ideas concerning the determination of interest rates. Perhaps like so many aspects of applied economics, the incorporation of conventional macro-economic intuition regarding the yield curve in the construction of these models will require a more precise description of macro-economists' priors.

NOTES

1. See Karatzas and Shreve (1988) for an extensive discussion of Brownian motion and of most of the tools from probability which are applied to finance.

2. They are often called the *local* drift and volatilities as they apply only at time t and vary at each point in time according to the values of their arguments.

3. However, Ahn and Thompson (1988) and Babbs and Webber (1994) consider term structure models in which the state variables are modelled by Poisson jump diffusion processes.

4. The value of the portfolio changes with the value of its components but for notational convenience dependence on time is suppressed.

5. It should be understood that the portfolios weights $\{x_1, \ldots, x_{s+1}\}$ vary with time.

6. We also require $\mathrm{Lim}_{T \to \infty} P(S, t, T) = 0$.

7. A version of the Feynman–Kac result applicable to the above is as follows. Under certain regularity conditions for a function f,

$$v(\tau, s) = E\left(f(S_T) \exp\left(- \int_\tau^T q(S_t) \, dt \, | S_\tau = s \right) \right)$$

then

$$\frac{\partial v}{\partial t} + \sum_{i=1}^{s} \mu_i(S_t) \frac{\partial v}{\partial S_i} + \sum_{j=1}^{s} \sum_{i=1}^{s} \frac{\sigma_{i,j}^2(S_t)}{2} \frac{\partial^2 v}{\partial S_i \partial S_j} - q(S_t) v = 0$$

where $\{S_t, t \geq \emptyset\}$ is an s-dimensional Itô process given by:

$$dS_{i,t} = \mu_i(S_t) \, dt + \sum_{i=1}^{s} \sigma_{i,j}(S_t) \, dB_{i,t} \qquad i = 1, 2, \ldots, s$$

See also Oksendal (1988, p. 108) and Karatzas and Shreve (1988, p. 366) for further details.

8. Harrison and Pliska (1981) shows that the existence of a no-arbitrage equilibrium corresponds to the existence of an adjusted state variable process (as in (4.13) above) under which the process $\{Z_t, t \geq 0\}$ given by

$$Z(S_t, t, T) = \exp\left(- \int_0^t r_s \, ds \right)$$

is a martingale, i.e. $Z_t = E(Z_s | Z_t)$, $s \geq t$, where the expectation is taken with respect to this risk-adjusted version of the state variable process. In fact, the Feynman–Kac result shows that no-arbitrage is equivalent to the existence of a state variable process under which the price process of any security discounted by the factor Z_t is a martingale.
If we rewrite (4.12) as

$$dS_{i,t} = \alpha_i(S_t, t, T) \, dt + \sum_{j=1}^{s} \beta_{i,j}(S_t, t, T)(dB_{j,t} - \lambda \, dt) \qquad i = 1, 2, \ldots, s$$

and define

$$d\tilde{B}_{i,t} = dB_{j,t} - \lambda_j \, dt \qquad j = 1, 2, \ldots, s$$

then no-arbitrage is equivalent to the existence of a probability measure under which this new vector process is a standard Brownian motion.

Girsanov's theorem allows us to construct the equivalent martingale measure from the original probability measure (see Harrison and Pliska, 1981). It is more common, in the jargon, to speak of the existence of *equivalent martingale measures* rather than risk-adjusted state variable processes as being equivalent to the absence of arbitrage (see Harrison and Kreps, 1979).

9.   In fact, CIR (1985b) give a simple generalization of their model with where the asymptotic mean of the short rate is given as $\varphi(t)$, making it time-varying — this increases the flexibility of the functional form for the discount function.

10.   In this chapter, evolutionary models are models which start with a price process for discount bonds in a risk-neutral world. Therefore the market prices of risk are not identified in these models.

11.   However, their model does not quite fit the definition of an evolutionary model given earlier in the sense that in their set-up they still need to identify the market prices of risk.

12.   Markov processes are processes for which the future motion of the process does not depend on its past history, *only* the current level. For example, (4.26) is a Markov process, since the motion of the short note depends on the drift and volatility terms which depend only on the current short rate and not on the path of the short rate prior to time t.

13.   One generalization of (4.26), due to Longstaff and Schwartz (1992), allows the short rate and its volatility to be generated by two processes of the (CIR) 'square-root' type.

14.   That said, comparing the models in terms of effective 'degrees of freedom' generally assumes that both models are calibrated to the current term structure at a single point in time. In contrast, some authors (e.g. Longstaff and Schwartz) intended their equilibrium models to be calibrated on the basis of historical estimates of the parameters in their model.

REFERENCES

Ahn, C. M. and Thompson, H. (1988) Jump-diffusion processes and the term structure of interest rates, *Journal of Finance*, **1**.

Babbs, S. and Webber, N. (1994) A theory of the term structure with an official short rate, Financial Options Research Centre, University of Warwick, 94/49.

Backus, D. and Zin, S. (1994) Reverse engineering the yield curve, NBER Working Paper, no. 4676.

Bick, A. (1990) On viable diffusion price processes of the market portfolio, *Journal of Finance*, **2**.

Black, F., Derman, E. and Toy, W. (1990) A one-factor model of interest rates and its application to Treasury bond options, *Financial Analysts Journal*.

Black, F. and Scholes, M. (1973) The pricing of options and corporate liabilities, *Journal of Political Economy*, **81**.

Brennan, M. and Schwartz, E. (1979) A continuous-time approach to the pricing of bonds, *Journal of Banking and Finance*, **3**.

Carverhill, A. (1991) The term structure of interest rates and associated options; equilibrium vs evolutionary models, Financial Options Research Centre, University of Warwick, 91/21.

Chan, K., Karolyi, A., Longstaff, F. and Sanders, A. (1992) An empirical comparison of alternative models of the short-term interest rate, *Journal of Finance*, **3**.

Cohen, H. and Heath, D. (1992) A new method of testing pricing models as applied to forward interest rate models, Federal Reserve Bank of Atlanta, working paper 92–16.

Cox, J., Ingersoll, J. and Ross, S. (1981) A re-examination of traditional hypotheses about the term structure of interest rates, *Journal of Finance*, **4**.

Cox, J., Ingersoll, J. and Ross, S. (1985a) An intertemporal general equilibrium model of asset prices, *Econometrica*, **53**.

Cox, J., Ingersoll, J. and Ross, S. (1985b) A theory of the term structure of interest rates, *Econometrica*, **53**.

Duffie, D. (1992) *Dynamic Asset Pricing Theory*, Princeton University Press, Princeton, NJ.

Duffie, D. and Kan, R. (1992) A yield-factor model of interest rates, Graduate School of Business, Stanford University.

Fama, E. (1976) Forward rates as predictors of future spot rates, *Journal of Financial Economics*, **3**.

Fama, E. (1984) The information in the term structure, *Journal of Financial Economics*, **13**.

Friedman, M. (1958) *Essays in Positive Economics*, Phoenix Books, University of Chicago Press.

Harrison, M. and Kreps, D. (1979) Martingales and arbitrage in multi-period securities markets, *Journal of Economic Theory*, **20**.

Harrison, M. and Pliska, S. (1981) Martingales and stochastic integrals in the theory of continuous trading, *Stochastic Processes and Their Applications*, **11**.

Heath, D., Jarrow, R., and Morton, A. (1992) Bond pricing and the term structure of interest rates: a new methodology for contingent claims valuation, *Econometrica*, **60**.

Ho, T. and Lee, S. (1986) Term structure movements and the pricing of interest rate contingent claims, *Journal of Finance*, **5**.

Hull, J. and White, A. (1990) Pricing interest rate derivative securities, *Review of Financial Studies*, **3**.

Ingersoll, J. (1987) *The Theory of Financial Decision Making*, Rowman Littlefield.

Jamshidian, F. (1987) Pricing of contingent claims in the one-factor term structure model, Merrill Lynch Capital Markets Working Paper.

Karatzas, I. and Shreve, S. (1988) *Brownian Motion and Stochastic Calculus*, Springer-Verlag, New York.

Longstaff, F. and Schwartz, E. (1992) Interest rate volatility and the term structure: a two-factor general equilibrium model, *Journal of Finance*, **47**.

Merton, R. (1990) *Continuous-time Finance*, Basil Blackwell, Oxford.

Murphy, G. (1995) Generalised methods of moments estimation of the short process in the UK, forthcoming Bank of England working paper.

Oksendal, B. (1985) *Stochastic Differential Equations*, Springer-Verlag, Berlin.

Nielson, L. and Saá-Requejo, J. (1992) Exchange rate and term structure dynamics and the pricing of derivative securities, INSEAD working paper.

Schaefer, S. and Schwartz, E. (1987) Time-dependent variance and the pricing of bond options, *Journal of Finance*, **42**.

Steeley, J. (1990) Modelling the dynamics of the term structure of interest rates, *The Economic and Social Review*, **21**, No. 4.

Strickland, C. (1994) A comparison of models of the term structure, Financial Options Research Centre, University of Warwick, 94/46.

Strickland, C. and Kin, P. (1994) Comparisons of term structure models for pricing interest rates derivatives, Financial Options Research Centre, University of Warwick, Annual Conference 1994.

Varian, H. (1987) The arbitrage principle in financial economics, *Economic Perspectives*, **1**, 2.

Vasicek, O. (1977) An equilibrium characterization of the term structure, *Journal of Financial Economics*, **5**.

CHAPTER 5

The effects of taxation

5.1 INTRODUCTION

The term structure estimation methods described in Chapter 2 are implicitly based on the assumption that a bond's price depends only on the term structure of interest rates. If this were the case then, given a term structure, it would be possible to determine *exactly* the price of every bond in the market. However, as described in Chapter 3, there are a number of characteristics of bond markets that can also play an important part in the relative valuation of bonds. By far the most important of these is the existence of tax regimes. Different regimes can impact on bond prices in different ways: *investor-specific* tax rules cause different investors to value the same bond differently because they receive different cashflows net of tax[1]. On the other hand, *bond-specific* tax rules exist that cause an investor to value two bonds differently on an after-tax basis even though they provide similar gross cashflows.

A possible course is to treat the effects of tax regulations as 'noise' — measurement error that means a term structure has to be statistically fitted to observed bond prices instead of it being possible to simply 'join the dots' to obtain a smooth term structure. This would be reasonable if such effects were evenly spread along the length of the curve, so that the fitted curve that essentially averages over measurement errors actually coincided with the true term structure. However, if this were not the case, such an assumption would bias the estimated term structure. Suppose, for example, that tax regulations cause shorter maturity bonds to trade at a premium relative to both longer maturity bonds and to the term structure. The yields on these shorter maturity bonds will therefore generally lie below the term structure. A curve fitted using observed bond prices and ignoring this effect would therefore produce an estimated term structure below the true one at shorter maturities, causing any inferences drawn from such a term structure to be similarly biased. Many studies have been carried out that find that the distortionary impact of tax regimes has a significant impact on term structure estimation. Litzenberger and Rolfo (1984) report that introducing a parameter to cater for tax effects in econometric models of the term structure can substantially decrease the variation exhibited by these models when applied to some of the major bond markets. Jordan (1984) reports a 'statistically significant tax-induced bias in [the] non-tax-adjusted equation'. Schaefer (1981) demonstrates that different classes of tax-paying investors in the UK government bond market face significantly different term structures, a situation that has persisted — see Derry and Pradhan (1993). It is important therefore to consider all the possible complications — and perhaps augment the methodologies described in Chapter 2 — to obtain an unbiased estimate of the term structure of interest rates.

5.2   TAX RULES IN DIFFERENT BOND MARKETS

Tax rules vary across bond markets, but several common features can be identified. In some countries the tax rules are such that their impact on different bonds is approximately even, but in many countries tax rules can cause two apparently similar bonds to be valued differently by different market participants. This section outlines the various kinds of taxation rules to be found, and describes the effects they can have on relative valuation.

5.2.1   TAX RULES AND GOVERNMENT BOND MARKETS

The general taxation regime of many countries distinguishes between *income* and *capital gain*. Income can broadly be defined as the regular receipt of money — an individual's wage, for example, or the interest earned on a deposit held in a bank. A capital gain, in contrast, is a one-off receipt of cash — money received from the sale of a work of art (less the purchase price) would be an example of a capital gain. A distinction is often made between income and capital gain for tax purposes — the tax payable on a sum of money received as a salary payment would in general be different from the tax due if the same amount was raised by selling a work of art.

Although it can sometimes appear a little artificial, the same distinction is often made for the taxation of financial assets. In particular, an individual investing in a government bond will often be liable to both income tax and capital gains tax. Several countries treat the coupon receipts from a bond as income, but the difference between the price at which the bond was sold and that at which it was bought is defined to be capital gain. Any difference between the income and capital gains tax rate will therefore cause an investor to consider not only the term structure of interest rates before buying a bond but also the proportion of return that is due to capital gain (and taxed as such) and that due to income.

Corporations are usually treated differently from individual investors for the purposes of taxation. In many countries, any return from the purchase or sale of a government bond by a corporation — be it capital gain or income — is treated as a profit (or loss), and is entered into the profit and loss statement and taxed at the appropriate corporate tax rate. It is often the case (particularly for companies that actively trade financial instruments) that, for tax purposes, profits can be offset against any losses the firm may have incurred. So not only will corporations view the return from various bonds differently from individuals, but it is also not entirely clear what proportion (if any) of the return received by a corporation is subject to tax.

A further complication arises from the fact that tax payments due on bonds issued by many governments are deducted at source. This feature is referred to as *withholding tax*, since the amount due is simply withheld by the tax authority rather than the payment being made gross and the investor later paying any amount due in taxes. In some countries withholding tax is applied to both income and capital gains, whereas in others it is applied only to income payments — more specific details on the rules in different countries are given below. This can affect the valuation of a bond in a number of ways, essentially because the timing of cashflows is often altered by withholding tax rules. For example, most individual investors in UK government bonds are subject to a 25% withholding tax on coupon payments[2]. Consider an individual investor who faces a 40% marginal rate of income tax and therefore will be due to pay 40% tax on each coupon payment. In reality he or she will pay 25% (the amount withheld) as soon as the coupon payment is made, but will not be due to pay the remainder (15% of the coupon income) until the end of the tax year when tax payments become due. This 15% could be reinvested until the date on which the tax is due — effectively increasing the return.

Some countries also tax transactions of financial instruments, employing a *transactions* or *turnover* tax. Where such a tax rule exists, a small percentage of the total value traded becomes liable to be paid as tax. In Italy, for example, a tax on all transactions of government bonds is currently imposed at a rate of 0.9% of the value traded[3]. Although it is hard to assess the overall impact of the existence of such a tax on financial markets, it seems likely that the main price effect will be to widen the 'bid–ask spreads' — the difference between the prices at which a trader is willing to buy and sell — rather than the absolute level of the price and so, assuming such a tax is applied equally to all bonds in the market, the effect on relative bond prices should be minimal[4,5].

The existence of such diverse tax rules has numerous effects on the relative valuation of government bonds, but these can reasonably be divided into two main types: the creation of distinct classes of investor and the creation of distinct classes of instrument.

5.2.2   CONSEQUENCE 1: THE CREATION OF DIFFERENT CATEGORIES OF INVESTOR

Owning a fixed-income security entitles an investor to a set of fixed *gross* cashflows at different times in the future[6]. If a tax regime exists that distinguishes between different classes of investor, these classes will not (except by coincidence) receive the same *net* cashflows, and hence will value the instrument differently. Consider the following example.

An individual faces 40% (income) tax on coupon income but no tax on capital gain, while a trading company faces 33% (corporation) tax on both income and capital gain. Both agree that the term structure is flat at 10%, and want to value a two-year bond (to the nearest penny) that pays annual coupons at 8%, a redemption payment of £100 and that is currently trading at £92.00.

$$\text{Value to individual} = \frac{8.00(1 - 0.40)}{1.10} + \frac{8.00(1 - 0.40)}{1.10^2} + \frac{100}{1.10^2}$$

$$= \mathbf{£90.98}$$

$$\text{Value to company} = \frac{8.00(1 - 0.33)}{1.10} + \frac{8.00(1 - 0.33)}{1.10^2}$$

$$+ \frac{100.00 - ((100.00 - 92.00)0.33)}{1.10^2}$$

$$= \mathbf{£89.76}$$

Note how the cashflows are adjusted for tax in each of the cases — the final term in the second equation representing the redemption payment less capital gains tax. In this example (assuming no other bonds and no other classes of investor) the marginal investor who sets the trading price of this bond will be the individual, simply because he or she attaches a higher value than the company to its stream of cashflows.

It is generally the case that corporations face different tax treatment to individuals, and that within these broad categories there are more sub-divisions. Individuals often face different marginal rates of income tax — the 0%, 20%, 25% and 40% structure currently in force in the UK (applied to coupon income only) is an example — whereas different categories of companies face different tax treatments. In the UK a distinction is made between small, medium and large companies, while charities and pension funds (among others) are exempt from all taxation on government bonds[7]. France and Germany have similar regimes, although in France individuals face a flat 'investment tax' on all income and capital gain from investments — currently at 18.1% and non-profit organizations face a reduced (but non-zero) rate of tax. Italy is different, where all investors face a withholding tax (currently at 12.5%) on both income and capital gain[8], but companies can apply to have this refunded and have all profit and loss taxed at the appropriate corporate tax rate.

Furthermore, many countries also distinguish between domestic and non-resident investors, creating yet more classes of investor. In the French, German and Italian bond markets non-residents (domiciled in countries that have a tax treaty with the country in question) can apply for exemptions from the taxes faced by domestic investors in those markets. In the UK, although they are not formally exempt from taxation on all bonds, facilities exist whereby non-residents can claim tax exemption in many circumstances. Those resident in countries with a full double-taxation agreement with the UK can apply to receive coupon payments gross, as can non-residents purchasing gilts that are designated Free Of Tax to Residents Abroad (FOTRA)[9]. In all such cases, non-residents are taxed according to their domestic tax rules.

So when analysing a single government bond market, it is necessary to consider not only the different categories of investors that might exist due to the domestic tax rules but also those rules faced by non-resident investors. Moreover, non-residents may behave differently because, although technically exempt from tax, they may experience a delay in recovering the taxable amount. An investor who receives a gross coupon directly will obviously value a bond more highly than one who technically receives it gross but in reality receives only a net payment on the coupon date and the refund with some delay.

5.2.3 CONSEQUENCE 2: THE CREATION OF DIFFERENT CATEGORIES OF INSTRUMENT

In certain countries tax rules cause instruments with the same *gross* return to be valued differently by the same investor, simply because the instruments face different tax treatments. One example of such a structure is the withholding tax rules applicable to Italian government debt. Originally there was no withholding tax on government securities, but a rate of 6.25% was introduced on 20 September 1986 and then was increased to 12.5% on 1 September 1987, since when it has remained at this level. Government securities are taxed at the withholding tax rate applicable at their issue date, so bonds issued before 20 September 1986 that have yet to mature remain exempt from withholding tax, and those issued between that date and 1 September 1987 are still only taxed at 6.25%. A similar situation exists in the USA, where the tax treatment of financial instruments has changed several times in the past few decades (Dermody and Rockafellar, 1994, give an overview of these changes), but all instruments retain the treatment that was applied at issue. If two government bonds exist that have identical terms[10] except for the fact that they were issued under different tax regimes, then an investor subject to tax will always prefer the bond with the lower associated tax rate(s). This increase in demand will drive its price up relative to that of the more heavily taxed bond.

The UK gilt market provides another example of such effects. Until the tax reforms come into force in 1996[11], individual investors in government bonds are taxed at their marginal income tax rate on any coupon income received, but are exempt from tax on any capital gain they earned. Bonds with high coupons provide more of their return in the form of coupon income than do bonds with lower coupons. Therefore any individual paying income tax will — other things being equal — prefer low coupon bonds, while those investors paying the same rate of tax on income and capital gains will be indifferent to the size of the bond's coupon.

For example, consider two annual bonds trading in the market with the same maturity (1 year) but different coupon payments (3% and 9%), and assume that all investors again agree on a flat gross yield curve of 10%. Suppose the bonds are priced such that they reflect the valuation of a tax-exempt investor (such as a charity or a pension fund), both having a gross redemption yield of 10%. Then their prices (P_3 and P_9) are simply given by:

$$3\% \text{ bond: } P_3 = \frac{3.00}{1.10} + \frac{100.00}{1.10} = £93.64$$

$$9\% \text{ bond: } P_9 = \frac{9.00}{1.10} + \frac{100.00}{1.10} = £99.09$$

Suppose an individual facing 40% tax on coupon income has to buy one of the two bonds at these prices — which will they prefer? They will choose the bond that gives them the highest (net) redemption yield:

$$3\% \text{ bond: } \frac{3.00(1 - 0.40)}{(1 + y_3^N/100)} + \frac{100.00}{(1 + y_3^N/100)} = £93.64 \qquad y_3^N = 8.718\%$$

$$9\% \text{ bond: } \frac{9.00(1 - 0.40)}{(1 + y_9^N/100)} + \frac{100.00}{(1 + y_9^N/100)} = £99.09 \qquad y_9^N = 6.367\%$$

The effect of differential tax treatment of income and capital gains in this case is to make the 3% bond far more attractive to a taxpayer than the higher-coupon bond because of the higher net yield, while a tax-exempt investor is indifferent between two bonds offering the same gross yield.

This type of situation is clearly not stable. In the above case, a taxpaying investor would pay above the market price to obtain the low coupon bond (or would sell the high coupon bond below the market price). If there is a significant number of taxpaying investors, such behaviour will drive the net yields closer together, forcing the gross yields — and therefore the tax-exempt investor's valuations — apart. Bond yields therefore contain information about these effects as well as about the term structure of interest rates, meaning that any term structure estimation technique that ignores such effects runs the risk of producing significantly biased estimates.

5.3   MODELLING TAX EFFECTS[12]

Several models have been proposed that describe tax effects in bond markets and thereby attempt to remove any distorting factors when estimating the term structure of interest rates. In this section the theoretical properties of three such models are described — McCulloch (1975) and Schaefer (1981) from the academic literature, and the model currently used by the Bank of England described in Mastronikola (1991). Two of the three models were developed particularly for UK government bonds which, until recently, were subject to differential taxation of coupon income and capital gain along with a withholding tax on coupon payments. However, tax changes announced in July 1995 to take effect by May 1996 remove this distinction for most investors, taxing capital uplift as income[13]. These changes mean that the models described in the rest of the chapter may no longer be directly applicable to the UK market. However, they still could be applied to other countries where such a distinction persists (such as Germany and the USA, for example), and they will still be useful for historical analysis of the UK term structure of interest rates.

5.3.1   McCULLOCH (1975)

In his original work on term structure estimation, McCulloch (1971) overlooked the effects that tax rules might have on bond prices, but augmented his model to take account of tax rules in his second paper (1975). For a bond with n coupon payments of size c (payable at time t_j, $j = 1, \ldots, n$) and maturity t_m subject to income tax on coupon payments and capital gains tax on the difference between the purchase price and the redemption value R, its full price[14] P can be related to the discount function $\delta(.)$ by:

$$P = c(1 - \tau) \sum_{j=1}^{n} \delta(t_j) + [R - t_{CG}(R - p)]\delta(t_m) \qquad (5.1)$$

From this equation, a least squares estimation procedure similar to that described in Chapter 2 can be formulated. The problem is less straightforward because the above equation is non-linear in τ but, since the rest of the formulation is linear, it reduces to a one-dimensional non-linear search for an estimate of τ that minimizes the sum of squared residuals between observed and fitted prices. McCulloch calls τ the *effective* income tax rate, and describes it as 'the approximate rate at which the Treasury recaptures its interest payments when it floats new debt'.

5.3.2   SCHAEFER (1981)

Schaefer begins from a different perspective, using a simple example to demonstrate that, given a set of bond prices, it is impossible to derive a unique term structure using the bond price equation from Chapter 1 (which he calls the 'no-arbitrage' condition) if there exists more than one category of taxpayer in the market and the tax treatment of long and short positions is symmetric. His example is as follows:

Suppose there are two investors in the market — one tax-exempt and the other facing an income tax rate of 50% — and two one-period bonds with coupons 4% and 10%. Both bonds make payments only at maturity, when each pays a coupon and repays the principal (£100, say). Having computed the after-tax cash flows, the bond pricing equation implies the following equations for the tax-exempt investor:

$$P_1 = \frac{104}{(1+z_1)} \quad \text{and} \quad P_2 = \frac{110}{(1+z_2)} \tag{5.2a}$$

whereas, for the tax-paying investor:

$$P_1 = \frac{102}{(1+z_1')} \quad \text{and} \quad P_2 = \frac{105}{(1+z_2')} \tag{5.2b}$$

The two pairs of equations are evidently inconsistent: if P_1 and P_2 are fixed then z_1 and z_1' cannot be equal, implying that for given market prices the two classes of investors value the two bonds differently. In turn, this implies that costless arbitrage would be possible between the different categories of investor (at the cost of the tax authorities). Since this is inconsistent with the existence of equilibrium as well as being unrealistic, Schaefer assumes that short-sales of gilts are banned. This assumption implies (among other things) that no arbitrage is possible and hence that no bond can be underpriced. Therefore, for any given tax rate τ, the price equation becomes:

$$P \geq \frac{C}{(1+z_1)} + \frac{C}{(1+z_2)^2} + \cdots + \frac{R+C}{(1+z_n)^n} \tag{5.3}$$

where all the cashflows are post-tax and the term structure z_i is *specific* to the tax rate τ. For an investor facing an income tax rate τ, each bond in the market is either efficient (if its market price equates exactly to the investor's valuation) or inefficient (with a market price greater than the investor's valuation). Thus, Schaefer argues, there is no unique term structure of interest rates but rather a series of tax-specific term structures, each of which should be estimated using only those bonds which are efficient to the investors in that tax clientele. As he states[15] '... the problem has two parts: (i) finding which bonds are optimally held at a particular tax rate and then (ii) solving (5.3) with the strict equality for those bonds, while ensuring that the inequality holds for all remaining bonds' (page 418).

The estimation procedure involves one further (and essentially arbitrary) assumption about the series of cashflows required by investors, in order to determine those bonds that are optimally held at the chosen tax rate. Given these cashflows s_j ($j = 1, \ldots, T$, where T represents the number of periods of interest), the problem of finding the optimal portfolio[16] x^* (where x_i^* represents the holding of bond i ($i = 1, \ldots m$) — of maturity $M(i)$ — in the portfolio) can be expressed in terms of a linear program:

$$\min_{x_i} \sum_{i=1}^{m} P_i x_i$$

subject to:
$$\sum_{i=1}^{m} a_{ij} x_j \geq s_j \quad j = 1, \ldots, T \tag{5.4}$$

and

$$x_i \geq 0 \qquad\qquad i = 1, \ldots, m$$

where a_{ij} represents the after-tax payment from bond i in period j, P_i is the price of bond i and x_i is the number of units of bond i which are held. Schaefer notes that the dual values to (5.4) measure the cost (in current value) of a unit increase in the cashflow in each period. In other words, the dual value of each cashflow constraint in the above equation corresponds to the appropriate discount factor d_j. Transforming the above linear program to its dual problem:

$$\max_{d_j} \sum_{j=1}^{T} s_{ji} d_j$$

subject to: $$\sum_{j=1}^{T} a_{ij} d_j \leq P_i \qquad i = 1, \ldots, m \qquad\qquad (5.5)$$

and

$$d_j \geq 0 \qquad\qquad j = 1, \ldots, T$$

The above formulation can only be solved if there exists a bond that provides a cashflow in each of the periods $1, \ldots, T$. Since this is not usually the case[17] the discount function needs to be approximated as a linear combination of n continuous basis functions (as described in Chapter 2):

$$\delta(t) = \sum_{k=0}^{n} \alpha_k f_k(t) \qquad\qquad (5.6)$$

where α_k ($k = 0, \ldots, n$) are the weights attached to the functions $f_k(t)$. With this approximation, the model becomes:

$$\max_{\alpha_k} \sum_{k=0}^{n} \sigma_k \alpha_k$$

subject to: $$\sum_{k=0}^{n} b_{ik} \alpha_k \leq P_i \qquad i = 1, \ldots, m \qquad\qquad (5.7)$$

$$\sum_{k=0}^{n} \alpha_k f_k(1) \geq 0$$

and

$$\alpha_0 = 1, \alpha_k \geq 0 \qquad\qquad k = 1, \ldots, n$$

where

$$\sigma_k = \sum_{j=1}^{T} s_j f_k(t_j) \quad \text{and} \quad b_{ik} = \sum_{j=1}^{M(i)} a_{ij} f_k(t_{ij})$$

Schaefer's specification of the problem highlights a number of difficulties with McCulloch's approach. First, by definition, McCulloch's methodology will calculate the term structure for only one category of taxpayer (facing the effective tax rate). The effective tax rate calculated using McCulloch's regression methodology will be some kind of 'average' of all income tax rates faced by investors, rather than the rate applicable to the marginal investor. Second, this tax rate is (implicitly) assumed to apply to all bonds along the length of the curve, an unrealistic assumption if any of the categories of investor have preferences for the maturity of debt they want to hold.

The model specified by Schaefer is well suited to an individual institution making decisions about which bonds to hold, since the applicable tax rate is clear and the profile of cashflows required should also be known (or at least reasonably well approximated). However, problems arise when using this model to identify a (single) 'market' term structure. There are two possible ways forward:

(1) Simply select one of the tax specific term structures and use this as a 'representative' term structure, for example the term structure for 0% taxpayers. The problem with this approach is that it ignores information from all bonds other than those used to determine the particular term structure. It may also lead to a data shortage problem[18] which can be alleviated to some degree by also including 'near-efficient' bonds — those within a tolerance limit of being efficient bonds — and including these in a McCulloch-type regression[19]. However, some information is still being ignored and the term structure cannot be described as being representative of the whole market without further assumptions being made.

(2) Another method derives from a suggestion in Schaefer (1981), outlining how a representative par yield curve can be estimated from a set of tax-specific term structures. Using (1.27) and scaling by τ, the (pre-tax) coupon $C_{\tau,m}$ required by an investor facing tax rate τ to value an m-period bond at its face value R is:

$$C_{\tau,m} = \frac{R(1 - d_m)}{(1 - \tau)\sum_{i=1}^{m} d_i} \tag{5.8}$$

Since the market price of a bond is determined by the investor who attaches to it the highest value, the 'market par yield' $y(m)$ is given by the lowest coupon stock with maturity m that at least one class of investor will price at par:

$$y(m) = \min_{\tau}(C_{\tau,m}) \tag{5.9}$$

from which a representative zero-coupon curve and forward rate curve can be calculated using the relationships detailed in Chapter 1.

Approach (2) has the advantage over approach (1) that it does represent the whole market, rather than a specific category of taxpayer. However, to obtain an accurate term structure in this way requires the identification of all distinct tax categories (not an easy task) and the estimation of all their separate term structures. Both approaches suffer from two drawbacks when used to estimate market representative curves. First, both require a function specifying the cash-flows required in all future periods by at least one category of investor. This is essentially an arbitrary selection and it is not clear what effect different functional forms may have on resulting term structures. Second, the estimation method depends crucially on the assumption that no bonds are underpriced and so, as Schaefer states (1981, p. 429): 'To the extent that ... underpricing does occur, our estimates [of term structures] may be upward biased'.

5.3.3   MASTRONIKOLA (1991) — THE BANK OF ENGLAND MODEL

Mastronikola (1991) tackles the problem highlighted by Schaefer by noting that this tax effect manifests itself entirely through the bond coupons[20] and attempts to correct for it by modelling the relationship between yield and coupon, as well as that between yield and maturity, explicitly. A yield *surface* (yield as a function of coupon and maturity) is estimated, allowing the size of the coupon effect to vary with maturity (unlike McCulloch, 1975). The par yield curve can be obtained from such a surface by noting that a yield of a bond trading at par must equal its coupon (the same condition used to derive (1.27) and (1.28)); so the par yield curve can be thought of as the intersection between the yield surface and the 'yield = coupon' plane (see Mastronikola, 1991, diagram A).

The yield-coupon relationship *for a given maturity* is modelled using *capital–income curves* to describe the trade-off between capital gain (assuming the bond is held to maturity) and income. For a bond with coupon C and redemption payment R (equal to £1, say) trading at price P, the capital gain and income (the latter being defined as the bonds running yield — see Chapter 1) are given by:

$$\text{Capital gain} = \frac{1}{P} - 1 \qquad \text{Income} = \frac{C}{P} \qquad (5.10)$$

Note that, for a given maturity, describing the relationship between capital gain and income is equivalent to describing the relationship between yield and coupon since the only variables in (5.10) are coupon and price (the latter of which, if maturity is fixed, is itself a function of yield and coupon only). The relationship between capital gain and income can therefore be transformed to a relationship between yield and coupon.

For a particular (fixed) maturity m, a capital–income diagram describes the trade-off between capital gain and income received on a bond[21]. For a fixed yield y, capital gain CG can be shown to be a linear function of income r (see Mastronikola, 1991, equations (3) and (4) on p. 11):

$$\frac{1}{P} - 1 = A(y - r) \qquad (5.11a)$$

where

$$A = \frac{[1 + \frac{1}{2}y(1 - \tau)^m] - 1}{y} \qquad (5.11b)$$

This relationship is shown graphically in Figure 5.1(a). It is an indifference curve describing the various balances between capital gain and income to which an investor (facing tax rate τ — see below) is indifferent.

Note in Figure 5.1 the line $CG = 0$ is called the *par line* since a bond bought at par and held to maturity yields no capital gain. Figure 5.1(b) shows the

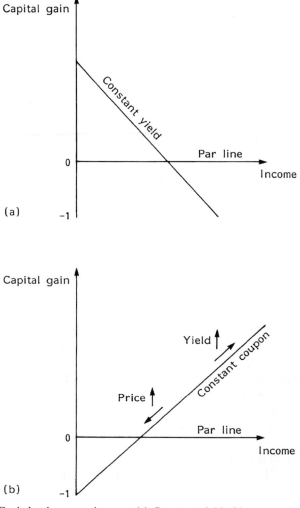

Figure 5.1   Capital gain versus income. (a) Constant yield; (b) constant coupon

relationship between capital gain and income if the coupon C is fixed; clearly (from equation (5.10)) as the price rises, both income and capital gain fall. The relationship is linear with slope $1/C$ since, from the definition of r:

$$r = \frac{C}{P} \qquad \text{and so} \qquad \frac{1}{P} - 1 = \frac{r}{C} - 1 \qquad (5.12)$$

For a fixed maturity and yield, A in (5.11b) depends only on the tax rate τ and therefore it is this income tax rate alone that determines the slope of the indifference line in Figure 5.1(a). Figure 5.2 illustrates this by displaying the indifference lines for two investors: a gross investor ($\tau = 0$) represented by the line GG$'$ and a tax-paying investor represented by the line HH$'$ ($\tau > 0$). In this scenario, since they pay tax on income but not on capital gain, the tax-paying investor requires a larger increase in income than gross investors to offset a unit decrease in capital gain — hence HH$'$ is less steeply sloped than GG$'$ in Figure 5.2.

Figure 5.3 illustrates how two bonds (1 and 2) with the same maturity m but different coupons C_1 and C_2 are priced in a market with these two categories of investors. The slopes of the constant coupon lines representing the two bonds (denoted C_1 and C_2 in Figure 5.3) are $1/C_1$ and $1/C_2$ (from (5.12)) and therefore since the gradient of C_2 is greater than the gradient of C_1 in Figure 5.3, $1/C_2 > 1/C_1$; i.e. the coupon C_1 must be larger than the coupon C_2. This illustrates the general property of such diagrams that constant coupon lines representing high coupon bonds are less steep than those representing low coupon bonds.

The intersections of C_1 and C_2 with GG$'$ (denoted $P_1(G)$ and $P_2(G)$) indicate how gross investors will value the stream of cashflows from bonds 1 and 2 respectively. Likewise, $P_1(H)$ and $P_2(H)$ represent the taxpayers' valuation of

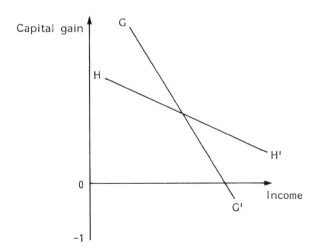

Figure 5.2 The effect of tax

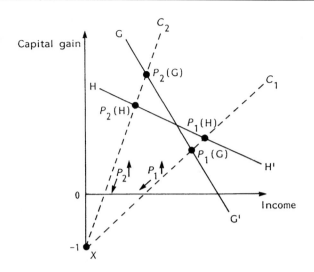

Figure 5.3   Capital gain versus income

the same two bonds. Clearly, the higher coupon bond's price will therefore be set by the tax-exempt investor, whereas the lower coupon bond's price will be determined by the tax-paying investor. Such a specification models a market assumed to be in 'equilibrium under switching' (Mastronikola, 1991, p. 10), in which no investor can switch from one stock to any combination of other stocks if such a switch results in:

• Higher capital gain and maintained income, or
• Higher income and maintained capital gain, or
• Both higher income and higher capital gain.

These conditions define an equilibrium equivalent to the 'no arbitrage' equilibrium in Schaefer's model[22] — for each bond it is the category of taxpayer who values it the highest who determines its price.

Figure 5.4(a) shows two extreme indifference lines, for a gross investor and a 100% income taxpayer. The line for an investor facing 100% income tax rate is horizontal since such an investor will only invest in bonds providing a pure capital gain. This model can easily be generalized to any number of categories of taxpayers, as illustrated in Figure 5.4(b). If the market is in equilibrium under switching, the prices of bonds in this diagram will lie on the heavy boundary (corresponding to an 'efficient frontier'). However, as mentioned earlier, it is difficult to specify a number of distinct categories of taxpayers because of the potential range of different tax treatments faced by domestic and overseas investors. For this reason, the model allows for a continuous spectrum

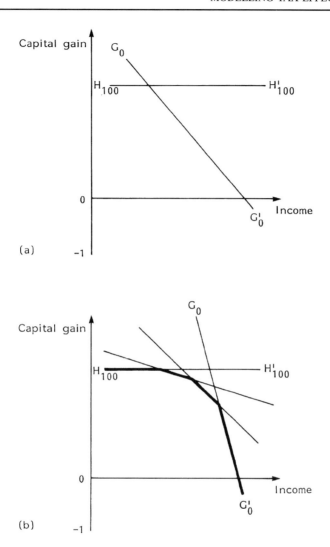

Figure 5.4   Capital gain versus income. (a) Extreme cases; (b) intermediate cases

of income taxpayers between the gross investor and the 100% tax rate payer, the
boundary in Figure 5.4(b) becoming the *capital-income curve* in Figure 5.5. So
although the theory behind Schaefer (1981) and Mastronikola (1991) is the same,
there is an important difference in implementation: Schaefer *a priori* determines
the specific rates for which term structures are required, whereas Mastronikola
defines how categories of taxpayers interact and thereby estimates a single term
structure representative of the market as a whole.

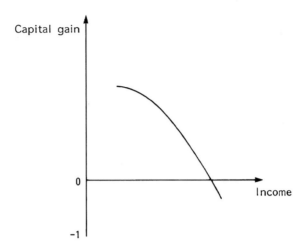

Figure 5.5   Capital income curve

The capital-income (Figure 5.5) curve is defined by[23]

$$CG = \begin{cases} \alpha(y(m) - r) & r \geq y(m) \\ \alpha(y(m) - r) + \lambda(m)(y(m) - r)^{\delta} & r < y(m) \end{cases} \qquad (5.13a)$$

where

$$\alpha = \frac{[1 + \frac{1}{2}y(1 - \tau(m))^{m}] - 1}{y(m)} \qquad (5.13b)$$

and $y(m)$ is the (given) par yield at maturity m^{24}. Here $\tau(m)$ represents the tax rate faced by gross investors and should therefore in theory equal zero, but in practice need not be constrained to do so. Deviations from zero can to some extent be explained by taxpayers holding high coupon bonds that are trading above par, but may also reflect underpricing in the market. A linear function is defined to specify how $\tau(m)$ varies with maturity m.

To specify the capital–income curve completely, specifications of δ and $\lambda(m)$ are required. The model assumes *a priori* that δ is fixed and also assumes that the capital–income curve is bounded by two extreme forms (Figure 5.6). The upper extreme curve in Figure 5.6 corresponds to the case where all bonds above the par line are held by gross investors, and can be represented by $\lambda(m) = 0$. Conversely, the lower extreme curve represents the largest tax effect. It is constructed by assuming that a 100% taxpayer is holding the lowest coupon bond in the market, so the capital income curve becomes horizontal as it crosses the constant coupon line representing the lowest coupon bond. The true curve lies between these two extremes (see Mastronikola for a full deviation).

The four parameters that specify the relationships between $\tau(m)$ and m, and $\lambda(m)$ and m (and hence how the yield–coupon relationship varies with maturity)

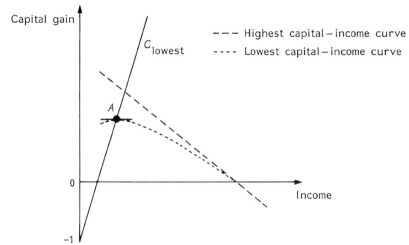

Figure 5.6   Extreme capital income curves

are combined with those that specify the yield–maturity relationship $y(m)$. A non-linear estimation technique that minimizes the sum of squared residuals between the observed and fitted yields is used to estimate the values of these parameters simultaneously[25]. In a sense this is the reverse of Schaefer's approach which, rather than finding a 'best-fit' curve, instead involves determining the optimal set of bonds for each category of taxpayer from which a tax-specific term structure is estimated.

5.3.4   OTHER TAX EFFECTS

The above discussion has concentrated on the distinction between income and capital gains tax, but many other effects can be incorporated into the models described above if felt to be significant. One example is that proposed in Vasicek and Fong (1982) to capture all distortions caused by the existence of bonds with different coupons. Their approach is to augment the bond price equation as shown in (5.14)[26]:

$$P = c \sum_{j=1}^{n} \delta(t_j) + R\delta(t_m) - q\frac{C}{P}\left(\frac{\partial P}{\partial Y}\right) \tag{5.14}$$

where Y is the gross redemption yield of the bond corresponding to the (dirty) price P. Note how this is similar to the approach used by Mastronikola (1991) in using the running yield C/P to represent the income from a bond. However, Vasicek and Fong's approach is less rich because the additional parameter is designed to capture all 'coupon effects' without distinguishing between them, although the negative sign on the additional term reflects the authors' belief that high-coupon bonds will be valued lower than low-coupon bonds[27]. Although it is very similar to (5.1), it has the advantage that the bond price equation is linear, meaning that standard linear regression techniques can be used rather than resorting to non-linear iteration techniques.

Mastronikola (1991) takes a more detailed approach to model the various tax effects. In this study, not only are the effects caused by the differential taxation of income and capital gain modelled thoroughly, but the proposed model also takes account of two other tax effects. The first derives from the presumption that, because taxpayers want to avoid coupon income, they will buy bonds as early as possible in the coupon cycle and then sell before the date on which they would be registered to receive a coupon payment. Although the payment of tax cannot be avoided entirely in this manner, it can certainly be delayed. To capture this effect, the dirty price P in the price equation is written as:

$$P = p + \beta ai \tag{5.15}$$

where p is the bond's clean price. Since accrued interest accumulates from zero through the coupon cycle, the parameter β will capture any relative valuation effect caused by increased demand at particular points in the coupon cycle[28].

This study also takes account of another feature of the UK gilt market caused by the tax system — again one that is likely to disappear following the 1996 tax reforms. As mentioned earlier, some gilts are designated to make coupon payments Free Of Tax to Residents Abroad (FOTRA), making them more desirable to foreign investors than non-FOTRA bonds simply because their coupons are paid gross and so a foreign investor does not have to wait for a tax reimbursement. Lacking a detailed model of how a non-resident would value a FOTRA bond relative to other non-FOTRA bonds, a dummy variable[29] is included in the bond price equation. Although undoubtedly crude, using a dummy variable in such instances is a simple and often very effective way of accounting for such effects in the absence of a more detailed model.

Another way in which tax rules can affect the valuation of bonds is the manner in which the *timing* of cashflows is affected. For example, consider a gross investor in Italy who is exempt from withholding tax on government bonds but still receives the coupon payment net of tax and must apply to have the tax payment reimbursed[30]. Such an investor will clearly receive all the coupon payments eventually, but the proportion withheld by the authorities will be received only with a delay. Suppose, on average, this delay is estimated to be x years, then the bond price equation can be written:

$$P = c(1 - \tau) \sum_{j=1}^{n} \delta(t_j) + c\tau \sum_{j=1}^{n} \delta(t_j + x) + R\delta(t_m) \tag{5.16}$$

Of course, such a model relies on being able to estimate reasonably the delay with which the tax payment will be reimbursed.

It is very difficult to account for all possible taxation effects that may affect the valuation of government bonds, and studies that try to do so formally can get extremely complicated — for example, Dermody and Rockafellar (1994) present a thorough but very complex model of the US government bond market. However, it is important to identify the most significant effects for each particular market, since ignoring them can bias term structure estimates (e.g. Jordan, 1984).

5.4 CONCLUSIONS

Choosing a method to model tax effects is to some degree independent of the choice of method to model the term structure as described in Chapter 2. For example, there is no reason why the model described by Mastronikola (1991) for estimating the coupon effect cannot be used in conjunction with a model that fits a discount function rather than a par yield. Indeed, this is exactly what was done to produce the data used in the empirical comparisons described in Chapter 3.

McCulloch (1975) introduced the methodology for adjusting yield curves for taxation effects, and demonstrated that adjusting for tax using his technique is substantially better than not adjusting at all — verified more formally by Jordan (1984). However, his approach for handling tax has a number of disadvantages; in particular, it is unclear what the 'effective tax rate' actually represents — and yet it is assumed constant along the length of the curve. Vasicek and Fong (1982) describe a variation on this approach that has a linear formulation, but one that is subject to the same problems when trying to interpret the estimated parameters.

Schaefer (1981) notes that there are in fact multiple term structures, one for each distinct category of taxpaying investors — highlighting the drawback with McCulloch's approach. Schaefer's suggested method of estimating a separate term structure for each category of taxpayer is useful for an individual institution attempting to decide which bonds are efficient to hold and thereby assessing its term structure of interest rates, but causes problems when trying to estimate a single 'market' yield curve. It is necessary either to identify all distinct categories of taxpayer, something that could easily change on a daily basis, or to assume that one particular term structure is somehow representative of the market and, in the process, discard information from all bonds that are inefficient for that particular category of investor. The assumption that no bond is underpriced also leaves open the possibility that the estimated term structure is biased.

Mastronikola (1991) attempts to model both the yield–maturity and the yield–coupon relationships of the bond market and, in a way different from that adopted by Schaefer, models the category of investor determining the marginal price of each bond (see Mastronikola, 1991, or Deacon and Derry, 1994). The model therefore estimates a gross investor's par yield curve using information from all bonds in the market, rather than just the efficient subset. Although not so rigorous theoretically, it does resolve a number of the practical estimation problems inherent in Schaefer's approach — primarily because it uses information from all the bonds in the market to construct a single market curve.

NOTES

1. Indeed, as described in Chapter 3, such rules alone can cause a bond market to become *segmented* — a situation in which different classes of bonds are held and traded by distinct categories of investors.
2. Once the proposed tax reforms to the UK government bond market have taken effect — due to be implemented by May 1996 — tax will not be withheld on strippable or stripped gilts. Since January 1996 investors lending gilts as part of a repurchase ('repo') agreement have received coupon payments gross. Also, withholding tax will be reduced from 25% to 20%.
3. This tax is not applied to foreign investors.
4. The existence of a transactions tax may induce investors to 'buy and hold' longer-dated bonds rather than rolling over shorter-dated instruments.
5. Although it may, of course, make security markets less attractive to international investors than those in other countries.
6. In the absence of any complicating factors such as embedded optionality, indexation to retail prices, etc.
7. Again, this distinction is likely to disappear following the changes in tax rules proposed in May 1996.
8. In Italy, an official issue price is declared and, for bonds issued at a discount, the redemption payment is reduced by an amount dictated by the witholding tax rate. For example, if a bond is issued at $90.00 (per $100.00 face value) and the witholding tax rate is 12.5%, then the redemption payment for all investors will be: $100.00 − 0.125 × ($100.00 − $90.00) = $98.75. Investors exempted from this tax must apply for the $1.25 to be refunded.
9. Details of how tax is reclaimed under a double-taxation agreement or to register for gross payment of coupons on a FOTRA stock are given in Bank of England (1993).
10. Both bonds having the same maturity date, coupon payments, liquidity, etc.
11. A full description of these changes is given in Bank of England (1995).
12. This section is taken largely from Deacon and Derry (1994, Sections 4 and 5).
13. Although proposals announced in the 1995 Budget suggest that the income-capital gain distinction will remain in place for UK individual investors.
14. $P = p + ai$ where p represents the bond's quoted (or *clean*) price and ai its accrued interest. See Chapter 1 for a discussion of clean/dirty prices and accrued interest.
15. Schaefer, 1981, page 418
16. Defined as the portfolio '... which results in cashflows $s_1, s_2, \ldots, s_T$ in periods $1, 2, \ldots, T$ and provides those cash flows at *minimum cost*' (Schaefer, 1981, page 418).
17. As described in Chapter 2, even some of the most developed government bond markets have gaps in the maturity spectrum.

18. In the study carried out by Derry and Pradhan (1993), typically only six to eight bonds from a universe of 40 to 60 were found to be efficient on any particular date.
19. A suggestion made to the authors by Professor Schaefer.
20. Assuming that investors are exempt from paying tax on capital gains.
21. Here m is defined as the number of half-years to maturity, reflecting the application of this model to the gilt-edged market in which nearly all bonds pay semi-annual coupons.
22. Therefore this model also depends on the assumption that short-sales are restricted.
23. Again, m defined as maturity measured in half-years.
24. This comes directly from the definition of A in (5.11b). Note that δ here is not related to the discount function of previous chapters. δ can be thought of as the 'degree' of curvature of the capital–income curve above the par line (e.g. quadratic if $\delta = 2$, etc.) while $\lambda(m)$ can be thought of as a 'weight' that specifies how much this curvature comes into effect at maturity m.
25. Two other effects are modelled using dummy variables to represent whether or not a bond is trading ex-dividend (XD) and/or Free Of Tax to Residents Abroad (FOTRA).
26. This is not the full model proposed by the authors. It is simplified here to highlight how the model captures tax effects.
27. The scaling factor $(\partial p/\partial Y)$ results from the authors' assumption that any such coupon effect will be linear in the running yield (as opposed to price), and this factor serves to transform such a move in yield to a corresponding yield in price. It comes from noting that $dp = dY(\partial p/\partial y)$.
28. In the UK, holders of gilts become eligible to receive the next coupon 37 days before the coupon payment is due, and between this date and the coupon payment date the bond is said to trade *ex-dividend*. Since the effect described here will be largest at the beginning of this period, Mastronikola (1991) refers to this as the *ex-dividend (XD) effect*. The XD period will be reduced to 7 working days from January 1996.
29. Equal to unity if the bond is FOTRA, zero otherwise.
30. In Italy withholding tax is also payable on capital gains, but for simplicity this is overlooked here.

REFERENCES

Bank of England (1993) *British Government Securities: The Market in Gilt-Edged Securities* (May).
Bank of England (1995) *Gilts and the Gilt Market: Review 1994-5* (July).
Deacon, M. and Derry, A. (1994) Estimating the term structure of interest rates, Bank of England Working Paper 24 (July).

Dermody, J. and Rockafellar, R. (1994) Mathematics of debt instruments taxation, *Financial Markets, Institutions & Instruments* **3**, No. 2 (May).

Derry, A. and Pradhan, M. (1993) Tax specific term structures of interest rates in the UK government bond market, Bank of England Working Paper 11 (April).

Fage, P. (1988) *Yield Calculations*, CSFB Research, London.

Jordan (1984) Tax effects in term structure estimation, *Journal of Finance*, **XXXIX**, No. 2 (June), 393–406.

Litzenberger, R. and Rolfo, J. (1984) An international study of tax effects on government bonds, *Journal of Finance*, **XXXIX**, No. 1 (March), 1–22.

Mastronikola, K. (1991) Yield curves for gilt-edged stocks: a new model, Bank of England Discussion Paper (Technical Series), No. 49 (December).

McCulloch, J.H. (1971) Measuring the term structure of interest rates, *Journal of Business*, **XLIV** (January), 19–31.

McCulloch, J.H. (1975) The tax-adjusted yield curve, *Journal of Finance*, **XXX**, No. 3 (June), 811–30.

Schaefer, S. (1981) Measuring a tax-specific term structure of interest rates in the market for British government securities, *The Economic Journal*, **91** (June), 415–38.

Vasicek, O. and Fong, H. (1982) Term structure modelling using exponential splines, *Journal of Finance*, **XXXVII**, No. 2 (May), 339–56.

CHAPTER 6

Bonds with embedded options

6.1 INTRODUCTION

This chapter introduces bonds with embedded options to show why such instruments cannot readily be thought of in the same way as conventional bonds for valuation and yield curve estimation purposes. A description of the techniques for valuing such bonds is set within the theoretical framework of Chapter 4 and merits a separate volume in its own right, which is beyond the scope of this book. This chapter focuses on callable and convertible bonds in order to illustrate why bonds with embedded options deserve special treatment. There are, of course, myriad variations which one could introduce into the terms of a bond which might create additional option-like properties.

To value bonds with embedded options requires consideration of the level of yields and the volatility of the yield curve is required. Such bonds are very common among corporate debt issues. Where borrowers and lenders disagree on the appropriate level of yields for debt of a particular credit quality, they may still be able to arrange debt-based finance by trading a bond with embedded option characteristics which, in addition, factors the volatility of the yield curve into the price. Therefore, such bonds are often used as an alternative form of debt-based finance where the borrower and lender have different beliefs regarding the level of yields.

Bonds with embedded options can be thought of as having value which is the sum of a straight bond component and an option component. So the same price is consistent with different beliefs regarding the level of yields and the level of interest rate volatility. Where the borrower and lender differ on the appropriate level of yields for the debt in question, the fact that such bonds are issued is an indication of the fact that views on the yield levels have been traded against views on volatility.

In addition, the terms of these bonds might also allow the lender to signal to the borrower his or her beliefs regarding the level and direction of yields (an example of this will be given later in the chapter). This could be achieved by making adjustments to the strike price(s) of the option embedded in the bond.

This chapter discusses the two most common forms of option-bearing bonds issued by the UK government — callable and convertible bonds. In addition, the use of these bonds as instruments of government finance in other countries is briefly surveyed. Several of the pricing and yield curve estimation issues of such bonds are also explored.

6.2   CALLABLE BONDS

6.2.1   WHAT IS A CALLABLE BOND?

Callable bonds are securities which can be redeemed early (or called) at the discretion of the issuer, after a certain date which is specified at issue. The motivation behind issuing a callable bond rather than a standard bond is that if yield levels fall below the coupon of the callable, the issuer can call the bond and then refinance the debt with a bond of lower coupon. Thus the risk of yields falling in the future is reduced, albeit at the expense of selling the bonds for a lower price than conventional bonds without the call feature. In the case of governments an additional consideration for issuance of callables it may be that this can also be used as a signal to the market that the authorities view current yield levels as being too high and are unwilling to lock themselves into such high levels of funding costs.

6.2.2   SOVEREIGN CALLABLE BOND ISSUES

The earliest callable gilts that were issued had no final redemption dates, simply a date after which they could be called. The last issue of this type was in 1946, and all such bonds have very low coupons compared to current conventional gilts (see Table 6.1), reflecting the low level of yields when they were issued. Given

Table 6.1   UK irredeemable gilts

Coupon (%)	Stock name	Earliest call date	Nominal amount outstanding (£m)
4.00	Consols	1957	358
3.50	War Loan	1952	1909
3.50	Conversion	1961	115
3.00	Treasury	1966	56
2.50	Consols	1923	275
2.50	Treasury	1975	474
2.50	Annuities	1905	3
2.75	Annuities	1905	1

Source: Bank of England. Figures as at 20 March 1995.

that it will only become profitable to call these bonds if yield levels fall below the coupon rates on the bonds they are unlikely ever to be redeemed. Consequently they have become known as irredeemables.

Since 1946, *all* issues of callable gilts have had a definite final maturity date, in addition to an earlier call date. The first bond of this type was 4% Funding 1960/1990, which was issued in 1919. The two dates in the title of such bonds signify the period during which they may be redeemed — thus, 14% Treasury 1998/2001 may be redeemed on *any* date between 22 May 1998 and 22 May 2001. In the UK market, callables with a fixed final redemption date are sometimes referred to as either double-dated or split-maturity bonds — a full listing of stocks being given in Table 6.2. The UK last issued a callable bond in 1987. To redeem callables early, the authorities must provide 3 months' notice.

Although the terms of callable bonds can be such that they can be called at any specified price, early redemption in the gilt market has always been at par. For a given callable gilt, if after its earliest redemption date, yield levels fall below its coupon, there is an incentive for the authorities to call the bond since they could refinance the debt with a lower coupon. See Table 6.3.

For each of the more liquid double-dated gilts, Table 6.4 illustrates the expected par yield[1] on the call date, of maturity equal to the number of years between the call date and the redemption date. Comparing these par yields with the coupons on the bonds gives an indication of the likelihood of early redemption. Unlike some other governments that have issued callable bonds, the UK has in the past redeemed callable bonds early — an example of which is given below.

Table 6.2 UK double-dated gilts

Coupon (%)	Stock name	Earliest maturity date	Final maturity date	Nominal amount outstanding (£m)
3.00	Exchequer Gas	1990	1995	214
6.75	Treasury	1995	1998	1200
14.00	Treasury	1998	2001	970
12.00	Exchequer	1999	2002	105
13.75	Treasury	2000	2003	53
11.50	Treasury	2001	2004	1620
3.50	Funding	1999	2004	543
12.50	Treasury	2003	2005	2200
8.00	Treasury	2002	2006	2000
11.75	Treasury	2003	2007	3150
13.50	Treasury	2004	2008	1250
5.50	Treasury	2008	2012	1000
7.75	Treasury	2012	2015	800
2.50	Treasury	1986	2016	78
12.00	Treasury	2013	2017	1000

Source: Bank of England. Figures as at 20 March 1995. It should be noted that this is a *full* listing of double-dated gilts, and as such, includes several illiquid issues which are rarely traded.

Table 6.3 Summary of countries' experience of callable government bond issuance

Country	Comment
Austria	Recent move away from issuing callables
Belgium	Most recent issues have carried annual call options after their first four years
Canada	Has just one callable bond
Ireland	Callables are identical to UK callables
Japan	All Japanese bonds are callable. However, none have ever been redeemed early despite the fact that most are valued in excess of par at present.
Netherlands	During 1985–87 many callables were redeemed early. No new callable bonds have been issued in recent years. Early redemption is against a given (descending) penalty expressed as a redemption price above par.
Norway	Callables are similar to Belgian and Dutch issues
Switzerland	About 80% of Swiss federal government bonds are callable. Issues have 10–15 year maturities and are callable two or three years before final maturity
USA	Callable issues are mainly concentrated in the 10–15 year maturity range. This means that there are few conventional bonds with which to estimate this sector of the yield curve.

Sources: D'Andrea and Mahoney (1994), ISSA (1994) and McLean (1993).

Table 6.4 Implied refinancing rates

Stock	Call window (years)	Implied forward par yield* (%)
6.75% Treasury 1995/98	3	8.46
14.00% Treasury 1998/01	3	9.17
11.50% Treasury 2001/04	3	8.92
3.50% Funding 1999/04	5	8.96
12.50% Treasury 2003/05	2	8.57
8.00 Treasury 2002/06	4	8.59
11.75% Treasury 2003/07	4	8.50
13.50% Treasury 2004/08	4	8.33
5.50% Treasury 2008/12	4	8.13
7.75% Treasury 2012/15	3	8.24
12.00% Exchequer 2013/17	4	8.32

*This is the par yield when of maturity equal to the length of the call window which is implied by the yield curve for bonds issued on the initial call date of the callable.

From Table 6.4 we would conclude that those bonds with coupons which are significantly less than the implied par yield at their call date are unlikely to be redeemed early.

6.2.3   EXAMPLE

The last UK callable gilt to be redeemed early was 9% Treasury Loan 1992/96, which had a final redemption date of 15 March 1996 and a first redemption date of 15 March 1992. This was redeemed on 28 January 1993, notice of redemption being given on 23 October 1992. Figure 6.1 illustrates the price history for the stock as it approached redemption — the vertical line denoting the date on which early redemption was announced. In the Bank of England press notice announcing the early redemption, the Bank declared 'gilt yields having fallen, a cost saving for the government can be achieved by redeeming this stock now and replacing it with cheaper finance. The issue of a new stock, 7.25% Treasury 1998, is being simultaneously announced' (Bank of England, 1992)[2].

Because 3 months' notice of early redemption must be given for callable gilts, the authorities need to make an assessment of future yield levels before they can make the decision to exercise the call. It is not sufficient for the bond to be trading above par today. The calling of 9% Treasury 1992/96 illustrates two features of callable bonds that differ from conventional bonds. First, the government chose to refinance this debt by locking into lower yields. Figure 6.1 shows that the price of the bond had crossed its par value in September 1992 and remained above this level for the remainder of the year. Second, in the months after 'Black Wednesday' (16 September 1992) base rates were progressively reduced. The early redemption of 9% 1992/96 may have been due to the authorities belief that yields were on a downward path since base rates were falling and because a new regime for monetary policy had been announced. Alternatively, one might argue that if rates were falling, the redemption of the callable was 'too early' or suboptimal from the point of view of refinancing at the lowest possible rates. In weighing up these views, it is useful to remember that optimal exercise of the call option must be weighed against other constraints which bind on the borrower.

6.2.4   PRICING CALLABLE BONDS

The main aim of this section is to illustrate market conventions for pricing such bonds and show how to decompose the bond into its conventional and option components. A market convention which overly simplifies the computation of the value of a callable bond is to price the bond using the par rule, also referred to as pricing on a yield-to-worst basis. For the purposes of this section, an example of a callable bond with a European-style embedded option is given. There is no limit to the further complications that one can introduce to the structure of the

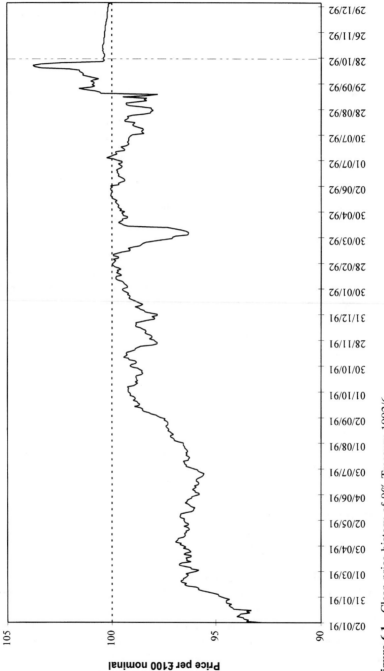

Figure 6.1   Clean price history of 9% Treasury 1992/6

option embedded in the bond, of which American-style call features and non-par exercise prices are but two. Consider a 7-year callable bond with a coupon of 6% which is (1) issued on 28 March 1995, (2) callable on 28 March 1999, otherwise (3) redeemable at par on 28 March 2002. The coupon is paid semi-annually. If it were known with certainty that on 28 March 1999 the value of 3-year bullet bonds with coupons of 6% will be in excess of par, then the bond will be called. This course of action minimizes the issuer's borrowing liability. In such a situation, the callable would be currently priced as a 4-year bullet bond since the certain knowledge that the bond will be called means that it is no different from a conventional bullet bond. Conversely, if it were known for certain that the value of the remaining uncalled payment streams will be less than par on 28 March 1999 (whence the bond will not be called) then the callable would be priced as if it were a 7-year conventional bond. The par rule for pricing callable gilts simply assumes that if a callable is trading above par it will be called, and if it is trading below par it will not be called:

$$\text{`Value' of callable under par rule} = \begin{cases} \text{price of long} & \text{if price} < 100 \\ \text{price of short} & \text{if price} > 100 \end{cases}$$

where 'long' denotes the series of payment streams if the callable runs to maturity (28 March 2002) and 'short' denotes the series of payment streams if the callable is called on the call date (28 March 1999).

Figure 6.2 shows the price/yield relationship for the short and the long bond at the issue date. The solid kinked line indicates the price/yield relationship for the callable bond when it is priced using the par rule. Observe that at any given price level, the yield on the callable corresponds to the bond with the lowest yield: hence the term 'yield-to-worst'.

This pricing rule can lead to substantial errors both in the price of the callable and in the computation of gross redemption yields implied from the bond. In the case of the latter, it may happen that when a callable is trading at a price which frequently moves above and below par due to slight changes in the yield curve, the implied yields may change in excess of 50 bp due to the disparity between the yield on the short bond and the yield on the long bond. Clearly, the par rule is greatly affected by the variation in the yield curve between the call date and the maturity date, and by the size of the gap between these two dates.

To clarify this, it is helpful to decompose the callable into its bullet bond and option components. In this case, two such decompositions are possible. First, continuing with the example provided above, the callable bond may be viewed as an obligation on the issuer to pay £3 every six months from 28 September 1995 until 28 September 1998. On 28 March 1999, the issuer then pays £3. If the value of the remaining coupon streams is in excess of par, then the bond is called and a further £100 is paid, thereby dispensing with the issuer's liability to the lender. If the bond is not called — due to the fact that the remaining payment streams are cheap relative to par — then the bond runs to maturity. In the case

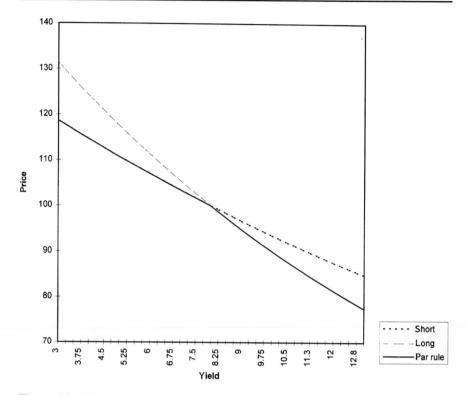

Figure 6.2 Price/yield relationship

where the bond is called, the gain due to calling the bond is the difference between the value of the long bond (on the call date, which excludes the coupon paid at that date) and £100. Thus, the issuer may be viewed as having sold a long bond and bought a European option on the long bond which is exercisable on the call date at a price of £100:

Price of callable = price of long bond − price of call option on long bond

From this it can be concluded that when the callable is trading below par, and the par rule determines the price of the callable as that of the long bond, this price overstates the value of the callable since the value of the option is positive.

The callable bond can also be viewed in terms of the short bond and an option. Consider the situation where the callable is trading above par. In this situation, the issuer pretends that he or she is meeting the obligation corresponding to a short bond and 'redeems' the callable at the call date. However, when the callable is trading below par, the issuer effectively exercises the right to sell a 6% bond redeemable on 28 March 2002 for £100. In this sense, the issuer has exercised a put option on the long bond at 28 March 1999 with a strike price of £100. So by selling the callable, the issuer has sold a short bond and purchased a European put option:

Price of callable = price of short bond − price of put option on long bond

Therefore, when the callable is trading above par, and the par rule determines the price of the bond to be equal to that of the short bond, then the price of the callable will be overstated since the put option will have positive value.

6.2.5 WHAT RISKS DO CALLABLES HEDGE?

The previous section demonstrates that the call feature of the callable bond is captured by a call or put option on the value of the (remaining payment streams of the) long bond at the call date. The option has an exercise price of £100. Thus in effect, the option hedges against the risk that the 3-year yield on 28 March 1999 will fall below 6%. To put this another way, the option allows the issuer to refinance the borrowing at a lower rate, if in fact, 3-year yields are lower at the call date. Since the yield in question is a gross redemption yield, which is, in effect, an average of zero-coupon rates up to 3 years, the option protects against a combination of parallel shifts, steepening slopes and inverted twists in the yield curve over the maturity range between the call date and the maturity date.

6.2.6 PUTTABLE BONDS

In essence, puttable bonds are identical to callable bonds, except that it is the investor rather than the issuer that has the right to exercise the option — in this case to *sell* the bond back to the issuer at a predetermined price. The similarity between callables and puttables means that exactly the same techniques for valuation can be employed. Although puttable bonds provide the issuer with more revenue than callable or conventional bonds — since the investor is paying for the right to sell the bond back to the issuer — the trade-off is an inevitable loss in funding control for the issuer since not all investors will sell (exercise the put option) the bonds when it is optimal to do so. This may help to explain why puttable government bonds are far rarer than their callable counterparts.

Puttable bonds allow the purchaser of the bond to sell the bond at a future date at some pre-specified price, usually the par value of the bond. Thus the option will be exercised if the value of the outstanding cash flows on the bond is less than the exercise price of the put option embedded in the puttable bond. Italy began issuing puttable government bonds (CTOs[3]) in 1988 — these typically being of 6-year maturity, with the option giving the investor the opportunity of early redemption, at par, at the end of the third year.

Generally, options are exercisable upon notice to the Bank of Italy during a specified period — normally one month before the exercise date. Issues of CTOs have been suspended since May 1992. Other countries with puttable government bonds include Belgium and Norway (whose bonds are both callable and puttable), the Netherlands, and Portugal (whose puttables have coupon resets and are hybrids between fixed and floating-rate bond).

6.3   CONVERTIBLE BONDS

6.3.1   WHAT IS A CONVERTIBLE BOND?

A convertible bond offers the investor the option to convert into another security or securities at predetermined conversion rates on predetermined dates. This chapter focuses on convertible bonds in which a conventional bond (the 'short' or convertible stock) may be converted into another conventional bond (the conversion stock or 'long') which matures at a later date than the original stock. Convertible bonds are normally encountered in corporate finance as instruments providing the option to exchange debt for equity rather than debt for debt. Attention here is restricted to financial instruments whose value is solely related to the term structure of interest rates.

6.3.2   CONVERTIBLE BOND ISSUES

Convertible bonds are sold less widely by sovereign issuers than callables. Unlike corporate issues of convertibles where an option is sold giving the right to exchange the bond for equity, sovereign convertible issues confer the right to exchange a bond for another bond at a later date. The French government bond market currently has eight issues known as 'emprunts' or 'échangeables'. These are fixed-rate bonds that can be exchanged for floating-rate bonds at a date specified at issue. The Netherlands also has convertible bonds — these are known as extendible bonds and give the holder the option, during a certain period of time, to convert into longer-maturity bonds at a par conversion rate. These bonds were mainly issued during the 1980s and have since largely been converted. Poland has also issued convertible bonds.

Convertible gilts were first issued in the UK in 1981, and have typically been short-dated issues which could be converted into long-dated stocks. Investors are offered several dates on which they may convert their holdings — these dates are usually six months apart and are always dividend dates. The terms for conversion are expressed as the nominal amount of the conversion bond received per £100 nominal of the convertible bond — these terms deteriorating progressively for later conversion dates. For example, 7% Treasury Convertible 1997 may be converted into 9% Treasury 2012 on a conversion term of £86 on 6 February 1996. This means that on 6 February 1996 a holder of 7% Treasury Convertible 1997 *may* exchange £100 nominal of stock for £86 nominal of 9% Treasury 2012.

Although most UK convertible issues have been of the form of short fixed interest gilts with an option to convert into long fixed-interest gilts, there have been some exceptions. For instance, 10% Treasury Convertible 1991 offered

Table 6.5 Conversion Terms for 10% Treasury Convertible 1991

Conversion stock	Date of conversion	Conversion terms
9.5% Conversion 2001	12 July 1987	102.00
	12 January 1988	101.00
	12 July 1988	100.00
	12 January 1989	99.00
	12 July 1989	98.00
9.0% Conversion 2011	12 July 1987	105.00
	12 January 1988	103.00
	12 July 1988	101.00
	12 January 1989	99.00
	12 July 1989	97.00

Source: Belchamber (1988, p. 208).

options to convert into a medium stock — 9.5% Conversion 2001 — *or* a long stock — 9% Conversion 2011. Details of these conversion options are given in Table 6.5. Also, in 1983 the Bank of England issued an index-linked gilt that could be converted into a conventional fixed interest gilt — this was almost all converted six months after issue.

Convertibles are an attractive source of funding for the authorities since, potentially, they can provide long-term funding at long-term yield levels below those at the time of issue. This is possible because the issuance of convertibles enables the authorities to set lower coupons on the conversion bonds than the market would have been prepared to accept had direct funding of long maturity bonds been undertaken instead. Convertible gilts also appeal to investors, since if yield levels fall they can convert into the long-dated bond, while if yield levels rise they are only exposed to the fall in prices of short-dated bonds. One problem with convertibles is that if a significant part of the issue is converted, the remaining stock becomes illiquid.

6.3.3 PRICING CONVERTIBLE BONDS

An earlier section introduced a simple market convention often used to value callable bonds. In the case of convertible bonds, even the simplest pricing method requires a substantial amount of computation. Consider, for example, the issue of 7% Treasury Convertible 1997 on 25 May 1994. This bond contains options which entitle the holder to exchange the bond for a quantity[4] of 9% Treasury 2012 on four different dates[5]. In order to obtain an estimate for the value of the convertible assume that interest rates follow a deterministic pattern which is embedded in the current yield curve. This implies that future rates are implied forward rates. For those who prefer to think of the term structure in terms of the forward curve, this amounts to chopping off the short end of the forward curve as time elapses. Therefore, in a deterministic world, the forward curve in

Table 6.6   Prices and implied yields of convertible and conversion stocks at conversion dates

Date	Price of short bond (£)	Yield (%)	Price of long bond (£)	Yield (%)	Short/long ×100
6 Aug. 1994	98.78	7.46	107.07	8.24	92.26
6 Feb. 1995	97.84	7.97	105.36	8.41	92.86
6 Aug. 1995	95.55	8.36	104.33	8.51	93.50
6 Feb. 1996	97.75	8.63	103.79	8.57	94.18

six months' time is simply the curve obtained when the first six months of the current forward curve is deleted. Table 6.6 gives the prices and yields of the long and short bonds at the conversion dates, based on the yields implied by the yield curve as at 24 May 1994.

Suppose, for simplicity, that the terms of the convertible bond stipulated that on the conversion date, 200 convertible bonds could be exchanged for 185 of the conversion stock, implying a 'conversion ratio' of 92.5. It would be optimal to exchange the short bond for the long only if the price of the short was less than 0.925 times the price of the long, that is,

$$100 \times \frac{\text{Price of short bond}}{\text{Price of long bond}} < \text{conversion terms } (= 92.5)$$

From Table 6.6 it can be seen that this condition — which is necessary but not sufficient for conversion — only holds in the case of the first conversion date, where the price of the long bond is sufficiently high relative to the short to make it profitable to convert at the specified conversion ratio. In a deterministic world, the optimal strategy would be to hold the short bond until the first conversion date (thereby collecting the coupon on the short bond at that date), then exchange the short bond for the long bond at that date. With this conversion strategy, one can easily compute the value of the convertible as the discounted present value of the payment streams which in this case is simply the price of the long bond minus the present value (as of 25 May 1994) of £0.6625[6] paid on 6 August 1994, giving the bond a value of £101.59.

This is a 'cross-over' method for pricing convertible stock since the decision when to exercise is determined by the date at which the short/long ratio crosses the conversion ratio. However, it suffers from some simple drawbacks. For example, it is possible that the short/long ratio starts above the level of the conversion ratio, falls below this level and then rises above it again. This suggests two possible conversion dates and therefore two possible series of payment streams to be valued. The cross-over method does not resolve this ambiguity.

Such ambiguities aside, suppose that the conversion terms were set to be 89, 88, 87 and 86 for each of the respective conversion dates[7]. In our deterministic world, the conversion option would not be exercised since on none of the conversion dates does the short/long ratio fall below these terms on any given date. The cross-over method would imply that the convertible has a value equal to that of the short bond, which is £99.32. However, the convertible actually traded at a price far in excess of £101 after it was auctioned, implying that the market attached a value of more than £1.50 to the conversion option. Clearly, the cross-over method is seriously deficient because it can lead to substantial pricing errors. To price a bond such as this properly, dynamic programming must be used with a stochastic model of the term structure. Chapter 4 provided an outline of the Ho and Lee (1986) model, the simplest tree-based term structure model suitable for this purpose. As with the previous section on callable bonds, the price of this convertible bond can be decomposed as follows:

Price of convertible = price of short bond + price of (compound) option

The option in this case is quite complicated since it has the American-style feature of multiple call dates and coupons are paid on each conversion date. Geske (1979) provides a method for valuing American call options on dividend paying stock. Suppose the terms of the convertible were such that there was only one conversion date, namely the last date (6 February 1996), so that the option in question would simply be a European option. The option payoff on the conversion date would be equal to

$$\max\{0.86 \times (\text{long}-\text{short}), 0\}$$

This resembles the payoff of an option to exchange one asset for another (see Margrabe, 1978), but is still a non-trivial option pricing problem since the maturity of the option was such that the behaviour of the term structure cannot easily be ignored.

6.3.4   WHAT RISKS DO CONVERTIBLES HEDGE?

The option embedded in a convertible bond owes its value to variations in the price ratio between the long and the short bonds brought about by variations in the term structure. Suppose a flat yield curve at 7.5% is subjected to three types of changes — which will enable us to distinguish the effects of yield curve behaviour on the moneyness of the option. First, a parallel shift in the forward curve by ±50 bp and ±100 bp; second, changes in the slope of the forward curve which are captured by a step jump (by ±50 bp and ±100 bp) in the forward curve between 6 August 1996 and 6 February 1997; and, third, changes in the slope of the forward curve after 1997 captured by a step jump (by ± 50 bp and ±100 bp) in the forward curve between 6 February 1999 and 6 August 1999[8]. In effect, this isolates changes to the short/long ratio due to the term structure movements which impact on the short and long bonds before and after the conversion dates.

As Table 6.7 shows, the third effect has the greatest impact on the short/long ratio. The intuition behind this is simply that the short/long ratio responds most to shocks which affect the value of the short and the long bonds

Table 6.7

Short/long as at 6 August 1994 (bp)	(1)	(2)	(3)
−100	0.8033	0.8033	0.7903
−50	0.8333	0.8334	0.8267
0	0.8637	0.8637	0.8637
+50	0.8943	0.8942	0.9012
+100	0.9251	0.9249	0.9393

asymmetrically — the asymmetry in this case being due to the fact that the change in this change in the term structure only affects cash flow of the long bond. The similarity between the first and second effects shows that asymmetry is most important. Since the discount factors for the payments on the short bond are common to those of the long bond, it will be those changes to the term structure which impact the valuation of the latter payment streams of the long bond that will have the greatest effect. Therefore, the convertible hedges risk due mainly to a fall in the yields on the long bond around the time of the conversion dates. The value of the option is most sensitive to twists in the yield curve in the maturity range after the redemption of the short bond.

6.4   OTHER ISSUES

6.4.1   OPTION-ADJUSTED YIELDS

Where a bond with an embedded option has a bullet bond/option decomposition and the relevant bullet bond can be easily priced, it is common to quantify the effect of the embedded option on the bond in terms of an adjustment to the yield. For instance, in the case of the callable example given earlier — the hypothetical 6% Callable 1999–2004 — suppose that the price of the short is £98, implying a yield of 7.09% and that the price of the callable is £97. Treating the callable as a short bullet bond would imply a yield of 7.66%. Thus, the effect of the call option gives rise to a 57 bp adjustment to the yield on the short. The utility of this approach (as with the previous rules of thumb) relies heavily on the assumption that callable bonds will not be called, the gain in yield only being of value if the call option is not exercised — or on some explicit modelling of the option-adjusted yield itself.

6.4.2   USING BONDS WITH OPTIONS IN THE ESTIMATION OF THE YIELD CURVE

Table 6.2 shows that the UK gilt market has a significant number of callable bonds in the maturity range 2000–2010, several of which are quite large issues of stock. Exclusion of such bonds from the estimation of the term structure (using methods such as those described in Chapter 2) leaves 'gaps' in the spectrum of market information which means that the estimated level of yields in this maturity range is particularly sensitive to yields on those few conventional bonds in this region[9]. On the other hand, inclusion of these bonds raises pricing issues that are as complicated as the task of yield curve estimation itself. As a simplistic compromise some practitioners opt to include callables by employing the par rule — this will however, systematically bias the yields. Given this, it is common for callables to be excluded altogether from the estimation of the yield curve.

NOTES

1. These rates are derived from the yield curve of 10 March 1995.
2. On redemption, in addition to the principal, holders of 9% Treasury 1992/96 received the proportion of the dividend which had accrued to that date.
3. CTO denotes Certificati del Tesoro con Opzione or Treasury certificates with option.
4. The quantity is determined by the conversion terms specified for that date.
5. The four dates were 8 August 1994 and 1995, and 8 February 1995 and 1996.
6. This is calculated as follows: £0.6625 = $\{0.925 \times (9/2)\} - (7/2)$.
7. These are in fact the conversion terms set for this particular gilt.
8. Four possible jumps are considered of differing magnitudes: ± 50 bp and ± 100 bp. The changing slope of the term structure is modelled by assuming that the forward curve is broken into two flat pieces where the break occurs at the point where the change in slope is desired.
9. It should be noted that this phenomenon is not unique to the UK market — the medium sector of the US market is even more heavily dominated by callable issues.

REFERENCES

Bank of England (1992) Redemption of 9% Treasury Loan 1992-1996, Press Notice, 23 October.

Bank of England (1994) 7% Treasury Convertible Stock 1997, Prospectus, 17 May 1994.

Belchamber, C. (1988) "The UK Government Bond Market", CSFB.

D'Andrea, A. and Mahoney, S. (eds) (1994) The 1995 International Guide to Government Securities and Derivatives, IFR.

Geske, R. (1979) A note on an analytic valuation formula for unprotected American call options on stocks with known dividends, Journal of Finance, 7, 375-80.

Ho, T. and Lee, S. (1986) Term structure movements and the pricing of interest rate contingent claims, Journal of Finance, 31, 33-71.

ISSA (1994) *The International Society of Securities Administrators, 1994 Handbook.*

Margrabe, W. (1978) The value of an option to exchange one asset for another, *Journal of Finance*, **33**, 177–86.

McLean, S. (ed.) (1993) *The European Bond Markets* (5th edition), Probus, Cambridge.

Mobbs, S. (1986) *Evaluating Callable Bonds*, CSFB Research, London.

CHAPTER 7

Index-linked debt

7.1 INTRODUCTION

This chapter introduces the concept of index-linked or indexed bonds — bonds whose cash flows are linked to some measure of inflation in order to provide a guaranteed real return. In addition to providing details of the mechanics of indexed bonds and the reasons governments issue them, examples are given from index-linked markets. Of these, the UK, Australian and Swedish markets are looked at in depth. The second half of the chapter examines a number of possibilities for extracting information on inflation expectations by comparing the prices of indexed and non-indexed bonds.

Index-linked bonds are securities whose payments of income and/or principal are tied to a particular price index, and hence are protected against inflation. There are basically four types of index-linked bonds (ILBs): (1) 'indexed-principal' ILBs — both coupons and principal are adjusted for inflation; (2) 'indexed-coupon' ILBs — only the coupons are scaled for inflation; (3) 'zero-coupon' ILBs — these pay no coupons but the principal is scaled for inflation; (4) 'indexed-annuity' bonds — these pay inflation-adjusted coupons, but no principal on redemption.

The most common index used is the Consumer Price Index (CPI) for the respective country of issue, though others used include commodity price indices (e.g. gold) and stock market indices. This chapter focuses on indexed bonds issued by governments — for information on private sector index-linked issuance see Page and Trollope (1974). For convenience, for the rest of the chapter non-indexed bonds are referred to as conventionals.

Index-linking of financial instruments can be traced back to at least 1742, when the state of Massachusetts issued bonds whose value was linked to commodity prices. In the UK, Joseph Lowe advocated the use of index-linked debt after the Napoleonic wars, and Jevons in 1875 and Marshall in 1886 were proponents of the use of a standard unit of purchasing power in contracts for deferred payments. In this century, support for indexation has come from prominent economists such as Keynes and Irving Fisher. Fisher (1963) thought that both debtor and creditor should be protected from the adverse effects of inflation: 'The ideal is that neither debtor nor creditor should be worse off from having been deceived by unforeseen changes'. Despite such support for indexed debt, it is only really in the second half of this century that it has come to prominence.

As part of their price-stabilization programmes after the Second World War both France and Finland issued index-linked debt. These programmes were

Table 7.1   Summary of countries' experience of indexing government* bonds

Country	Issue date	Index used
Argentina	1972–	Non-agricultural wholesale prices
Australia	1983–	Consumer prices
	1991	Average weekly earnings
Austria	1953	Electricity prices
Brazil	1964–1980	Wholesale prices
Canada	1991–	Consumer prices
Chile		Consumer prices
Denmark	1982–	Consumer prices
Finland	1945–1967	Wholesale prices
France	1952, 1973	Gold price
	1956	Level of industrial production
	1956	Average value of French securities
	1957	Price of equities
Iceland	1955	Consumer prices
	1964–1980	Cost of Building Index
	1980–	Credit Terms Index[†]
Ireland	1983–	Consumer prices
Israel	1948–	Consumer prices
Italy	1983	GDP prices at factor cost
Mexico	1989–	Consumer prices
New Zealand	1979–1984, 1995–	'All Groups' consumer prices
Poland	1992–	Consumer goods and service price growth indices
Sweden	1952	Consumer prices
	1994–	Consumer prices
UK	1975–	Retail prices[‡]
	1981–	Retail prices[§]
USA	1742	Commodity prices

*Though the rest of this chapter is devoted almost exclusively to 'pure' government debt, for completeness this table also includes issues by public corporations and semi-government authorities, and those that carry a government guarantee.

[†]The CTI was introduced in 1979, and at this time was composed of two indices, the cost of living index (CLI) — carrying a weight of two thirds — and the building cost index (BCI). In February 1989 the composition of the CTI was changed to include the wage index (WI) in addition to the CLI and BCI — each index being given equal weight. Finally, in February 1995 it was agreed to redefine the CTI solely in terms of the CPI. For more details see Central Bank of Iceland (1991, 1995).

[‡]National Savings certificates.

[§]Gilt-edged securities.

Sources: BZW (1993), D'Andrea and Mahoney (1994), ISSA (1994), McLean (1993) and Page and Trollope (1974).

discontinued upon devaluation of the respective currencies — France in 1958 and Finland in 1967 — reflecting concern that higher import prices coupled with index-linking would create further inflationary pressures. More recently, several countries experiencing hyperinflation such as Argentina, Brazil and Israel[1] have issued indexed debt as a means of maintaining the acceptability of long-term debt contracts. The last fifteen years have seen index-linked markets established in the UK, Australia, Canada and Sweden — the most significant of these being the UK market. Also, the New Zealand government has returned to index-linked issuance in 1995. Table 7.1 provides a list of major countries that have issued indexed government debt.

7.2 HOW DO INDEX-LINKED BONDS WORK?

The Fisher identity postulates that the nominal yield on a conventional bond can be decomposed into several components. One of the more commonly used interpretations of the Fisher identity[2] states that the nominal yield y can be thought of as having three components, the *ex ante* real yield r, the average annual expected inflation rate over the life of the bond π^e and a risk premium ρ, that reflects the uncertainty of inflation:

$$\left(1 + \frac{y}{N}\right) = [(1 + \pi^c)(1 + \rho)]^{1/N} \left(1 + \frac{r}{N}\right)$$

where N is the number of coupons payable per year (e.g. $N = 2$ for the UK, since the market convention is to use semi-annual compounding).

Given the difficulty in estimating the inflation risk premium, most studies attempting to infer inflation expectations from bond prices assume there are no risk premia — the validity of this is discussed later. Under the assumption of zero risk premia, the Fisher identity simply reduces to:

$$\left(1 + \frac{y}{N}\right) = (1 + \pi^e)^{1/N} \left(1 + \frac{r}{N}\right)$$

In fact, market practitioners often employ a further simplified version, which states that the nominal yield is simply the real yield plus an expected inflation rate[3], i.e. $y = r + \pi^e$.

Now consider a simple example based on this formula. Suppose that the level of nominal yields is 6% — of which 4% can be attributed to real yields and 2% to expected inflation. Compare two bonds of the same maturity — a conventional and an index-linked bond. If over their lifetime inflation actually turns out to be higher than anticipated at, say, 4%, then the real yield on the indexed bond will still be 4% while the real yield on the conventional will *ex post* be only 2%. Conversely, if inflation was lower than had been expected at, say, 1%, then the real yield on the conventional would have been 5% while that on the indexed bond would still have been 4%. This simple example serves the purpose of demonstrating the key attribute of index-linked bonds, namely that they offer real value certainty.

As stated, index-linked bonds are designed to give the investor a real return that is known with certainty and is independent of the inflation rate — this being achieved by adjusting the cash flows to keep pace with inflation, thus preserving their real value. However, indexed bonds do not offer *complete* real value certainty, since there will always be some form of lag in the indexation, due to the time that it takes to compile and publish the relevant inflation index. Lags vary from two weeks (Mexico) to 13 months, though the latter reflects more than just a publication delay.

7.3   MOTIVATION FOR INDEX-LINKED ISSUANCE

This section examines the arguments in favour of governments issuing indexed debt.

7.3.1   REDUCING DEFICIT FINANCING COSTS

There are three aspects to this. In periods when governments view nominal yields as excessively high, they may be loath to lock into these rates by issuing conventionals and so will look at other forms of issuance such as indexed or convertible bonds. *Ex post*, if actual inflation over a period proved to be lower than the rate discounted in bond prices, then issuing index-linked bonds would have provided a cheaper form of funding than conventionals.

By issuing index-linked bonds rather than conventionals, governments can save on the inflation risk premium component of nominal bond yields — this premium reflects investors' uncertainty about future inflation. In offering almost complete real value certainty, the inflation premium that index-linked bonds attract should be negligible compared with that on conventionals[4].

Finally, by offering different types of bonds to the market — rather than all conventionals — governments should attract a wider range of investors, and consequently lower the yield that they have to pay at issue.

7.3.2   IMPROVING ANTI-INFLATION CREDIBILITY

An important problem for governments is how to convince agents in the economy that they are seriously committed to reducing inflation and subsequently keeping it low. A commonly held view is that governments can boost their anti-inflation credibility by issuing index-linked debt, since by taking a tough stance against inflation they can then reduce their future nominal costs of financing. However, there is a school of thought that argues that, by issuing indexed debt, a government is admitting defeat against inflation and effectively acknowledging that it cannot be eradicated.

7.3.3   PROVIDING A MEASURE OF INFLATION EXPECTATIONS

If a financial market trades both indexed and non-indexed bonds it is possible, subject to some assumptions about risk premia and liquidity premia, to derive estimates of market inflation expectations from the prices of these instruments. This provides a further incentive for governments to issue indexed bonds. In the USA, the Treasury has been looking at issuing indexed bonds for some time, one of the main benefits being seen as the information that this would provide on inflation expectations (Connor, 1994).

There are several reasons why knowledge of inflation expectations is useful. By comparing market expectations of inflation with the government's inflation targets, it is possible to gauge financial markets' perceptions of the credibility of monetary policy — Svensson (1994a) discusses this in detail. As mentioned earlier, knowledge of markets' inflation expectations can also assist decisions on whether to issue indexed or conventional debt. For instance, one of the reasons given for the 1994 Swedish indexed bond issue was that the Riksbank[5] believed that market inflation expectations were above the likely outturn for inflation, making indexed bonds a cheaper source of funds than conventionals.

7.3.4   FLEXIBILITY OF FUNDING

One of the reasons given for the establishment of an index-linked market in the UK was that it would allow improved monetary control due to increased flexibility gained from an additional type of funding instrument (Rutterford, 1983). Index-linked issues provide the authorities with an instrument that they would be able to sell in times of uncertainty about inflation, when the conventional market would be weak.

7.3.5   MAINTAINING THE VALUE OF CONTRACTS

The motives for indexed debt issuance will vary from country to country. One of the main reasons countries such as Argentina, Brazil, Israel and Mexico embarked on index-linked issuance was as a means of maintaining the acceptability to investors of long-term debt contracts under conditions of hyperinflation. Clearly, in such an environment any lag in indexation is particularly undesirable. For example, in Mexico, the CPI is published every two weeks (a reflection of high inflation in the past) and becomes available with a lag of only about 10 days. This is the indexation lag that is applied to Mexico's indexed bonds.

7.4   THE UK INDEX-LINKED GILT MARKET

7.4.1   INTRODUCTION

The announcement in the March 1981 budget of the government's plan to issue index-linked gilts, with purchases being restricted to pension funds, followed the publication in 1980 of the Wilson Report on the functioning of financial institutions. The official reasons given for issuing indexed bonds (HMT (1983)) were:

(1)   To reinforce belief in the government's anti-inflation policy
(2)   To reduce the cost of funding by reducing inflation risk
(3)   To improve monetary control by increasing the flexibility of funding.

de Kock (1991) reports that these advantages were partially offset by a number of disadvantages including the concern that issuing bonds that were much closer in characteristics to equities than were conventional bonds might depress equity prices and reduce corporate financing opportunities.

7.4.2   MARKET STRUCTURE

The first UK issue was made by tender on 27 March 1981. However, the index-linked market proper dates from March 1982, with the removal of all restrictions regarding who could hold index-linked gilts. By the end of 1995, the index-linked market consists of 13 stocks (see Table 7.2) with total face value of £25 billion, compared to a conventional market of almost £200 billion[6]. All index-linked gilts are of the 'indexed-principal' variety, the longest dated maturing in 2030, currently thirteen years after the longest conventional.

Capital and semi-annual interest payments are derived using the RPI with an 8-month lag. The reason for such a long lag is the method employed in the UK to calculate accrued interest on gilts. For this calculation, the size of each dividend must be known 6 months before the payment is due; as this is linked to the

Table 7.2   UK index-linked gilts

Coupon (%)	Maturity date	Date of first issue	Nominal amount outstanding (£m)
2.000	16/09/1996	27/03/1981	1200
4.625	27/04/1998	18/09/1992	800
2.500	24/09/2001	26/08/1982	1700
2.500	20/05/2003	27/10/1982	1700
4.375	21/10/2004	22/09/1992	1000
2.000	19/07/2006	08/07/1981	1950
2.500	20/05/2009	19/10/1982	2050
2.500	23/08/2011	28/01/1982	2500
2.500	16/08/2013	21/02/1985	2450
2.500	26/07/2016	19/01/1983	3050
2.500	16/04/2020	12/10/1983	3000
2.500	17/07/2024	30/12/1986	2700
4.125	22/07/2030	12/06/1992	1300

Source: Bank of England. As at 12 December 1995, in addition to the bonds listed there was also a 2.5% Index-Linked Treasury 1999 stock — though this is very small and rarely traded.

RPI, a lag of at least 6 months must be used. However, even a 6-month lag is impractical since the RPI figures themselves are only available with a lag, the figure for a particular month typically being available only in the second week of the next month. A further month's lag is allowed because coupon payments on different stocks are made at different times of the month — ensuring that *at all times* and for all bonds the RPI figure fixing the next coupon payment is known.

Capital and interest values are adjusted by the ratio of the RPI 8 months prior to the month in which the amount is paid, to the base RPI — the base RPI being the RPI level 8 months prior to the month in which the bond is issued. Mathematically, standard[7] interest payments are calculated from the formula:

$$\frac{c}{2} \cdot \frac{RPI_{M-8}}{RPI_{I-8}}$$

and the redemption proceeds from:

$$100 \cdot \frac{RPI_{R-8}}{RPI_{I-8}}$$

where

c = annual coupon rate
RPI_X = published RPI that relates to month X
I = month in which the stock is issued
M = month in which the interest payment falls
R = month in which the stock redeems

The formula employed by the Bank of England for calculating the real redemption yield on an index-linked gilt is given by:

$$\text{Price per £100 face value} = (uw)^{t_1} \left[D_1 + \frac{c}{2}\alpha a_n \right] + 100\alpha u^{t_1} w^n$$

where

D_1 = next receivable dividend
$\quad = \dfrac{RPID_1}{RPIB} \cdot \dfrac{c}{2}$
$RPIB$ = base RPI for the stock
$RPIL$ = latest RPI
$RPID_1$ = RPI defining the next receivable dividend
c = annual coupon rate (%)
r = real yield (%)[8]
$w = \left(1 \left/ 1 + \dfrac{r}{200} \right. \right)$, the half-yearly real discount factor
π^e = assumed annual inflation rate (%)
$u = \left(1 \left/ 1 + \dfrac{\pi^e}{100} \right. \right)^{1/2}$, the half-yearly inflation discount factor

$$\alpha = \frac{RPIL}{RPIB} u^{-(k/6)}$$

$k =$ number of months from the latest RPI to the RPI defining the next receivable dividend (k will be positive if the RPI defining this dividend is not yet known)

$t_i =$ time to the ith remaining dividend in half-years

$n =$ number of dividends remaining

$$a_n = w + w^2 + \cdots + w^{n-1} = 200 \left(\frac{1 - w^{n-1}}{r} \right)$$

7.4.3 AN ALTERNATIVE PROPOSAL FOR INDEXATION

Barro (1994) suggests a modification that could be made to the indexation procedure used in the UK in order to provide better protection against inflation. Of necessity this method uses an indexation lag of 8 months but for ease of explanation a 6-month lag is used (as in Barro, 1994).

Consider an n-period index-linked gilt that is issued at date 0, with semi-annual coupon payments at $1, 2, \ldots, n$. Let c be the annual coupon rate and π_i be the inflation rate for the RPI between dates $i - 1$ and i, as shown in Figure 7.1. Ignoring the RPI's 2-month publication lag ensures that π_i will be known at the start of period i.

The schedule of cash flows under the method of indexation employed by the Bank of England is given in the second column of Table 7.3. Column 3 of the table illustrates what the cash flows would be under perfect indexation — that is, the hypothetical ideal with no inflation lag. A comparison between these two sets of cash flows shows that the errors under the current system derive from the lag by one period in each of the terms $1 + \pi_i$ — for example, the second coupon is defined as $(c/2)(1 + \pi_0)(1 + \pi_1)$ compared to the ideal of $(c/2)(1 + \pi_1)(1 + \pi_2)$. The mistake in the last $1 + \pi_i$ term in each expression — that is, the one furthest to the right — is inevitable since the nominal payments have to be expressed one period in advance. More generally, in the formula for coupon t in column 3, the term $1 + \pi_t$ is unknown at the time that the nominal value of this coupon is announced and so $1 + \pi_{t-1}$ is used instead. Thus the formula for coupon t in column 2 commits a string of errors in that the earlier $1 + \pi_i$ terms are also

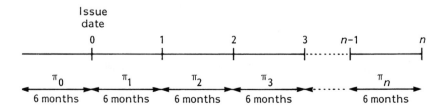

Figure 7.1

Table 7.3 Payment schedules under different indexation schemes

Payment	Current system	Perfect indexation	Barro proposal
Coupon 1	$\frac{c}{2}(1+\pi_0)$	$\frac{c}{2}(1+\pi_1)$	$\frac{c}{2}(1+\pi_0)$
Coupon 2	$\frac{c}{2}(1+\pi_0)(1+\pi_1)$	$\frac{c}{2}(1+\pi_1)(1+\pi_2)$	$\frac{c}{2}(1+\pi_1)(1+\pi_1)$
Coupon 3	$\frac{c}{2}(1+\pi_0)(1+\pi_1)(1+\pi_2)$	$\frac{c}{2}(1+\pi_1)(1+\pi_2)(1+\pi_3)$	$\frac{c}{2}(1+\pi_1)(1+\pi_2)(1+\pi_2)$
$\ldots$	$\vdots$	$\vdots$	$\vdots$
Coupon t	$\frac{c}{2}(1+\pi_0)(1+\pi_1)\ldots(1+\pi_{t-1})$	$\frac{c}{2}(1+\pi_1)(1+\pi_2)\ldots(1+\pi_t)$	$\frac{c}{2}(1+\pi_1)\ldots(1+\pi_{t-2})(1+\pi_2)(1+\pi_{t-1})$
$\ldots$	$\vdots$	$\vdots$	$\vdots$
Coupon n	$\frac{c}{2}(1+\pi_0)(1+\pi_1)\ldots(1+\pi_{n-1})$	$\frac{c}{2}(1+\pi_1)(1+\pi_2)\ldots(1+\pi_n)$	$\frac{c}{2}(1+\pi_1)\ldots(1+\pi_{n-2})(1+\pi_2)(1+\pi_{n-1})$
Redemption	$100(1+\pi_0)(1+\pi_1)\ldots(1+\pi_{n-1})$	$100(1+\pi_1)(1+\pi_2)\ldots(1+\pi_n)$	$100(1+\pi_1)\ldots(1+\pi_{n-2})(1+\pi_2)(1+\pi_{n-1})(1+\pi_{n-1})$

lagged by one period relative to those shown in column 3. Barro's proposal is to use the indexation method illustrated in column 4 of the table.

The first coupon payments shown in columns 2 and 4 — $(c/2)(1 + \pi_0)$ — are the same; each deviates from the ideal value shown in column 3 because $1 + \pi_0$ appears instead of $1 + \pi_1$. However, since π_1 is known when the nominal value of the second coupon payment is set, Barro reasons that it is unnecessary to allow this mistake to persist for the second (and subsequent) payments. Thus, column 4 uses $(c/2)(1 + \pi_1)(1 + \pi_1)$, instead of $(c/2)(1 + \pi_0)(1 + \pi_1)$ from column 2, to determine the second payment. The substitution of $(1 + \pi_1)$ for $(1 + \pi_0)$ means that the initial error — created by the gap between π_1 and π_0 — does not persist beyond the first payment. The second $1 + \pi_1$ term for the second coupon in column 4 necessarily still differs from the ideal value in column 3, which contains $1 + \pi_2$.

Barro's proposal is equivalent to saying that, for a given point in time, inflation over the preceding 6 months should, on average, provide a better predictor of inflation over the subsequent 6 months than inflation from an earlier period, i.e. for any t, π_{t-1} should be a better predictor of π_t than π_0.

7.5   THE AUSTRALIAN COMMONWEALTH GOVERNMENT TREASURY INDEX BOND MARKET

7.5.1   INTRODUCTION

The first Australian index-linked issue was of a CPI linked capital indexed bond by the State Electricity Commission of Victoria in August 1983. This was followed by several issues of capital indexed and interest indexed bonds by the Commonwealth Government during 1985. From 1987 onwards, the frequency and types of indexed issues increased as several semi-government authorities joined the market. In the late 1980s, annuity-style indexed securities were introduced, a move which helped to further accelerate the growth in the market. However, when the government moved into public sector surplus, the Reserve Bank of Australia bought in some of the indexed bonds as part of its debt-reduction policy.

7.5.2   MARKET STRUCTURE

Index-linked bonds constitute about 4% of total Commonwealth Government issues. The total size of the Australian indexed bond market stood at A\$5.3 billion at the end of 1992, of which only about 25% represents Commonwealth Government issues, the rest being issues largely by semi-government authorities such as the South Australian Government Financing Authority and the Tasmanian Public Finance Corporation. All indexed securities bar one are linked to the CPI — the exception being an Australian Overseas Telecommunications Corporation issue which is linked to Average Weekly Earnings. The four main classes

Table 7.4   Australian commonwealth government treasury indexed bonds

Type of bond	Coupon (%)	Maturity date	Date of first issue	Nominal amount outstanding (A$m)
CIB	4.00	20/08/1998	10/02/1987	126.4
IIB	4.65–5.75	20/08/1998	10/02/1987	2.4
CIB	4.00	20/08/2005	30/07/1985	531.8
IIB	4.25–5.80	20/08/2005	30/07/1985	0.1
CIB	4.00	20/08/2010	09/02/1993	1452.0
CIB	4.00	20/08/2015	17/05/1994	669.7

Source: Reserve Bank of Australia Figures as at 14 December 1995

of index-linked securities are:

- Capital Indexed Bonds (CIBs)
- Interest Indexed Bonds (IIBs)
- Indexed Annuity Bonds (IABs)
- Credit Foncier Bonds (CFBs)[9]

Since this chapter focuses on 'pure' government bonds and the Commonwealth Government has only issued CIBs and IIBs, details on CFBs and IABs are not provided here. For comprehensive coverage of these, refer to BZW (1993). Table 7.4 provides a listing of the current Commonwealth Government issues.

Capital Indexed Bonds are of the 'indexed-principal' type of ILBs and so are comparable with UK index-linked gilts. The main differences are that coupons are payable on a quarterly basis and that the indexation lag is, in essence, between 3 and 6 months, reflecting the fact that the CPI is only published quarterly[10]. For details on how to calculate interest payments, capital payments and real yields on CIBs see Appendix A.

Interest Indexed Bonds are of the 'indexed-coupon' variety of ILBs and have found only a limited market in Australia. Like the Commonwealth Government CIBs, the IIBs pay coupons quarterly but are generally considered more akin to a floating rate note than to an index-linked bond. For more information on IIBs refer to BZW (1993).

7.6 THE SWEDISH INDEX-LINKED TREASURY BOND MARKET

7.6.1 INTRODUCTION

Sweden briefly experimented with indexation in 1952, when a public corporation offered a partially indexed bond with less than 50% compensation (Page and Trollope, 1974). However, in 1994 the Swedish National Debt Office (NDO) embarked on a programme of index-linked issuance. The main technical interest in the Swedish market stems from the fact that the two indexed stocks issued to date have been zero-coupon bonds — one of the few markets to have introduced such instruments. One advantage of a zero-coupon bond is that it is not subject to reinvestment risk — the risk that the holder of a bond will not be able to reinvest coupon payments at the internal rate of return.

7.6.2 MARKET STRUCTURE

Sweden auctioned its first real zero-coupon bond in April 1994 — SEK 3.5 billion of a 20-year bond, with principal linked to the Swedish CPI. Although the auction was covered, the NDO judged that the yields bid were too high, and consequently over two thirds of the stock remained unissued. The NDO brought four more auctions of the same stock during 1994 — however, these proved equally disappointing. Possible explanations for these poor results include the very long duration of the bond (20 years as opposed to 8 years maximum for conventional bonds) and the apparent lack of a serious commitment by the NDO to establish liquid issues for a range of maturities.

Towards the end of 1994 the NDO announced that it proposed to issue shorter maturity indexed bonds, and in January 1995 SEK 500 million of a 9-year real zero-coupon bond was auctioned, together with a further SEK 500 million of the longer stock. Although the latter was well received by the market and was fully allocated, half of the shorter-maturity stock remained unissued.

Following the auctions in January, the NDO has adopted a policy of holding weekly auctions of small quantities of stock, in an attempt to tease the market along. The NDO believe that this demonstration of commitment to establishing and maintaining a liquid market will reassure investors, and will in the long term facilitate the return to larger auctions. Despite this, the 9-year bond has continued to be less popular than the longer stock, and has in fact been withdrawn from auction on more than one occasion, following a lack of demand. Table 7.5 provides details on the two Swedish issues.

Swedish indexed bonds are traded on a real yield basis — that is, they are bought at a discount that is determined by the real interest rate — with the principal indexed by the CPI, lagged by 3 months. Though the real return at which the investor purchases the bond will not always be the same as the real *ex post*

Table 7.5 Swedish index-linked treasury bonds

Coupon (%)	Maturity date	Date of first issue	Nominal amount outstanding (SEK million)
0.00	01/04/2004	16/01/1995	$378
0.00	01/04/2014	19/04/1994	29529

Source: Reuters. Figures as at 8 December 1995.

return, they will be close. For details on how to calculate capital payments and real redemption yields on Swedish indexed bonds see Appendix B.

7.7 SIMPLE MEASURES OF INFLATION EXPECTATIONS

As has already been explained, there are several reasons why knowledge of inflation expectations is useful. Traditionally, information on inflation expectations has been obtained by either survey or theory-based methods. However, these have shown themselves to be fairly unreliable — possibly because survey respondents have no incentive to answer accurately.

More recently, efforts have been made to extract expectations from asset prices. For example, between 1985 and 1987 the New York Coffee, Sugar and Cocoa Exchange traded a futures contract on the US CPI-W[11] price index (see Petzel and Fabozzi, 1988). Using the prices of these contracts, it was straightforward to obtain estimates of inflation expectations. The CPI futures failed to take off and were abandoned in 1987, this failure generally being attributed to the fact that US inflation (and inflation expectations) was relatively stable over the period they were traded, and because of the absence of an underlying asset. Since then — as far as the authors are aware — no futures markets have traded contracts of a similar nature, and so some alternative means of deriving inflation expectations from the prices of financial assets must be considered. For instance, Mishkin (1990) considers the possibility of extracting information from futures prices along the lines of extracting information from the nominal yield curve.

If a financial market trades both indexed and non-indexed securities it is possible, subject to some assumptions about risk and liquidity premia, to derive estimates from the prices of these instruments. The Bank of England has regularly published such estimates of inflation expectations since May 1993 (Bank of England, 1993b). This section considers two simple techniques frequently used by market practitioners to achieve this, along with their shortcomings. Both these and the subsequent technique discussed exploit the Fisher identity.

7.7.1 THE 'SIMPLE' APPROACH

Here, average expected inflation is calculated using the simplest interpretation of the Fisher identity — as the difference of the real yield on an index-linked bond (calculated using some assumed average inflation rate) from the nominal yield on a conventional bond of similar (preferably identical) maturity. The assumptions implicit in this calculation are discussed in the following section. For example, by subtracting the real yield on a 5-year index-linked stock from the nominal yield on a 5-year conventional this method gives an estimate of *average* expected inflation over the next 5 years. This measure is often misinterpreted as an expectation of inflation in 5 years' time. Since the real yield on an indexed bond is dependent on an assumed average rate of inflation, the inflation expectation produced by this method depends directly on the original inflation assumption; effectively an inflation expectation is being used to estimate an inflation expectation.

To illustrate this with an example from the UK, compare the real yield on 2% Index-Linked Treasury 1996 with the nominal yield on 10% Conversion 1996 for 20 January 1995. The yield on the conventional was 7.941%, while the real yield on the index-linked bond was *4.777%* using a 3% inflation assumption and *4.095%* using a 5% inflation assumption. Using the method outlined above produces inflation expectations of 3.164% and 3.846% respectively. This discrepancy between assumed and estimated inflation rates is referred to as a lack of internal consistency, and becomes more pronounced, the longer the lag in indexation.

7.7.2 BREAK-EVEN INFLATION RATES

The method of calculating 'break-even' inflation rates is more sophisticated, and eliminates the problem of consistency. Again, *average* inflation expectations are estimated by comparing the return on a conventional bond with that on an index-linked bond of similar maturity, but this time by application of the compound form of the Fisher identity, i.e.

$$\left(1 + \frac{y}{N}\right) = (1 + \pi^e)^{1/N}\left(1 + \frac{r}{N}\right)$$

where y is the nominal yield, r is the real yield, π^e is the annual inflation rate and N is the number of coupons payable per year.

Implicit in the break-even methodology (and the simple approach) is the assumption that investors are risk-neutral (i.e. that they will require no (inflation) risk premium for holding either index-linked or conventional bonds)[12]. This implies that in a no-arbitrage equilibrium a conventional and an index-linked stock will have the same expected nominal rate of return. This equality of the nominal rates means that the nominal yield on the conventional bond can be used in place of the nominal yield on the index-linked bond in the calculations. This leaves two relationships — the price/yield equation for an index-linked bond and the Fisher identity, to solve for the expected inflation rate and the real yield. In addition, as the price of a bond is a function of the investor's marginal income tax rate, an estimate for this must be provided exogenously. Given this, it is straightforward to solve the equations by the use of an iterative procedure.

Figure 7.2 shows how the UK break-even inflation rate (for an investor facing 0% income tax) derived from maturity matching 2.5% Index-Linked Treasury 2003 varied during 1993. One consequence of matching the index-linked stock with the conventional of closest maturity is that the conventional selected can change over time, as new bonds are issued. For instance, in this particular example although 10% Treasury 2003 was the closest maturity match to 2.5% Index-Linked Treasury 2003 for the first half of 1993, part-way through the year 8% Treasury 2003 — which is closer in maturity — was issued[13], and so this was used to generate the break-even rates for the second half of 1993. Examples of

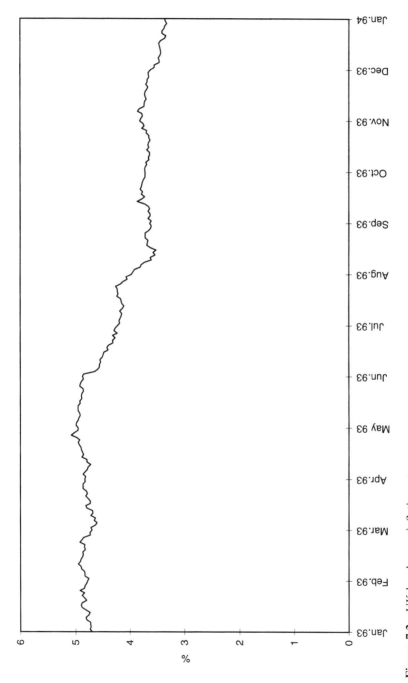

Figure 7.2 UK break-even inflation rates

Canadian break-even inflation rates are provided in Duenwald (1993) and for Australia in Heenan (1991).

Early work of a similar nature from the academic literature appears in Arak and Kreicher (1985). Here, the authors employ essentially the same method, but as a simplification they estimate and use a linear approximation to the price/yield equation. All their analysis is based on the 1996 index-linked bond and assumes 0% tax. Although a risk premium of zero is assumed, they do consider the likely effect that a non-zero risk premium would have on their results. Unfortunately, the results are distorted, since their calculations incorrectly assume that the base date for indexation of coupon and principal on indexed gilts is the stock issue date, rather than 8 months prior to the issue date. Break-even inflation rates are also discussed in some detail in Bootle (1991).

One variation of the break-even methodology involves matching the conventional and index-linked stocks by duration rather than by maturity. Duration provides a means of normalizing for the different risk characteristics of high and low coupon bonds. Bootle (1991) expresses reservations about matching conventional and index-linked bonds by duration — a point that is reiterated in Woodward (1990). They argue that normalizing for interest rate risk by duration matching is 'ill-conceived' in this context, since investors in conventionals face nominal interest rate risk (the risk of a change in real rates *or* inflation expectations) while index-linked investors are subject to real rate risk — only a change in the underlying level of real yields affects both types of stock in the same way. Duration matching should only be applied to instruments exposing the holder to the same type of risk. These issues are considered further in Deacon and Derry (1994a).

7.7.3 PROBLEMS WITH BREAK-EVEN INFLATION RATES

There are clearly several deficiencies with the break-even inflation rate methodology, whether matching by maturity or duration. First, the assumption that government bonds carry no risk or liquidity premia is unlikely to be realistic (a point discussed in more detail in Chapters 8 and 9). Also, it will often only be possible to find pairs of bonds which match *approximately* by maturity, introducing inaccuracies into the calculated values for the real rate and the expected inflation rate. More seriously, there may not even be an index-linked stock maturing at or near a relevant date. Another problem is that the marginal tax rate on holding bonds has to be supplied exogenously in order to solve for the break-even inflation rate. As a consequence, each market will have its convention regarding the tax rate to employ — for instance, at present the UK convention is to use tax rates of 0%, 25% and 40%. The level of a given break-even inflation rate time series is very sensitive to the tax assumption, as demonstrated in Figure 7.3[14]. Without a clear view on the appropriate tax rate to apply, it would appear that little useful information can thus be gained from the *level* of a break-even rate series. Empirically, however, it would seem that the *changes*

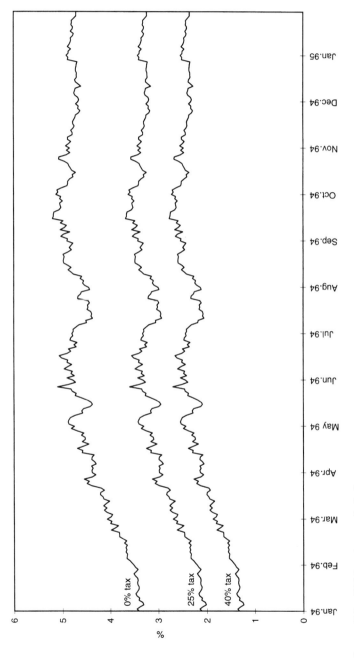

Figure 7.3   UK break-even inflation rates

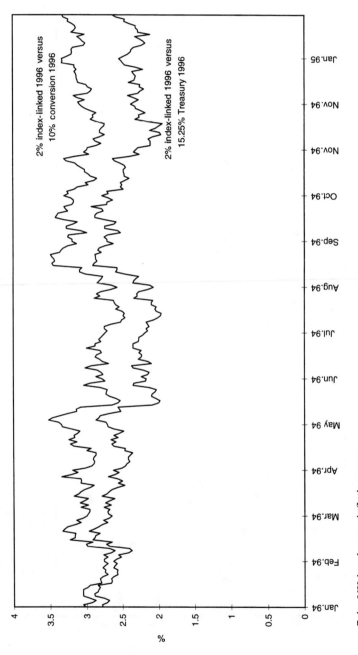

Figure 7.4   UK break-even inflation rates

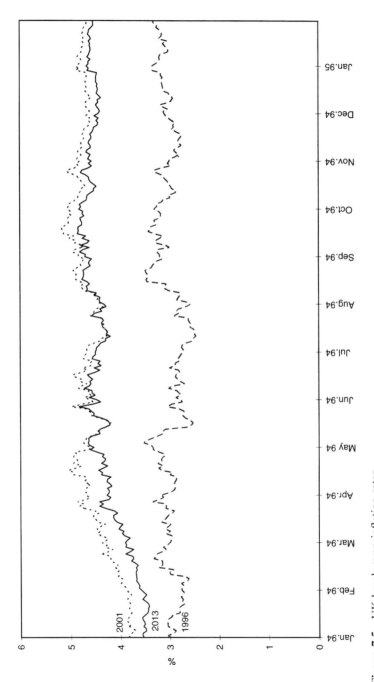

Figure 7.5   UK break-even inflation rates

in the series vary little with tax, i.e. there is a fairly stable differential between break-even time series of different tax rates.

The fact that a break-even inflation rate is derived from only two bond prices means that it is particularly vulnerable to distortions produced by the specific stocks selected. For instance, when matching stocks by maturity there may be conventionals of roughly equal maturity but widely differing coupons; the difference in the break-even rates that this would produce is likely to be significant[15], as demonstrated by Figure 7.4. Also, by concentrating on only two stocks this approach ignores any inflation information contained in other bonds.

It is possible to calculate a break-even inflation rate for each index-linked bond in a given market and hence to build up a picture of market expectations of average inflation over different time horizons (see Figure 7.5). However, even the UK index-linked market — which is the largest — consists of only 13 stocks spread over a maturity range of 1 to 35 years and so will not produce a particularly detailed picture[16]. The only way to back out a term structure of future inflation rates from these break-even rates would be to fit a curve to them, and then use this to estimate an implied forward inflation rate curve. Derivation of future inflation rates in such a way uses only the information contained in the pairs of bonds used to create the break-even inflation rates, thus both unnecessarily restricting the dataset used and leaving the resulting estimates dependent on any bond specific features in the chosen dataset — in particular, coupon effects. The resulting forward inflation rate curve is likely to be volatile, and one in which little confidence could be placed. One advantage in calculating break-even rates for the Swedish market is that there should be no such distortions in the indexed side of the calculation due to the zero-coupon nature of the bonds.

To conclude this section; although little can be learnt about the *level* of inflation expectations from break-even inflation rates, they can be useful as time series to show how expectations have *changed*. In the next section, an alternative approach is examined that eliminates several of the problems discussed above and facilitates the calculation of implied forward inflation rates.

7.8   THE TERM STRUCTURE OF IMPLIED FORWARD INFLATION RATES

Given the limited number of index-linked bonds in most markets, fitting a yield curve model to the data in order to produce a real yield curve would be implausible/unwise. But this is feasible in the particular case of the UK market and there is no reason why the general approach used could not be applied to other markets — given sufficient bonds.

7.8.1   THE TERM STRUCTURE OF REAL INTEREST RATES

Using index-linked bond prices, it is possible to estimate a term structure of real interest rates. The estimation of such a curve provides the 'real' counterpart to the nominal curves discussed in Chapter 2. In particular, it enables the derivation of a real forward rate curve. In practice, however, there are two factors which complicate such estimation: there is the lag in indexation and, in most markets, there are typically far fewer index-linked bonds than conventionals. The first means that, without some measure of expected inflation, real bond yields and hence term structures derived from real yields are dependent to some degree upon the assumed rate of inflation[17].

Despite these problems, the discount function-based approach to yield curve estimation discussed in Chapter 2 and pioneered by McCulloch (1971) can be amended to produce a real curve dependent upon an assumed rate of inflation. The tax treatment suggested in his second paper (1975) can also be included, but, for reasons outlined later, may not be appropriate for index-linked markets.

It can be shown (see Appendix C for a full derivation) that, when using McCulloch's methodology to fit a discount function using index-linked bonds, (2.2) need only[18] be amended by a scaling factor (Λ_{il}) that is known for each payment on each bond once an assumption has been made about future inflation expectations. So if $\delta_r(m)$ is the real discount function, defined by

$$\delta_r(m) = 1 + \sum_{j=1}^{k} a_j f_j(m)$$

where $f_j(m)$ is the jth basis function, the coefficients a_j are estimated from:

$$y_i = \sum_{j=1}^{k} a_j x_{ij}$$

where

$$y_i = p_i + ai_i - \frac{c_i}{2} \sum_{l=1}^{n} \Lambda_{il} - \Lambda_{in} R_i$$

$$x_{ij} = \frac{c_i}{2} \sum_{l=1}^{n} \Lambda_{il} f_j(l) + \Lambda_{in} R_i f_j(n)$$

$$u = (1 + \pi^e)^{-(1/2)}$$

$$\Lambda_{il} = \begin{cases} [u^{td_l}]_i \cdot \dfrac{RPID_l}{RPIB_i} & \text{if } RPID_l \text{ is known} \\[3mm] \left[u^{td_1 - (L/6)}\right]_i \cdot \dfrac{RPIL}{RPIB_i} & \text{otherwise} \end{cases}$$

Here p_i, c_i, ai_in and R_i are the clean price, coupon, accrued interest number of outstanding (semi-annual) coupon payments and real redemption payment of the ith indexed bond. Λ_{il} is the scaling factor for the lth cash flow on the ith bond, and depends on the ratio of the RPI defining each dividend to the bond's 'base'

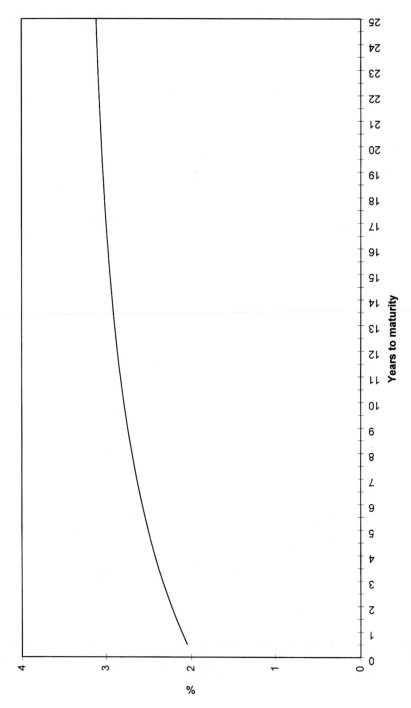

Figure 7.6 Real spot curve for 18 January 1994

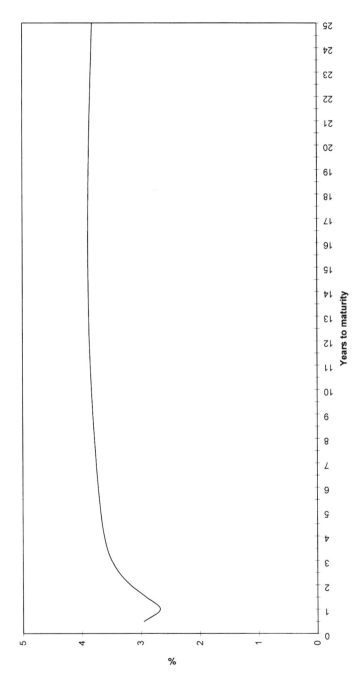

Figure 7.7 Implied forward inflation rates for 18 January 1994

RPI level. If the RPI setting a given coupon is unknown then we must estimate it using the latest available RPI figure in conjunction with some assumption about π^e, the path of future inflation.

7.8.2   THE TERM STRUCTURE OF INFLATION EXPECTATIONS

From term structure models for nominal and real spot interest rates it is possible to construct respective curves for nominal and real implied forward rates (Chapter 1). The term structure of implied forward inflation rates can then be obtained using the Fisher identity:

$$\left(1 + \frac{y}{2}\right) = (1 + i)^{1/2} \left(1 + \frac{r}{2}\right)$$

where y is the implied nominal forward rate, r is the implied real forward rate and i is the implied forward inflation rate.

Like the term structure of real spot rates, the real implied forward rate curve will depend on an inflation assumption. In order to make this assumption consistent with the implied forward inflation rates that are calculated, it is necessary to iterate on the assumed inflation rate, as illustrated by Deacon and Derry (1994a). In simple terms, for each iteration the real yield curve is re-estimated[19] until there is consistency between the assumed implied forward inflation rates and the estimated implied forward inflation rates. Figures 7.6 and 7.7 provide, respectively, illustrations of the real spot curve and implied forward inflation rate curve for 18 January 1994.

An alternative technique for deriving implied forward inflation rates is employed by Wilcox and Zervos (1994). Here, the authors express the prices of index-linked bonds solely in terms of nominal implied forward interest rates and implied forward inflation rates. Once the nominal forward interest rate curve has been estimated using smoothing splines, Wilcox and Zervos then apply a spline function directly to the implied forward inflation rate curve. This approach inevitably produces more flexible curves than the method outlined earlier due to the curve-fitting technique employed.

7.8.3   ESTIMATION PROBLEMS

The following section briefly examines some of the complications that arise in estimating implied forward inflation curves. For a more comprehensive exposition see Deacon and Derry (1994a).

7.9   TAX EFFECTS

In the UK, the range of coupons on index-linked bonds is not large and so tax rules are unlikely to affect prices of indexed bonds with the same maturity but different coupons to the extent observed in the conventional market. However, indexed bonds with different maturities may be attractive to different categories of investor. Anecdotal evidence suggests that high-rate income taxpayers, who are attracted to index-linked gilts because of the advantageous ratio of capital to income, prefer short-dated securities for reasons of liquidity and reduced price volatility. In contrast, long-dated index-linked gilts are favoured by pension funds, which are exempt from income tax.

Estimation of the implied forward inflation rate curve relies on a no-arbitrage condition, and it is therefore necessary to produce nominal and real curves for the same category of investor. The current methodology outlined here involves modelling both nominal and real curves from the perspective of a zero-rate taxpayer, the nominal curve by modelling the tax effect on the prices of those bonds not naturally held by such investors and thereby adjusting them to be comparable with the remainder, while the prices of indexed gilts are explicitly assumed to be set by 0% taxpayers, implying that any distortions are likely to be at the short maturities. This makes it possible to apply the no-arbitrage condition, since the comparison is between the index-linked and conventional markets from the perspective of the same (possibly hypothetical) investor paying no income or capital gains tax[20].

7.10   TERM PREMIA

In order to interpret implied forward inflation rates as 'true' market expectations of inflation it is necessary to assume that the estimated forward *interest* rates are expected future short rates. However, in practice there are several factors which are likely to lead to a difference between the two. These factors can be grouped into three categories: inflation risk premia, liquidity premia and Jensen's inequality[21] — which Chapter 8 discusses in depth.

Most academic studies of inflation expectations regard the estimation of the inflation risk premium as an intractable problem, either assuming it to be zero (Robertson and Symons, 1993) or taking it as given and estimating inflation expectations under alternative assumptions about its size. For instance, Arak and Kreicher (1985) generate results for inflation risk premia of 0% and 2%, while Woodward (1990) looks, in addition, at the case where the risk premium is 1%.

Only Levin and Copeland (1993) manage to produce an estimate for the inflation risk premium. Thanks to the lag in indexation on index-linked gilts they show that it is possible to derive estimates of expected inflation and real interest rates from a comparison of two indexed bonds of different durations, without recourse to any information from conventional gilts. It is then possible to combine the information from the prices of conventional bonds with these estimates for inflation expectations and real interest rates to derive an estimate for the inflation risk premium[22]. In fact, the results obtained by Levin and Copeland are for the net effect of the inflation risk premium and Jensen's inequality — over the estimation period 1982 to 1991 the largest estimate being 32 basis points for Q1 1990 and the smallest zero. When interpreting these results, it is important to bear in mind

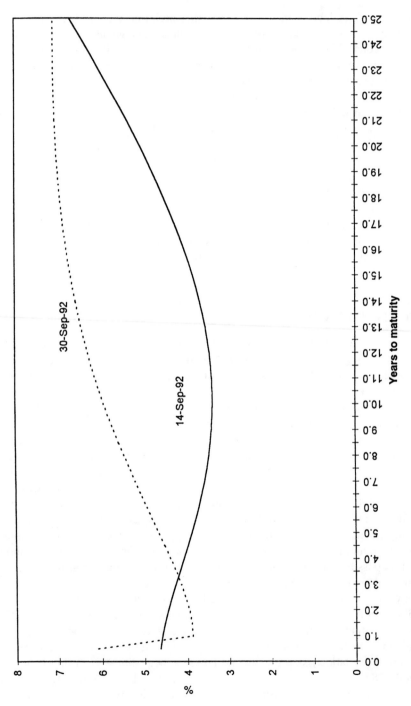

Figure 7.8 Implied forward inflation rates

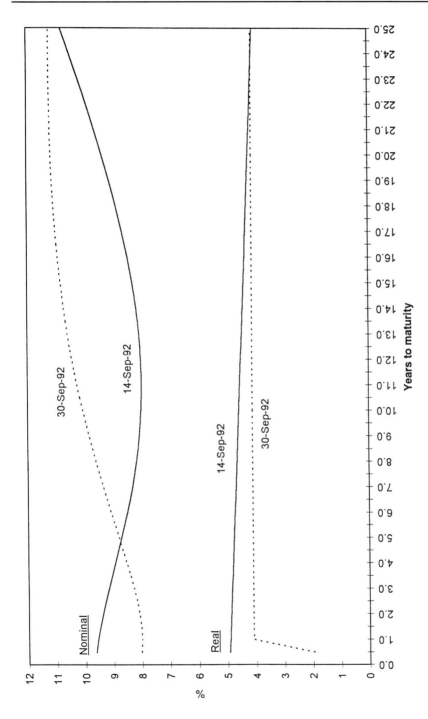

Figure 7.9 Implied forward interest rates

the simplifying assumptions that the authors had to impose in order to obtain solutions — namely a simplistic functional form for the inflation term structure and a single tax rate for all maturities. On the practitioner side, Cullen and Roberts (1994) report that the usual approximation for the inflation risk premium is 25 basis points on short-dated gilts and 50 basis points on longer stocks.

Barr and Pesaran (1995) apply a vector autoregression to decompose the causes of unanticipated movements in bond prices into news about fundamentals (expected future real interest and inflation rates) and expected future risk premia, concluding that though risk premia are present in both conventional and index-linked bond prices they have little influence on *relative* prices. This strengthens the case for looking at *changes* in the levels of the implied forward inflation rate curves rather than at the levels themselves.

7.10.1   AN EVENT STUDY OF INFLATION EXPECTATIONS

Given the method for deriving inflation expectations outlined in the preceding sections, it is useful to examine how these expectations responded to a recent monetary event. The example chosen is sterling's exit from the Exchange Rate Mechanism (ERM) on 16 September 1992 'Black Wednesday' — see figures 7.8 and 7.9.

APPENDIX A: CALCULATION OF INTEREST PAYMENTS, CAPITAL PAYMENTS AND REAL REDEMPTION YIELDS ON AUSTRALIAN CAPITAL INDEXED BONDS

The quarterly interest payments I_t are calculated as:

$$I_t = \frac{c}{4} \times \frac{K_t}{100}$$

where

c = annual coupon rate (%)

K_t = nominal value of the principal at the date of the next interest payment

$$= K_{t-1} \left[1 + \frac{i}{100} \right]$$

K_{t-1} = nominal value of the principal at the date of the previous interest payment. If there is no previous interest payment $K_{t-1} = 100$ (the face value of the bond)

i = the average percentage change in the CPI over the two quarters ending in the quarter which is two quarters prior to that in which the next interest payment falls. For example, if the next interest payment is in November 1995, i is based on the average movement in the CPI between December 1994 and June 1995.

$$i = \frac{100}{2}\left[\frac{CPI_t}{CPI_{t-2}} - 1\right]$$

where

CPI_t is the CPI for the second quarter of the relevant two quarter period
CPI_{t-2} is the CPI for the quarter immediately prior to the relevant two quarter period

The Reserve Bank of Australia price/yield formula for a capital indexed bond is given by:

$$\text{Price per \$100 face value} = w^{f/d}\left[\frac{c}{4}(x + a_n) + 100w^n\right]K_t\frac{\left(1 + \dfrac{i}{100}\right)^{-(f/d)}}{100}$$

where

r = real yield (%)

$$w = \left(1\Big/1 + \frac{r}{400}\right)$$

$$x = \begin{cases} 1 & \text{if there is an interest payment at the next payment date} \\ 0 & \text{if there is no interest payment at the next payment date} \end{cases}$$

f = the number of days from the settlement date to the next interest payment date
d = the number of days in the quarter ending on the next interest payment date
n = the number of full quarters between the next interest payment date and the maturity date

$$a_n = w + w^2 + \cdots + w^n = 400\left(\frac{1 - w^n}{r}\right)$$

APPENDIX B: CALCULATION OF CAPITAL PAYMENTS AND REAL REDEMPTION YIELDS ON SWEDISH INDEXED BONDS

The redemption payment is calculated as: Face value × (Final index/Base index). For example, in the case of the 2014 stock issued in April 1994 and redeeming in April 2014, the base index is the CPI for January 1994 and the final index is the CPI for January 2014.

At auction investors state the real yield that they require. This is converted into a price using the convention[23]:

$$P = \frac{I \cdot F}{(1 + r)^t}$$

where

t = remaining maturity in years
I = index factor
F = face value
r = *required* real yield (per cent per annum)

The index factor is a measure of accrued inflation and is calculated as follows:

$$I = \frac{\text{Reference Index}_{\text{Settlement day}}}{\text{Base Index}}$$

If the settlement date is the first of the month, the Reference Index is the CPI for the calendar month falling three months earlier, i.e. the Reference Index for 1 June corresponds to the CPI for March, etc. Reference Indices for other days in the month are obtained by linear interpolation, in which a month is deemed to have 30 days. For instance, the Reference Index for 5 June would be calculated as

$$\text{Reference Index}_{5 \text{ June}} = \text{Reference Index}_{1 \text{ June}}$$

$$+ \frac{4}{30} \cdot (\text{Reference Index}_{1 \text{ July}} - \text{Reference Index}_{1 \text{ June}})$$

The same convention — which ignores the indexation lag — is adopted for trading in the secondary market. For a more detailed explanation of how the interpolation operates see SNDO (1994).

APPENDIX C: DERIVATION OF THE MCCULLOCH REAL YIELD CURVE EQUATIONS

In order to estimate a real yield curve it is necessary to calculate a real redemption yield for each index-linked gilt. To do this, values must be estimated for the outstanding dividends and the corresponding discount rates for each such bond.

This appendix sets out how to produce these estimates for the net present value of each cash flow on a given index-linked stock, and how this makes it possible to produce a McCulloch real yield curve.

CALCULATION OF THE DIVIDENDS

For an index-linked gilt the lth remaining dividend payment[24] is half the coupon scaled by a factor:

$$\frac{RPID_l}{RPIB}$$

where

$RPIB$ = Base RPI level for the stock in question (the RPI level 8 months before the stock was issued).

$RPID_l$ = RPI value defining the lth remaining dividend payment (the RPI level 8 months before the date of the lth dividend).

For a given date it is likely that only $RPID_1$, the RPI defining the next dividend, is known with all subsequent dividends depending on yet-unpublished RPI values. In order to provide values for these dividends in the yield calculations the *latest* available RPI figure must be used in conjunction with some assumption about the path of future RPI inflation.

By way of example, consider a hypothetical index-linked gilt of 4% coupon, issued in January 1991 and paying dividends in September and March of each year. Suppose also that for a given settlement date in June 1994 the latest known RPI is for May 1994.

The base RPI value ($RPIB$) for the bond is the RPI level for May 1990, and $RPID_1$ — the RPI defining the next dividend (due in September 1994) is defined by the RPI for January 1994. Thus the next dividend is simply half the coupon multiplied by the RPI scaling factor:

$$\frac{RPID_1}{RPIB} \times \frac{4.0}{2}$$

and is a known quantity for the given settlement date.

However, the subsequent dividend, which is due in March 1995, will be defined by the RPI level for July 1994 which is as yet unknown. In order to estimate this dividend payment we use the latest known RPI (May 1994) and assume an inflation rate to bridge the 2-month gap between May and July 1994. For publication purposes, current market convention is to assume an inflation rate of either 3% or 5% for this period.

Let

π^e = the assumed annual inflation rate

t = time (in half-years) from the settlement date to the date of the latest RPI

td_l = time (in half-years) from the settlement date to the date of the RPI defining the lth remaining dividend

$u = (1 + \pi^e)^{-(1/2)}$

If $RPID_2$ is not yet known then we estimate it as:

$$RPID_2 = RPIL \times u^{t-td_2}$$

$RPIL \times u^{t-(td_1+1)}$ assuming that dividends are exactly 6 months apart

$RPIL \times u^{t-td_1} \times u^{-1}$

$RPIL \times u^{-L/6} \times u^{-1}$

In the above, the times between RPI dates — i.e. the terms $t - td_1$ and $t - td_2$ — are rounded to the nearest month, the UK convention for real yield calculations. L is defined to be $6(td_1 - t)$ — the *exact* number of months from the date of the latest RPI value to the date of the RPI defining the next dividend. L is usually negative, but may be positive when the stock is XD. Clearly, if $RPID_2$ is known we do not need to make such assumptions.

It can be shown that in the general case where the lth dividend is unknown the appropriate RPI level can be approximated by:

$$RPID_l = RPIL \times u^{-L/6} \times u^{-(l-1)}$$

CALCULATION OF THE DISCOUNT FACTORS

Let

r = the real yield

w = the real discount factor = $\left(1 + \dfrac{r}{2}\right)^{-1}$

Then, using the previous notation, the discount factor for the first dividend payment ($FACTOR_1$) is given by:

$$FACTOR_1 = (wu)^{td_1} = w^{td_1} \times u^{td_1}$$

Similarly, the discount factor for the second dividend payment ($FACTOR_2$) is defined to be:

$$FACTOR_2 = (wu)^{td_2}$$
$$= w^{td_2} \times u^{td_2}$$
$$= w^{td_2} \times u^{(td_1+1)}$$
$$= w^{td_2} u^{td_1} u$$

In general it can be shown that

$$FACTOR_l = w^{td_1} u^{td_1} u^{(l-1)}$$

CALCULATION OF THE CASH FLOW NET PRESENT VALUES

It is now possible to calculate the net present value of each cash flow. The net present value of the lth remaining dividend payment is given by:

$$\frac{RPID_l}{RPIB} \times \frac{c}{2} \times FACTOR_l$$

In the case where $RPID_l$ is *known* this reduces to:

$$\left(\frac{RPID_l}{RPIB} \times u^{td_l} \right) \times \frac{c}{2} \times w^{td_1}$$

When the value of $RPID_l$ is *unknown* the relation becomes:

$$\frac{RPIL}{RPIB} u^{-(L/6)} u^{-(l-1)} \times \frac{c}{2} \times w^{td_l} u^{td_1} u^{(l-1)}$$
$$= \left(\frac{RPIL}{RPIB} u^{td_1-(L/6)} \right) \times \frac{c}{2} \times w^{td_l}$$

Now define a term Λ_l to be:

$$\Lambda_l = \begin{cases} [u^{td_l}] \cdot \dfrac{RPID_l}{RPIB} & \text{if } RPID_l \text{ is known} \\[3mm] [u^{td_1-(L/6)}] \cdot \dfrac{RPIL}{RPIB} & \text{otherwise} \end{cases}$$

Then the net present value of the lth dividend payment reduces to

$$\Lambda_l \times \frac{c}{2} \times w^{td_l}$$

By defining $\delta_r(m)$ to be the real discount function at maturity m the above can be written as:

$$\Lambda_l \times \frac{c}{2} \times \delta_r(td_l)$$

Similarly, for an indexed bond with n cash flows the net present value of the real redemption payment R can be written as:

$$\Lambda_n \times R \times \delta_r(td_n)$$

In the case of an n-period conventional bond of (nominal) coupon c the present value of each dividend takes the form:

$$\frac{c}{2} \times \delta_N(td_l)$$

and the present value of the (nominal) redemption payment R the form:

$$R \times \delta_N(td_n)$$

where $\delta_N(m)$ is the nominal discount function at time m.

McCULLOCH REAL YIELD CURVE EQUATIONS

It follows that in order to adapt the McCulloch yield curve equations to generate a real yield curve, each cash flow of *each bond* must be scaled by the relevant Λ factor. Thus, the index-linked analogy of (2.1) is:

$$p_i + ai_i = \frac{c_i}{2} \sum_{l=1}^{n} \Lambda_{il}\delta_r(l) + \Lambda_{in}R_i\delta_r(n)$$

where p_i, c_i, ai_i, n and R_i are the clean price, accrued interest number of coupons outstanding (semi-annual) coupon payments and the real redemption payment of the ith bond.

Substituting the expression for the discount function (the real equivalent of (2.2)) into the ith price equation gives:

$$p_i + ai_i = \frac{c_i}{2} \sum_{l=1}^{n} \Lambda_{il} \left[1 + \sum_{j=1}^{k} a_j f_j(l) \right] + \Lambda_{in}R_i \left[1 + \sum_{j=1}^{k} a_j f_j(n) \right]$$

$$\Rightarrow p_i + ai_i = \frac{c_i}{2} \sum_{l=1}^{n} \Lambda_{il} + \frac{c_i}{2} \sum_{l=1}^{n} \Lambda_{il} \sum_{j=1}^{k} a_j f_j(l) + \Lambda_{in}R_i + \Lambda_{in}R_i \sum_{j=1}^{k} a_j f_j(n)$$

$$\Rightarrow p_i + ai_i - \frac{c_i}{2} \sum_{l=1}^{n} \Lambda_{il} - \Lambda_{in} R_i = \sum_{j=1}^{k} a_j \frac{c_i}{2} \sum_{l=1}^{n} \Lambda_{il} f_j(l) + \sum_{j=1}^{k} a_j \Lambda_{in} R_i f_j(n)$$

$$\Rightarrow p_i + ai_i - \frac{c_i}{2} \sum_{l=1}^{n} \Lambda_{il} - \Lambda_{in} R_i = \sum_{j=1}^{k} a_j \left[\frac{c_i}{2} \sum_{l=1}^{n} \Lambda_{il} f_j(l) + \Lambda_{in} R_i f_j(n) \right]$$

So the regression equation for the McCulloch real yield curve is defined by

$$y_i = \sum_{j=1}^{k} a_j x_{ij}$$

where

$$y_i = p_i + ai_i - \frac{c_i}{2} \sum_{l=1}^{n} \Lambda_{il} - \Lambda_{in} R_i$$

$$x_{ij} = \frac{c_i}{2} \sum_{l=1}^{n} \Lambda_{il} f_j(l) + \Lambda_{in} R_i f_j(n)$$

$$u = (1 + \pi^e)^{-(1/2)}$$

$$\Lambda_{il} = \begin{cases} [u^{td_l}]_i \cdot \dfrac{RPID_l}{RPIB_i} & \text{If } RPID_l \text{ is known} \\[2ex] [u^{td_1 - (L/6)}]_i \cdot \dfrac{RPIL}{RPIB_i} & \text{otherwise} \end{cases}$$

NOTES

1. In fact, it is only in the last few years that Israel has issued *non-indexed* debt.
2. This decomposition ignores any components due to liquidity premia.
3. In essence, this makes the assumption that yields are simple rates of interest rather than compound rates — a log-linear approximation to the previous formula.
4. However, given that index-linked markets are typically less liquid than their conventional counterparts, this is likely to be partially offset by a liquidity premium.
5. Although the Swedish National Debt Office and the Riksbank operate independently, and it is the former that decides on Sweden's issuance

programme, the latter's views on inflation carries some weight — as one would expect — in the decision-making process governing issuance.

6. Figures as at 12 December 1995. The figure for conventionals excludes irredeemable bonds.

7. Index-linked gilts are often issued part-way through a dividend period, and hence the size of the first dividend payment is adjusted accordingly. Also, index-linked gilts have in the past been issued in partly paid form, which adds further complications to the calculation of the first dividend.

8. Throughout the rest of this chapter r will be used to denote some form of *real* interest rate.

9. The cash flows on a CFB are identical to those on an equivalent IAB. However, while an *IAB* is viewed as a stream of revenue which has no principal attached, the whole of each payment being regarded as income resulting from the purchase of an annuity, in the case of a *CFB* the cash flows are considered a repayment of debt and hence each payment consists of principal and interest. Accordingly, the instruments are treated differently as regards taxation.

10. The measure of inflation used is actually an average rate. A full explanation is provided in Appendix A.

11. CPI-W is the Consumer Price Index for urban wage earners and clerical workers.

12. Any effects that might arise from differences in liquidity are also ignored.

13. In fact, 8% Treasury 2003 was issued in partly paid form and was only included in these break-even calculations after the last payment was made.

14. These break-even inflation rates were derived by matching 2.5% Index-Linked Treasury 2003 with the conventional of closest maturity.

15. In the light of the recently announced tax reforms this differential is now likely to be much reduced.

16. In fact, three index-linked stocks are beyond the maturity of the longest conventional, restricting the number of break-even pairings of observations to just ten.

17. This dependence can be important when calculating the yields on index-linked bonds approaching maturity, but becomes less important, the longer the maturity of the bond.

18. Since this derivation is specific to the UK it is assumed that coupon payments are received semi-annually rather than annually. So $c_i/2$ replaces c_i in the original McCulloch equations.

19. Only the real yield curve is re-estimated as part of the iteration, not the nominal curve — which is estimated only once.

20. These estimates can clearly be scaled in the usual way for investors facing other tax treatments.

21. There may also be some effect on both index-linked and conventional yield curves at specific maturities influenced by news about stock issuance.
22. It should be noted that Levin and Copeland ignore any inflation risk premium attached to index-linked gilts, arguing that it is likely to be second order relative to that on conventionals.
23. This approximation to the correct price/yield relationship avoids the need to make an assumption about future inflation.
24. This ignores the (obvious) adjustments that are required if the stock has not yet reached its first-ever dividend payment, since in general this will not simply be $c/2$ (in real terms).

REFERENCES

Arak, M. and Kreicher, L. (1985) The real rate of interest: inferences from the new UK indexed gilts, *International Economic Review*, **26**, No. 2 (June), 399–408.

Bank of England (1993) Chapter 5: Prospects for inflation, *Inflation Report*, May 182–3.

Barr, D.G. and Pesaran, B. (1995) An assessment of the relative importance of real interest rates, inflation and term premia in determining the prices of real and nominal UK bonds, Bank of England Working Paper No. 32, April.

Barro, R.J. (1994) A suggestion for revising the inflation adjustment of payments on index-linked bonds, mimeo 24 August.

Bootle, R. (1991) *Index-Linked Gilts — A Practical Investment Guide* (2nd edition), Woodhead-Faulkner, Cambridge.

BZW (1993) *Guide to Index-Linked Securities* (2nd edition), *BZW*, Australia.

Central Bank of Iceland (1991) Financial Indexation in Iceland, *Economic Statistics Quarterly*, **12**, No. 2 (May).

Central Bank of Iceland (1995) Changes in the indexation regime, *Economic Statistics Quarterly* (February).

Connor, J. (1994) US Treasury studies issuing bonds that protect investors from inflation, *Wall Street Journal*, 8 January.

Cullen, S. and Roberts, A. (1994) Index-linked gilts annual review 1994, *UBS Global Research*, 16 December.

D'Andrea, A. and Mahoney (eds) (1994) *The 1995 International Guide to Government Securities and Derivatives*, IFR, London.

Deacon, M.P. and Derry, A.J. (1994) Deriving estimates of inflation expectations from the prices of UK government bonds, Bank of England Working Paper No. 23 July.

de Kock, G. (1991) Expected inflation and real interest rates based on index-linked bond prices: the UK experience, *Federal Reserve Bank of New York Quarterly Review* Autumn.

Duenwald, C. (1993) British index-linked government bonds: a preliminary assessment of implicit inflation forecasts, Bank of Canada mimeo, 20 August.

Fisher, I. (1963) The purchasing power of money, *Augustus Kelly*, 210.

Heenan, D.A. (1991) Measures of expected inflation, *Reserve Bank of Australia Bulletin* April.

HMT (1983) *Economic Progress Report*, The Treasury, No. 133 (May).

ISSA (1994) *The International Society of Securities Administrators 1994 Handbook*.

Levin, E.J. and Copeland, L.S. (1993) Reading the message from the UK indexed bond market: real interest rates, expected inflation and the risk premium, *The Manchester School*, **LXI**, Supplement (June).

McLean, S.K. (ed.) (1993) *The European Bond Markets*, (5th edition), Probus, Cambridge.

McCulloch, J.H. (1971) Measuring the term structure of interest rates, *Journal of Business*, **XLIV**, (January), 19–31.

McCulloch, J.H. (1975) The tax-adjusted yield curve, *Journal of Finance*, **XXX**, No. 3 (June), 811–30.

Mishkin, F.S. (1990) Can futures market data be used to understand the behaviour of real interest rates? *Journal of Finance*, **XLV**, No. 1 (March).

New Zealand Treasury Debt. Management Office (1995) Inflation-indexed bonds: New Zealand government Inflation-Indexed Bond Prospectus.

Page, S.A.B. and Trollope, S. (1974) An international survey of indexing and its effects, *National Institute Economic Review*, No. 70 (November), 46–60.

Petzel, T.E. and Fabozzi, F.J. (1986) Real interest rates and CPI-W futures, *Advances in Futures and Options Research 1*, Part B, 225–70.

Reserve Bank of Australia (1994) *Treasury Capital Indexed Bonds Information Sheet*, August.

Robertson, D. and Symons, J. (1993) Real interest rates and index-linked gilts, Centre for Economic Performance, LSE, Discussion Paper No. DP 181.

Rutterford (1983) Index-linked gilts, *National Westminster Quarterly Review*, November.

Sibblies, B. (1992) Mexico: Government bonds ('Ajustabonas') instrument brief, *J.P. Morgan* 29 September.

Sibblies, B. (1994) Mexico: Ajustabonos instrument brief, *J.P. Morgan*, 19 August.

SNDO (1994) *Index-Linked Treasury Bonds*, The Swedish National Debt Office 30 March.

Svensson (1994) The simplest test of inflation target credibility, Centre for Economic Policy Research Discussion Paper No. 940 April.

Wilcox, D. and Zervos, D. (1994) Extracting real interest rates and inflation expectations from the UK gilt market, Federal Reserve Board mimeo October.

Woodward, G.T. (1990) The real thing: a dynamic profile of the term structure of real interest rates and inflation expectations in the United Kingdom, 1982–1989, *Journal of Business*, **63**, No. 3, 378–98.

CHAPTER 8

Term premia and the implied forward rate curve

8.1 INTRODUCTION

As noted in Chapter 1, the fact that bond prices have positive convexity with respect to yields complicates the relationship between these yields and market expectations of future interest rates. Put another way, the convexity of bond prices drives a wedge between *actual* expectations and the set of forward rates of interest *implied* by the current yield curve. Additional problems arise with the introduction of risk premia. In this chapter, via the expectations hypothesis, bond prices are derived as a function of market expectations — the convexity of these prices is then characterized by Jensen's Inequality.

The expectations hypothesis is based upon the general proposition that expectations about future interest rates affect the current level of long rates (see Fisher, 1896). Developed over the years by numerous researchers, most notably by Hicks (1939) and Lutz (1940–41), it offers a variety of equations linking unobservable expectations to observable bond prices. But if interest rates are stochastic, these equations are typically mutually inconsistent as a result of Jensen's Inequality. In fact, the only version of the expectations hypothesis to imply that forward rates accurately reflect expected future short rates is the 'pure unbiased expectations hypothesis'. Following Campbell (1986) the qualifier 'pure' is used to denote the absence of risk premia[1]. If actual expectations are implied by another version of the expectations hypothesis, there will be a *forward premium* which is characterized in terms of risk and Jensen's Inequality.

Cox, Ingersoll and Ross (1981) demonstrate that the only version of the expectations hypothesis consistent with a rational expectations equilibrium is the local expectations hypothesis. By definition, therefore, Jensen's Inequality drives a wedge between forward rates and actual expectations of future short rates. But Campbell (1986) argues that any forward premium arising solely from Jensen's

Inequality will typically be insignificant. Thus, in the absence of risk premia, forward rates are approximately equal to market expectations. More generally, any forward premium will be insignificant over and above the corresponding risk premium.

In this chapter we attempt to quantify an 'upper bound' upon the effect of Jensen's Inequality over the forward premium using empirical estimates of the Cox, Ingersoll and Ross (1985) model of the term structure. But the forward premium is also relevant to the technical exercise of estimating the yield curve. Expected future rates are likely to settle at a constant level as the expectations horizon increases — if the forward premium is well behaved, this constraint can be imposed during the estimation process. This issue is illustrated using two further models of the term structure, due to Merton (1973) and Vasicek (1977).

8.2   THE EXPECTATIONS HYPOTHESIS

Observed bond prices typically relate to coupon-bearing bonds which offer a variety of coupon rates at various payment dates. The returns on two bonds of the same maturity are therefore likely to differ. If coupon rates are known with certainty, however, any coupon bond may be constructed as a portfolio of zero-coupon (or pure-discount) bonds. Presented within a unified framework, the expectations hypothesis is concerned with the relationship between future short rates and the prices of these bonds[2].

8.2.1   DEFINITIONS AND NOTATION

Let $P(t, T)$ denote the time t price of a pure-discount bond paying a certain £1 at maturity T. The yield to maturity on the bond, $z(t, T)$, is its average (continuously compounded) rate of return and, in continuous time, is determined by the price–yield relationship:

$$P(t, T) = \exp\{-z(t, T) \cdot (T - t)\} \tag{8.1}$$

Both prices and yields are observable[3] at the current time t — the 'term structure of interest rates' is (often) defined as the set of bond prices, $\{P(t, T) : T \geq t\}$. Expressed in terms of bond yields, $z(t, T)$, this is referred to as the 'zero-coupon yield curve' and is calculated for each maturity T by:

$$z(t, T) = \frac{-\ln P(t, T)}{T - t} \tag{8.2}$$

According to the expectations hypothesis, both prices and yields are determined by unobservable market expectations of future interest rates. Reversing the logic implies that information about these expectations can be extracted from observable bond prices and/or the current yield curve.

To the extent that this is true, this information is reflected by the set of future rates of interest *implied* by the term structure, referred to as the 'implied forward rate curve'. These rates are determined in the price of a bond by:

$$P(t, T) = \exp\left\{-\int_t^T f(t, s)\,ds\right\} \tag{8.3}$$

where $f(t, s)$ is the forward rate of interest, contracted at time t, for instantaneous borrowing or lending at time s. If bond prices are differentiable with respect to T, each forward rate, $f(t, T)$, is calculated as:

$$f(t, T) = \frac{-\partial P(t, T)/\partial T}{P(t, T)} \tag{8.4}$$

and is defined as the implied instantaneous rate of return on the bond at the future settlement date T. If a bond is actually *defined* with only an 'instant' to maturity at time T it is referred to here as a 'single-period bond'. In this case, the yield on the bond is equal to its instantaneous rate of return which is given by the future rate of interest, r_T. At the current time t, the short rate of interest, r_t, defines the prevailing forward rate, $f(t, t)$. But the relationship between forward rates, $f(t, T)$, and *future* short rates, r_T, is uncertain for each future date T.

8.2.2   THE EXPECTATIONS HYPOTHESIS

As Cox, Ingersoll and Ross (1981) point out, there are four different formulations of the expectations hypothesis. In what follows, each is presented in its 'pure' form, that is, in the absence of risk premia[4].

The *unbiased expectations hypothesis* (UEH, subscript u), assumes that forward rates, $f(t, T)$, and expected future short rates, $E[r_T]$, are equal. Given equation (8.4), the UEH states that:

$$\frac{-\partial P_u(t, T)/\partial T}{P_u(t, T)} = E[r_T] \tag{8.5}$$

It therefore equates the future marginal rate of interest *implied* by observable bond prices, $P(t, T)$, with the *actual* expected rate, $E[r_T]$.

The *local expectations hypothesis* (LEH, subscript l) states that the expected instantaneous return on any $(T - t)$-maturity bond is equal to the current short rate, r_t:

$$E\left[\frac{dP_l(t, T)/dt}{P_l(t, T)}\right] = r_t \tag{8.6}$$

Since r_t is known with certainty and the choice of maturity date, T, is arbitrary, equation (8.6) implies that, at the current time t, expected short rates of return on bonds of all maturities are equivalent.

Over a longer period t to T the *returns to maturity hypothesis* (RTM, subscript r) equates the expected returns, inclusive of capital invested, from two alternative investment strategies: buying and holding a $(T - t)$-maturity bond and rolling over a series of single-period bonds:

$$\frac{1}{P_r(t, T)} = E\left[\exp\left\{\int_t^T r_s\,ds\right\}\right] \tag{8.7}$$

Notice that, since the pure-discount bond realizes a guaranteed payoff at maturity T, the return on the bond over the period t to T is also known with certainty at time t.

Similarly, by equating expected yields from the two investment strategies over the period t to T, the *yields to maturity hypothesis* (YTM, subscript y) states that:

$$\frac{-1}{T - t}\ln P_y(t, T) = E\left[\frac{1}{T - t}\int_t^T r_s\,ds\right] \tag{8.8}$$

By differentiating (8.8) with respect to T and comparing with equation (8.5), this relationship is shown to be identical to the unbiased expectations hypothesis. In other words, given market expectations of future interest rates, the two sets of bond prices, $P_u(t, T)$ and $P_y(t, T)$, are equal. These two relationships are therefore referred to exclusively as the UEH.

8.2.3   JENSEN'S INEQUALITY

Bond prices generated by the UEH, LEH and RTM will, in general, be mutually inconsistent. These prices are summarized in Table 8.1[5]. Differences between these prices arise from the uncertainty of future interest rates and are characterized by Jensen's Inequality, a well-known result from statistical theory. This states that, for a random variable X, if $g(X)$ is a strictly convex function, then[6,7]:

$$E[g(X)] > g[E(X)] \tag{8.9}$$

where the converse is true when $g(X)$ is a concave function of X. Thus for $X = \{-\int_t^T r_s\,ds\}$, the function $\exp(X)$ is convex and bond prices given by the local expectations hypothesis, $P_l(t, T)$, are larger than those generated by the UEH, $P_u(t, T)$. Meanwhile, for $X = \{\int_t^T r_s\,ds\}$, Jensen's Inequality implies that

Table 8.1

	$P_i(t, T)$
UEH	$\exp\left\{-E\left[\int_t^T r_s\,ds\right]\right\}$
LEH	$E\left[\exp\left\{-\int_t^T r_s\,ds\right\}\right]$
RTM	$1\bigg/E\left[\exp\left\{\int_t^T r_s\,ds\right\}\right]$

both sets of bond prices are larger than those generated by the return to maturity hypothesis, $P_r(t, T)$. Thus, given (the set of unique) market expectations of future short rates, $E[r_s]$:

$$P_l(t, T) > P_u(t, T) > P_r(t, T) \qquad \forall t < T \qquad (8.10)$$

As Cox, Ingersoll and Ross (1981) note, since we *observe* only one set of bond prices, only one of the bond-pricing relationships (equations (8.5) to (8.7)), can hold for a particular market. In other words, the three versions of the expectations hypothesis cannot simultaneously be responsible for generating bond price data from the set of expected future short rates.

8.3   TERM PREMIA

Given the set of observed bond prices, $\{P(t, T) : T \geq t\}$, the stochastic process followed by these prices defines expected holding period returns and (the set of) implied forward rates of interest. In each case there is a corresponding term premium: the instantaneous holding premium and the instantaneous forward premium. Different versions of the expectations hypothesis will imply different values for these premia.

8.3.1   STOCHASTIC BOND PRICES

This section describes a single-factor version of the bond pricing model presented in Chapter 4, where the only state variable is the current short rate of interest, r_t^8. This is assumed to follow an Itô process:

$$\mathrm{d}r_t = \alpha(r_t, t)\,\mathrm{d}t + \beta(r_t, t)\,\mathrm{d}\beta_t \qquad (8.11)$$

where the expected change in short rates over a period $\mathrm{d}t$ is given by the instantaneous (local) drift rate, $\alpha(r_t, t)$, while the instantaneous (local) volatility of r_t is determined by $\beta(r_t, t)$. The stochastic process followed by current bond prices, $P(t, T)$, is given by the analogous condition to equation (4.1):

$$\frac{\mathrm{d}P_t}{P_t} = \mu(r_t, t, T)\,\mathrm{d}t + \sigma(r_t, t, T)\,\mathrm{d}B_t \qquad (8.12)$$

where $\mu(r_t, t, T)$ is the expected instantaneous rate of return on the $(T - t)$-maturity pure-discount bond and $\sigma(r_t, t, T)$ measures the standard deviation of these returns. These parameters are derived according to equations (4.10a) and (4.10b) where the single factor, r_t, replaces the state variable, S_t, and $j = 1$.

8.3.2   INSTANTANEOUS HOLDING PREMIA

The instantaneous holding premium characterizes the excess return required by investors as compensation for the uncertainty of future rates of return[9]. It

Table 8.2

	$\mu(r_t, t, T)$
UEH	$r_t + \frac{1}{2}\sigma^2(r_t, t, T)$
LEH	r_t
RTM	$r_t + \sigma^2(r_t, t, T)$

describes the difference between the expected instantaneous holding return on the bond at time t, $\mu(r_t, t, T)$, and the current short rate, r_t[10]:

$$h(t, T) = \mu(r_t, t, T) - r_t \qquad (8.13)$$

Values for $\mu(r_t, t, T)$ implied by the three versions of the expectations hypothesis (equations (8.5), (8.6) and (8.7)) are summarized in Table 8.2[11].

Since the current short rate, r_t, is known at time t, different versions of the expectations hypothesis therefore imply different values for the instantaneous holding premium, $h(t, T)$, i.e.

$$h_l(t, s) < h_u(t, s) < h_r(t, s) \qquad \forall s \geq t \qquad (8.14)$$

By definition, as Table 8.2 shows, the local expectation hypothesis implies a holding premium, $h_l(t, s)$, equal to zero. Thus the remaining two hypotheses each correspond to strictly positive holding premia.

8.3.3   INSTANTANEOUS FORWARD PREMIA

For a given maturity, s, a positive forward premium, $\pi(t, s)$, at time t implies that the forward rate, $f(t, s)$, exceeds the expected short rate, $E[r_s]$, i.e.

$$\pi(t, s) = f(t, s) - E[r_s] \qquad (8.15)$$

Equation (8.3) shows that, in general, a higher forward rate, $f(t, s)$, corresponds to a lower bond price, $P(t, T)$. At the same time a (positive) holding premium, $h(t, s)$, lowers bond prices as future cashflows are discounted at a higher rate of return. In general, therefore, there is a positive relationship between forward rates and instantaneous holding period returns, i.e.

$$\frac{\partial f(t, s)}{\partial h(t, s)} > 0 \qquad (8.16)$$

Since the expected short rate, $E[r_s]$, is not specific to any version of the expectations hypothesis, inequality (8.14) is therefore redefined as:

$$\pi_l(t, s) < \pi_u(t, s) < \pi_r(t, s) \qquad (8.17)$$

In this case, the unbiased expectations hypothesis implies a zero instantaneous forward premium, $\pi_u(t, s)$. Thus the local expectations hypothesis corresponds to a negative forward premium, $\pi_l(t, s)$, while for the RTM, the premium, $\pi_r(t, s)$, is positive.

Notice that, by definition of the instantaneous holding and forward premia, $h_l(t, s) = 0$ and $\pi_u(t, s) = 0$ for all $s \geq t$. The mutual inconsistency of the UEH and LEH thus ensures that the two types of term premia, $h(t, T)$ and $\pi(t, T)$, cannot simultaneously equal zero.

8.4   BOND PRICING IN EQUILIBRIUM

Using the previous example, this section examines the sustainability of each version of the expectations hypothesis in equilibrium. Following Cox, Ingersoll and Ross (1981), this equilibrium is described in terms of instantaneous holding premia, $h(t, T)$. The equilibrium characterization of the instantaneous forward premium, $\pi(r_t, t, T)$, follows.

8.4.1   A NO-ARBITRAGE EQUILIBRIUM[12]

Suppose that pure-discount bond prices are generated by the return to maturity hypothesis and consider a portfolio consisting of s_i bonds of term to maturity τ_i for $i = 1, 2$. The value of this portfolio at time t, V_t, is given by:

$$V_t = s_1 P_r(t, T_1) + s_2 P_r(t, T_2) \tag{8.18}$$

where bond prices, $P_r(t, T)$, are generated according to equation (8.7). Defining weights, x_i, by $x_i = s_i P_r(t, T_i)/V_t$, the change in value of the portfolio over a period dt can be written as:

$$\frac{dV_t}{V_t} = x_1 \frac{dP_r(t, T_1)}{P_r(t, T_1)} + x_2 \frac{dP_r(t, T_2)}{P_r(t, T_2)} \tag{8.19}$$

Choosing weights $x_1 = \sigma(r_t, t, T_2)/\{\sigma(r_t, t, T_2) - \sigma(r_t, t, T_1)\}$ and $x_2 = 1 - x_1$ reduces the volatility of portfolio returns to zero. The instantaneous holding period return is given by $\mu_P(r_t, t, T_1, T_2)$ as follows:

$$\mu_P(r_t, t, T_1, T_2) = r_t - \sigma(r_t, t, T_1)\sigma(r_t, t, T_2) \neq r_t \tag{8.20}$$

The portfolio is therefore expected to earn a (guaranteed) riskless rate of return above (or below) the short rate, r_t. In other words, the RTM offers arbitrage opportunities between pure-discount bonds of differing maturities, τ_i.

Hence, the bond-pricing relationship implied by the return to maturity hypothesis is inconsistent with a no-arbitrage equilibrium and a similar argument applies to the unbiased expectations hypothesis. But for the local expectations hypothesis, Table 8.2 shows that expected instantaneous returns, $\mu(r_t, t, T)$, are equivalent to the short rate of interest, r_t. In other words, the LEH is consistent with zero instantaneous holding premia for bonds of all terms to maturity, $(T - t)$. Thus there are no arbitrage opportunities between bonds of differing maturities and, in the absence of risk premia, the LEH satisfies a no-arbitrage equilibrium of the term structure.

Suppose, then, that observed bond prices, $P(t, T)$, satisfy the local expectations hypothesis (equation (8.6)) for $P_1(t, T) = P(t, T)$. Inequality (8.10) shows that for a common set of market expectations of future interest rates, $E[r_s]$, each bond price, $P(t, T)$, will be higher than the theoretical price, $P_u(t, T)$, implied by the UEH. Therefore, inequality (8.14) holds for the observed forward premium, $\pi(t, s) = \pi_1(t, s)$, and for each future date s, forward rates of interest, $f(t, s)$, calculated from observed bond prices, $P(t, T)$, will underestimate expected future short rates, $E[r_s]$. Since there is a zero holding premium, $h(t, s)$, this forward premium arises solely from the inconsistency of the LEH and UEH, as characterized by Jensen's Inequality.

8.4.2   RISK PREMIA

By definition, the existence of risk premia contradicts the local expectations hypothesis equilibrium which requires that $\mu(r_t, t, T) = r_t$. However, Chapter 4 shows that there is a risk-adjusted version of the LEH which holds in a no-arbitrage equilibrium if the instantaneous holding premium, $h(t, T)$, is proportional to the volatility of bond returns, $\sigma(r_t, t, T)$, i.e.[13]:

$$h(t, T) = \lambda(r_t)\sigma(r_t, t, T) \tag{8.21}$$

where $\sigma(r_t, t, T)$ is the quantity of risk faced by a $(T - t)$-maturity pure-discount bond and $\lambda(r_t)$ is defined as the market price of risk, as was introduced in that chapter.

In this case, as demonstrated by equation (4.12), equilibrium bond prices are given by a risk-adjusted version of the local expectations hypothesis:

$$P(t, T) = E\left[\exp\left\{-\int_t^T r_s^m \, ds\right\}\right] \tag{8.22}$$

where the variable r^m is equal to the current short rate of interest at time t. But for each future date s, it is determined by the modified or risk-adjusted interest rate process:

$$dr_s^m = \{\alpha(r_t, t) - \lambda(r_t)\beta(r_t, t)\} \, dt + \beta(r_t, t) \, dB_t \tag{8.23}$$

which rather than replacing the 'true' diffusion process for short rates, r, simply defines a tool by which to determine risk-adjusted bond prices, $P(t, T)$[14]. Thus if the risk preferences of investors correspond to equation (8.21) while interest rates evolve according to (8.11) an equilibrium pricing relationship may be characterized by the risk-adjusted LEH, given by equations (8.22) and (8.23). Whether or not this characterization implies a negative forward premium, $\pi(t, T)$, as in the previous case, depends upon the magnitude of the holding premium, $h(t, T)$. For $h(t, T) = 0$, Jensen's Inequality drives forward rates below expected rates, yielding a negative forward premium. But, as previously noted, there is a positive relationship between instantaneous holding premia and forward premia. Thus, for $h(t, T) > 0$, the sign of the forward premium depends upon whether the holding premium is sufficiently large to outweigh the effect of Jensen's Inequality.

8.5   SOME PRACTICAL ISSUES

In theory, the implied instantaneous forward premium can be inferred from the short rate parameters, $\alpha(r_t, t)$ and $\beta(r_t, t)$, and from the market price of risk, $\lambda(r_t)$. But in practice, these values are unobservable and market expectations are inferred from the current yield curve. In doing so, a number of assumptions are implicitly made about the two types of term premia, $h(t, T)$ and $\pi(t, T)$. These assumptions imply a number of constraints upon the underlying parameters, $\alpha(r_t, t)$, $\beta(r_t, t)$ and $\lambda(r_t)$.

8.5.1   MODELLING THE YIELD CURVE

According to Chapter 3, Figure 3.3, competing methods of yield curve estimation generate inconsistent estimates of the implied forward rate curve. Given a unique set of market expectations of future interest rates, this implies that each model implicitly assumes a different form of the instantaneous forward premium, $\pi(t, T)$. Suppose, for example, following Svensson (1994), expectations of future interest rates are assumed to be constant beyond a certain settlement date, T. Then McCulloch's (1971, 1975) yield curve implies that the forward premium tends to infinity as the maturity of the bond, T, falls further into the future. Both the Nelson and Siegel (1987) and Svensson (1994) models, on the other hand, constrain the forward premium at the long end of the curve to flatten towards a constant value, $\pi(t, \infty)$. In other words, by constraining the forward rate curve under the assumption of constant expectations, each of these models implies that:

$$\lim_{s \to \infty} E[r_s] = c_1 \qquad (8.24)$$

$$\lim_{s \to \infty} f(t, s) = c_2 \qquad (8.25)$$

$$\lim_{s \to \infty} \pi(t, s) = c_3 \qquad (8.26)$$

where c_1, c_2 and c_3 are constants. Estimating either of these yield curves, under the assumption of constant expectations at the long end of the curve, implicitly constrains the short rate parameters, $\alpha(r_t, t)$ and $\beta(r_t, t)$, to satisfy equations (8.24) to (8.26).

Similarly, suppose that, in each case, the implied forward rate curve obtains a maximum (or minimum) at some term to maturity, $\hat{\tau}$, where τ is the term to maturity, $(T - t)$. For example, on the particular date given by Figure 3.3 in Chapter 3, there is a turning point in the forward curve at $\hat{\tau} \approx 4$ years. Then:

$$\frac{\partial f(t, \hat{\tau})}{\partial \tau} = 0 \tag{8.27}$$

where the forward rate, $f(t, \hat{\tau})$, is some function of the short rate parameters, $\alpha(r_t, t)$ and $\beta(r_t, t)$, and the market price of risk, $\lambda(r_t)$. These values are therefore implicitly constrained to satisfy equation (8.27).

8.5.2   TESTING THE EXPECTATIONS HYPOTHESIS

Campbell and Shiller (1991) test the validity of the expectations hypothesis by assuming that different types of term premia are constant across time. They show that, under this assumption, a constant risk premium interpretation of the unbiased expectations hypothesis is derived as a linear approximation to the non-linear relationship implied by the LEH. Thus, assuming that the instantaneous holding premium, $h(t, T)$, is constant, the equilibrium characterization given by equations (8.22) to (8.23) can be tested via the linear relationship between bond yields (or forward rates) and expected short rates implied by the UEH. Defining $h(t, T)$ by the term, $\lambda(r_t)\sigma(r_t, t, T)$, this approach implicitly places a restriction upon the short rate parameters, $\alpha(r_t, t)$ and $\beta(r_t, t)$, and the market price of risk, $\lambda(r_t)$.

Campbell (1986), for instance, provides a general equilibrium example for which these restrictions are satisfied and the two types of term premia, $h(t, T)$ and $\pi(t, T)$, are each constant functions of maturity, $h(T - t)$ and $\pi(T - t)$. Based upon the Vasicek (1977) model of the term structure, introduced in Chapter 4, his example assumes that the market price of risk, $\lambda(r_t)$, and the short rate parameters, $\alpha(r_t, t)$ and $\beta(r_t, t)$, are characterized by:

$$\lambda(r_t) = c_4 \tag{8.28}$$

$$\alpha(r_t, t) = c_5 + c_6 r_t \tag{8.29}$$

$$\beta(r_t, t) = c_7 \tag{8.30}$$

where each of the values c_4, c_5, c_6 and c_7 are assumed to be constant. In general, if two of these equations hold, the assumption of a constant risk premium is only valid if the remaining condition is satisfied. Thus, a test of the expectations hypothesis based upon the assumption of a constant holding premium, $h(t, T)$, may be biased if, for example, the volatility of short rates is some function of r_t. In fact, Campbell and Shiller (1991) conclude that their (disappointing) results may be interpreted to suggest the existence of time-varying risk premia.

8.5.3   UNDERESTIMATING MARKET EXPECTATIONS

Campbell (1986) also shows that differences between competing versions of the expectations hypothesis are of second-order importance with respect to bond yield variability. Thus, assuming that the volatility of bond prices is not too high, for empirical applications at least, these differences may largely be ignored. If risk premia are equal to zero, this implies that the 'pure' forms of the LEH and UEH are approximately equal and that the effect of Jensen's Inequality is negligible. Similarly, regardless of the precise nature of the holding premium, $h(t, T)$, the unbiased expectations hypothesis can be derived as a linear approximation to the local expectations hypothesis with $\pi(t, T) \approx h(t, T)$. In other words, the bias in forward rates arising from Jensen's Inequality is empirically insignificant over and above the bias caused by the instantaneous holding premium, $h(t, T)$.

The effect of Jensen's Inequality over the instantaneous forward premium, $\pi(t, s)$, is isolated by setting the market price of risk to zero. Then, as implied by the LEH, there will be a negative forward premium, $\pi(t, s)$, for all settlement dates s and:

$$f(t, s) < E[r_s] \qquad \forall s > t \tag{8.31}$$

In other words, forward rates are a biased predictor of expectations of future short rates and Jensen's Inequality measures the extent to which it is possible to *underestimate* these expectations from the implied forward rate curve.

According to Campbell's approximation, inequality (8.31) holds when the market price of risk is equal to zero, but by an empirically insignificant amount. Thus, in the absence of risk premia, the implied forward rate curve is assumed to be an unbiased indicator of market expectations of future short rates. Similarly, when investors are risk-averse, it is reasonable to assume that implied forward rates will *overestimate* these expectations. But the extent to which each of these assertions is true depends upon the variability of bond yields which, in turn, is determined by the underlying short rate parameters, $\alpha(r_t, t)$ and $\beta(r_t, t)$.

8.6   NUMERICAL EXAMPLES IN CONTINUOUS TIME

By way of example, three interest rate models, due to Merton (1973), Vasicek (1977) and Cox, Ingersoll and Ross (1985) (CIR) are considered. These are used to derive, in each case, an expression for the forward premium, $\pi(t, T)$. For the purposes of illustration, estimates of the market price of risk are derived with respect to equation (8.27) in each of the first two cases. By setting the market price of risk to zero for the CIR model an 'upper bound' is calculated for the effect of Jensen's Inequality over the instantaneous forward premium, $\pi(t, T)$. It should be stressed that these results typically rely upon the underlying (strong) assumption that the local expectations hypothesis generates observed bond prices for a single-factor model of the term structure.

Table 8.3

	α_0		α_1	β_0	β_1
Merton	$\mu =$	-0.00255	0	$\sigma = 0.02435$	0
Vasicek	$\kappa\varphi =$	0.03636	$\kappa = 0.33012$	$\sigma = 0.02451$	0
CIR	$\kappa\varphi =$	0.05784	$\kappa = 0.54810$	$\sigma = 0.07164$	$\frac{1}{2}$

8.6.1 THREE INTEREST RATE MODELS

For each of the three models, the short rate of interest is assumed to satisfy equation (8.11), following a stochastic process of the general form:

$$dr_t = \{\alpha_0 - \alpha_1 r_t\}\, dt + \beta_0 r_t^{\beta_1}\, dB_t \tag{8.32}$$

Parameter values for the three models are summarized by Table 8.3. Estimates are taken from Murphy (1995) and are derived from daily observations of three-month LIBOR over the period 1 January 1981 to 31 December 1993.

Each parameter is expressed in proportional terms at an annual rate. The Merton model is a random walk with an annual drift rate, μ, while each of the Vasicek and CIR models revert to a long-run mean, φ, at the annual rate, κ[15]. For the purposes of illustration, the current short rate, r_t, is proxied by the average rate of interest over the sample period, 0.11205.

8.6.2 THE IMPLIED FORWARD RATE CURVE[16]

Under the risk-adjusted LEH, the Merton model of the term structure implies equilibrium forward rates, $f(t, s)$, and instantaneous forward premia, $\pi(t, s)$, as follows:

$$f(t, s) = r_t + (\mu - \lambda\sigma)\tau - \tfrac{1}{2}\sigma^2\tau^2 \tag{8.33}$$

$$\pi(t, s) = -\lambda\sigma\tau - \tfrac{1}{2}\sigma^2\tau^2 \tag{8.34}$$

where τ is the term to maturity, $(s - t)$, and the market price of risk, $\lambda(r_t)$, is assumed to be a constant, λ. In this case, each of the conditions set out to satisfy Svensson's yield curve model (equations (8.24) to (8.26)) are violated. For a negative drift rate, μ:

$$\lim_{s \to \infty} E[r_s] = -\infty \tag{8.35}$$

while the converse is true for $\mu > 0$. Both the implied forward rate curve and the set of forward premia are also unbounded, i.e.

$$\lim_{s \to \infty} f(t, s) = -\infty \tag{8.36}$$

$$\lim_{s \to \infty} \pi(t, s) = -\infty \tag{8.37}$$

Thus, for long settlement dates, s, forward rates of interest will always underestimate market expectations of future interest rates.

The forward rate, $f(t, s)$, and instantaneous forward premium, $\pi(t, s)$, implied by the Vasicek model of the term structure are given by:

$$f(t, s) = Y + (r_t - Y)e^{-\kappa\tau} + \frac{\sigma^2(1 - e^{-\kappa\tau})e^{-\kappa\tau}}{2\kappa^2} \tag{8.38}$$

$$\pi(t, s) = \frac{-\sigma^2(1 - e^{-\kappa\tau})^2}{2\kappa^2} - \frac{\sigma\lambda(1 - e^{-\kappa\tau})}{\kappa} \tag{8.39}$$

where Y is the yield on a perpetuity and is defined with respect to the parameters, φ, σ, κ and λ^{17}. In this case, each of the limits for the expected short rate, forward rate and forward premium are bounded by the parameters of the model. Analogous expressions to equations (8.35) to (8.37) are given by:

$$\lim_{s \to \infty} E[r_s] = \varphi \tag{8.40}$$

$$\lim_{s \to \infty} f(t, s) = Y \tag{8.41}$$

$$\lim_{s \to \infty} \pi(t, s) = \frac{-\sigma^2}{2\kappa^2} - \frac{\sigma\lambda}{\kappa} \tag{8.42}$$

where, assuming that the short rate parameters, κ, φ and σ, are constant, the limit in each case is also constant. Thus, it is more likely that Svensson's estimate of the yield curve is described by the Vasicek model of the term structure than Merton's interest rate model.

For the purpose of comparison, suppose that, regardless of the method of estimation, the forward rate curve obtains a stationary point at $\tau \approx 4$ years. Condition (8.27) implies the market price of risk, λ, in each case. For the Merton model, by differentiating equation (8.33) for $\tau = 4$, the market price of risk is given by $\lambda = -0.2$. Vasicek's model, meanwhile, obtains a maximum for $\tau = 4$ if $\lambda = -0.08$. Each model therefore implies a different level at which investors price a unit of risk.

The implied forward rate curves generated by the two models are illustrated in Figure 8.1. The instantaneous forward premia pertaining to each are given in Figure 8.2. An interesting point to note is that each of the Vasicek curves approaches its limit after only 5 to 10 years. Thus, expectations of future short rates are also implicitly assumed to become constant within a relatively short period of time[18]. The random walk process, on the other hand, is clearly unrealistic as it implies a negative forward premium which increases rapidly as the maturity of the pure-discount bond increases.

8.6.3   AN UPPER BOUND FOR JENSEN'S INEQUALITY

As mentioned previously, the Vasicek model is consistent with a constant holding premium, $h(s - t)$. But suppose, as suggested by Campbell and Shiller (1991), this premium is actually time-variant, violating one of the conditions set out by equations (8.28) to (8.30). Consider, for example, the volatility of short rates,

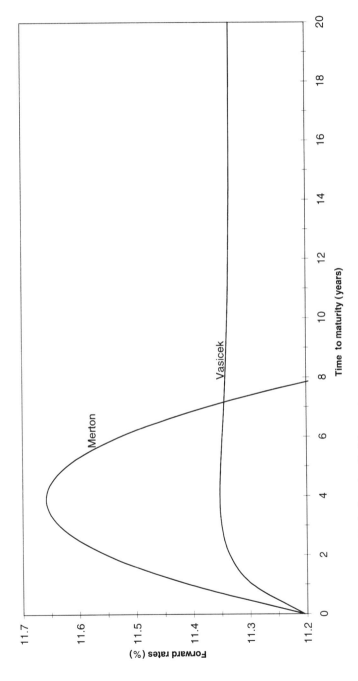

Figure 8.1 Merton versus Vasicek — implied forward rates

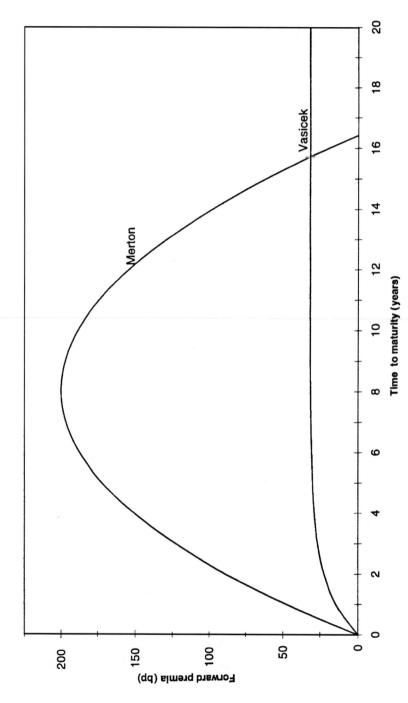

Figure 8.2   Merton versus Vasicek — instantaneous forward premia

$\beta(r_t, t)$. If this is constant interest rates can become negative, as discussed in Chapter 4. As Cox, Ingersoll and Ross point out, this possibility is precluded if $\beta(r_t, t)$ is a function of the current short rate, r_t. In this case, the instantaneous holding premium, $h(t, s)$, will also vary over time.

The Cox, Ingersoll and Ross model is described in Chapter 4. Forward rates and instantaneous forward premia are derived as functions of $B(s - t)$, (see Section 4.3), and the short rate (drift) parameters, κ and φ, i.e.:

$$f(t, s) = \kappa\varphi B(s - t) + r\frac{\partial B(s - t)}{\partial s} \tag{8.43}$$

$$\pi(t, s) = \kappa\varphi B(s - t) + r\frac{\partial B(s - t)}{\partial s} - \varphi - (r - \varphi)e^{-\kappa\tau} \tag{8.44}$$

Since $B(s - t) \neq e^{-\kappa\tau}$, $\pi(t, s)$ is a function of the current short rate r_t and therefore varies across time. Taking limits of (8.43) and (8.44) as τ tends to infinity, as with the Vasicek model, the CIR interest rate process implies a finite boundary for both the implied forward rate curve and instantaneous forward premia, namely:

$$\lim_{s\to\infty} f(t, s) = \frac{\varphi\kappa}{\omega} \tag{8.45}$$

$$\lim_{s\to\infty} \pi(t, s) = -\varphi + \frac{\varphi\kappa}{\omega} \tag{8.46}$$

where ω is a function of the short rate parameters, κ, φ and σ, and the market price of risk, λ[19]. Thus, as implied by the Svensson yield curve, as expectations of future short rates gravitate towards the long-run mean, φ, both the implied forward rate curve, $f(t, s)$, and the instantanous forward premia, $\pi(t, s)$, tend towards a constant as the settlement date, s, tends towards infinity.

In theory, assuming that the Cox, Ingersoll and Ross model accurately describes the evolution of future short rates, the effect of Jensen's Inequality is calculated by quantifying expression (8.44) with the parameter, θ, in $B(s - t)$, set to zero. But, in practice, the parameters of the model are difficult to estimate. It is useful, therefore, to consider a number of possible scenarios by allowing these parameters to vary, as summarized by Figure 8.3 to 8.7.

Using the benchmark parameters, the forward premium induced by Jensen's Inequality reaches a limit of around -9 basis points (bp) at the long end of the maturity range. As the curve falls most steeply in the earlier stages, the difference in expectations exceeds -5 bp after only 3 years. But increasing the value of σ increases the absolute value of the premium. A rise to $\sigma = 0.12$, for example, corresponding to an interest rate volatility of around 0.04 with r_t set at 0.11205, increases the 5-year premium from -8 to -22 bp. The limit at the long end of the maturity range is then around -24 bp. Suppose instead that the benchmark level for volatility is overestimated, its true level being 0.01, implying a value for σ of approximately 0.03. In this case, Jensen's Inequality never exceeds the insignificant level of approximately $-1\frac{1}{2}$ bp.

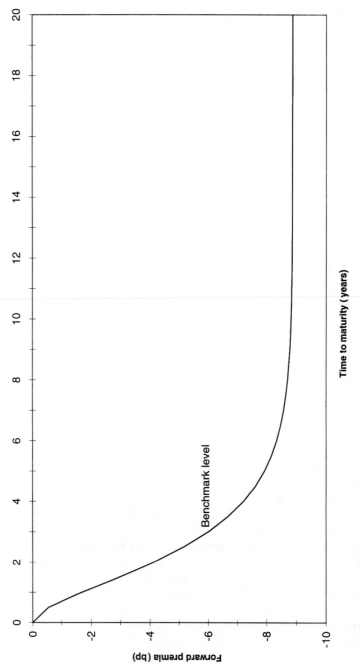

Figure 8.3   CIR forward premia — benchmark parameters

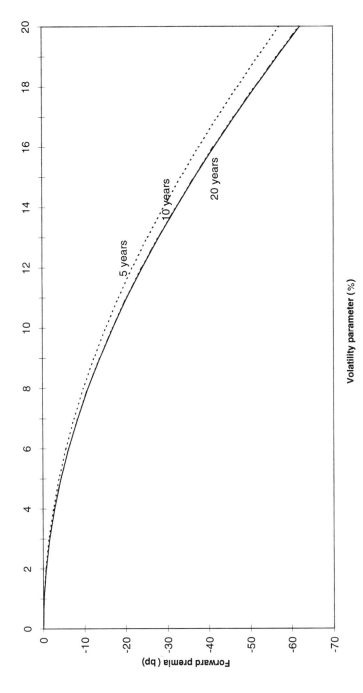

Figure 8.4   CIR forward premia — range for σ from 0 to 0.2

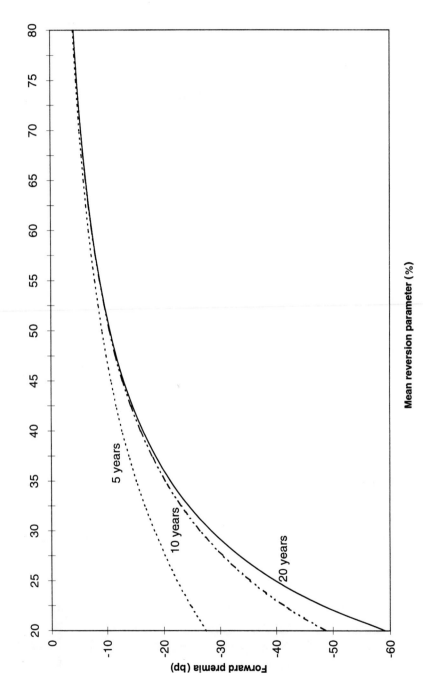

Figure 8.5   CIR forward premia — range for κ from 0.2 to 0.8

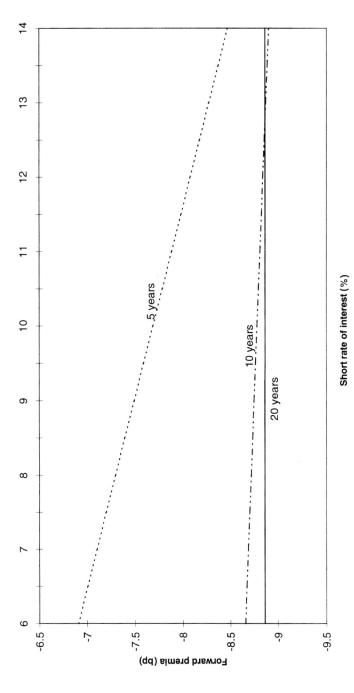

Figure 8.6   CIR forward premia — range for r_t from 0.06 to 0.14

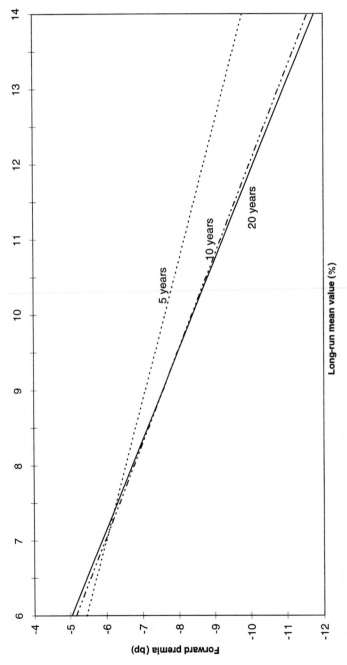

Figure 8.7 CIR forward premia — range for φ from 0.06 to 0.14

Now consider the coefficient of mean reversion, κ. Lowering its value from 0.55 to 0.3 has a dramatic effect, tripling the limit of the premium to nearly 30 bp. This is unsurprising as the lower κ is, the more the CIR interest rate process behaves like a random walk. Increasing the coefficient of mean reversion to 0.8 works in the opposite direction to generate a maximum for the difference in expectations of around -4 bp. Changing the value of the current short rate, r_t, meanwhile, has a very limited effect on the benchmark results. Decreasing it to 0.06 reduces the magnitude of the 5-year premium by about 1 bp, leaving the limit at the long end of the scale virtually unaffected. Similarly, increasing r_t from 0.11205 to 0.14 serves only to raise the difference in expectations at 5 years to maturity from -7.9 bp to -8.5 bp. Increasing the long-run level, φ, from 0.10552 to 0.14 has the effect of raising the limit of the effect of Jensen's Inequality from around -9 bp to -12 bp. At the short end the difference in expectations rises by about 2 bp. Similarly, as φ falls to 0.06, the absolute value of the premium drop to -5 bp at 20 years to maturity while the difference at the shorter end falls to around $-5\frac{1}{2}$ bp.

8.7 CONCLUSION

Jensen's Inequality is important in so far as it drives a wedge between alternative versions of the expectations hypothesis. Given the parameter estimates for the Cox, Ingersoll and Ross interest rate model, however, its empirical significance in relation to inferences about interest rate expectations is rather more doubtful[20] as, at benchmark level, the premium never exceeds -10 bp. Even with a high value for σ at 0.12 or a low rate of mean reversion, κ, at 0.3, the premium is confined to around -30 bp.

It is important to note, however, that these results are based upon the assumption that the yield curve is generated by only one factor, the short rate of interest. Several studies (e.g. Litterman and Scheinkman, 1991) have shown that the yield curve is more likely to be driven by two or three factors, one of which may or may not be the short rate of interest. In a multi-factor model, it is not clear to what extent the local expectations hypothesis is more likely to be consistent with a no-arbitrage equilibrium than its competing hypotheses. Even if the LEH is the 'true' data-generation process, there is no guarantee that the forward premium induced by Jensen's Inequality will be as insignificant with more than one factor.

APPENDIX

Consider the returns to maturity hypothesis given by equation (8.7). Differentiating (8.7) with respect to the current time t gives:

$$E\left[\frac{\mathrm{d}(1/P(t,T))}{P(t,T)}\right] = -r_t\,\mathrm{d}t \qquad (A8.1)$$

Applying Itô's Lemma to the general equation for bond prices (equation (8.12))
yields a stochastic process for $1/P(t, T)$:

$$\frac{d(1/P_t)}{1/P_t} = \{-\mu(r_t, t, T) + \sigma^2(r_t, t, T)\} \, dt - \sigma(r_t, t, T) \, dB_t \qquad (A8.2)$$

Equating (A8.1) and (A8.2) for the terms in dt implies that the instantaneous
holding period return is:

$$\mu(r_t, t, T) = r_t + \sigma^2(r_t, t, T) \qquad (A8.3)$$

i.e. under the returns to maturity hypothesis, instantaneous holding returns are
expected to be in excess of the risk-free rate of interest.

Now consider the unbiased expectations hypothesis in the form given by the
YTM (equation (8.8)). Differentiating (8.8) with respect to time t and taking
expectations:

$$E[d \ln P(t, T)] = r_t \, dt \qquad (A8.4)$$

By applying Itô's Lemma to equation (8.12) the stochastic process followed by
$\ln P(t, T)$ is:

$$d(\ln P_t) = \{\mu(r_t, t, T) - \tfrac{1}{2}\sigma^2(r_t, t, T)\} \, dt + \sigma(r_t, t, T) \, dB_t \qquad (A8.5)$$

Equating terms in dt, from equations (A8.4) and (A8.5):

$$\mu(r_t, t, T) = r_t + \tfrac{1}{2}\sigma^2(r_t, t, T) \qquad (A8.6)$$

i.e. as with the returns to maturity hypothesis, the bond is expected to earn a
return in excess of the risk-free rate.

NOTES

1. It is shown in Section 8.3 that different versions of the expectations hypothesis are in fact consistent with an *implicit* risk premium. By the absence
   of risk premia, we mean to convey that if investors price bonds according
   to a particular version of the expectations hypothesis, there is no *explicit*
   allowance for risk.
2. In effect, these prices are equivalent to the discount functions introduced
   in Chapter 1. Thus, the expectations hypothesis describes the relationship
   between future short rates of interest and the discount rate at which future
   cashflows are discounted.
3. By observable, we mean that these prices and yields may be inferred from
   coupon bond prices via the estimation techniques described in Chapter 2.
4. Equivalently, the expectation is taken with respect to the 'true' stochastic
   process governing future short rates, as opposed to the 'risk-adjusted'
   process (see Chapter 4).

5. Prices for the UEH and RTM are simply found by rearranging equations (8.5) and (8.7). As Cox, Ingersoll and Ross (1981) note, deriving the expression for prices generated by the LEH from equation (8.6) relies 'on the isomorphic relation between differential and integral equations' — the reader is referred to Cox, Ingersoll and Ross (1980) for a formal proof.

6. For this purpose $g(x)$ is defined as a convex function if $\partial^2 g(x)/\partial x^2 > 0$.

7. See Williams (1991), for example, for a proof of Jensen's Inequality.

8. In other words, all information regarding the level of current and future interest rates is assumed to be summarized by the current short rate, r_t.

9. As Section 4.1 shows, this premium is determined by the market prices of risk due to the random processes underlying the term structure. In this case, there is only one source of risk — the uncertainty of future short rates of interest.

10. Notice that, by definition:

$$\mu(r_t, t, T) = E \left[\frac{dP(t, T)/dt}{P(t, T)} \right]$$

11. See the Appendix for a derivation of values for $\mu(r_t, t, T)$ for the RTM and UEH. The result for the LEH is found by definition.

12. Notice that a more general version of the following argument is used in Chapter 4 to derive the equilibrium characterization of the term structure, a risk-adjusted version of the LEH. Assuming a zero market price of risk, this section shows why 'pure' forms of the other two hypotheses fail to hold in equilibrium. Equivalently, since each version implicitly defines an instantaneous holding premium, $h(t, s)$ it demonstrates that, as derived in Chapter 4, this premium must take a particular form to be consistent with a risk-adjusted equilibrium. This is further addressed in the next section.

13. See equation (4.7) for $i = 1$ and $\lambda = \lambda(r_t)$.

14. See Duffie (1993) for further explanation as to the set of modified interest rates, $r^m(s)$.

15. See Section 4.2 for a more detailed discussion of the properties of these models.

16. In each case, only expressions for forward rates, $f(t, s)$, and forward premia, $\pi(t, s)$, are given. The reader is referred to the original papers for a derivation of each of these expressions.

17. In particular,

$$Y = \varphi - \frac{\partial \lambda}{\kappa} - \frac{\sigma^2}{2\kappa^2}$$

18. The exact timing of this reversion to the mean is, of course, determined by the value of the parameter, κ.

19. In particular, $\omega = \frac{1}{2}(\kappa + \gamma + \theta)$ where $\gamma = \sqrt{(\kappa + \theta)^2 + 2\sigma^2}$ and $\theta = \lambda\sigma/\sqrt{r}$.

20. Of course, any inference about the significance of this bias is dependent upon the purpose for which information about market expectations of future interest rates are extracted from the implied forward rate curve.

REFERENCES

Campbell, J. (1986) A defense of traditional hypotheses about the term structure of interest rates, *Journal of Finance*, **XLL**, No. 1, March.

Campbell, J. and Shiller, R. (1991) Yield spreads and interest rate movements: a bird's eye view, *Review of Economic Studies*, **58**, 495–514.

Cox, J., Ingersoll, J. and Ross, S. (1980) A theory of the term structure of interest rates, unpublished working paper, Stanford University.

Cox, J., Ingersoll, J. and Ross, S. (1981) A re-examination of traditional hypotheses about the term structure of interest rates, *Journal of Finance*, **4**.

Cox, J., Ingersoll, J. and Ross, S. (1985) A theory of the term structure of interest rates, *Econometrica*, **53**.

Duffie, D. (1992) *Dynamic Asset Pricing Theory*, Princeton University Press, Princeton, NJ.

Hicks, J. (1939) *Value and Capital*, Oxford University Press, London.

Fisher, I. (1896) *Appreciation and Interest*, Publications of the American Economic Association.

Litterman, R. and Scheinkman, J. (1991) Common factors affecting bond returns, *Journal of Fixed Income*, **1**, No. 1, June, 54–61.

Lutz, F. (1940–41) The structure of interest rates, *Quarterly Journal of Economics*, 36–63.

McCulloch, J. H. (1971) Measuring the term structure of interest rates, *Journal of Business*, **XLIV** (January), 19–31.

McCulloch, J. H. (1975) The tax-adjusted yield curve, *Journal of Finance*, **30**, 811–830.

Merton, R. C. (1973) Rational theory of option pricing, *Bell Journal of Economics and Management Science*, **4**, 141–83.

Murphy, G. (1995) Generalised methods of moments estimation of the short rate process in the UK, Bank of England, mimeo.

Nelson, C. R. and Siegel, A. F. (1987) Parsimonious modeling of yield curves, *Journal of Business*, **60**, 473–89.

Svensson, L. E. O. (1994) Estimating and interpreting forward interest rates: Sweden 1992-94, International Monetary Fund Working Paper No. 114, September.

Vasicek, O. (1977) An equilibrium characterisation of the term structure, *Journal of Financial Economics*, November, 177–88.

Williams, D. (1991) *Probability with Martingales*, Cambridge University Press, Cambridge.

CHAPTER 9

Empirical evidence on the expectations theory of the yield curve

9.1 INTRODUCTION

Chapter 8 showed how the pure form of the expectation theory, where forward rates are exactly equal to expected future spot rates, cannot hold in practice. It demonstrated that a combination of risk and Jensen's Inequality — the term premium — will tend to drive a wedge between observed forward rates and market expectations of spot rates. The form of this term premium is an important aspect of yield curve analysis since it determines the relationship between observed forward rates and the underlying market expectation which is of fundamental importance both to policy-makers (who wish to monitor market expectations) and market practitioners (who wish to determine if the current yield curve reflects fair value).

Although the previous chapter also demonstrated that many models of the interest rate process predict that these term premia will be relatively small and stable over time, such models are widely accepted to be unrealistic in their assumptions and are unlikely to hold in practice. This chapter uses a different approach to analysing term premia: it looks at empirical studies which have tested the ability of the yield curve to predict future interest rates. If term premia are small, or even if they are just stable over time, *changes* in the yield curve should be purely determined by *changes* in expectations of future interest rates. Equation (9.1) shows this simple version of the expectations theory with a constant term premium[1] (in this chapter we define a constant term premium as one which is constant over time but which need not be constant across different maturity bonds). It is clear from this equation that as long as the term premium is constant over time, only changes in expectations of future short rates can induce changes in the current long rate:

$$R_t = \sum_{i=0}^{k-1} E_t r_{t+si} + V \qquad k = l/s \qquad (9.1)$$

where

R = longer-term l-period rate at t
r = shorter-term s-period rate at t
V = term Premium

(Note: R and r will be used to denote a long-term and short-term interest rate respectively throughout this chapter.)

If equation (9.1) holds, then understanding the link between market expectations and current interest rates is simple. If, on the other hand, the term premium varies significantly over time in an unpredictable way, it becomes difficult to discern whether the yield curve is changing because of changing expectations or because of changing term premia. This chapter reviews the evidence on the simple version of the expectations theory shown in equation (9.1) against the alternative that V varies significantly and unpredictably.

The chapter is divided into four further sections. Section 9.2 gives a brief survey of the literature on testing the expectations theory. Section 9.3 outlines the methodology. Section 9.4 presents a more detailed evaluation of the techniques used to test equation (9.1) and Section 9.5 a short conclusion.

9.2   TESTING THE EXPECTATIONS THEORY: A SURVEY

9.2.1   EARLY TESTS OF THE EXPECTATIONS THEORY

Almost invariably, modern tests of the expectations theory have been based on a rational expectations version of equation (9.1) which involves replacing $E_t(r_{t+i})$ with its subsequent outcome r_{t+i}. This is based on the concept of unbiased expectations implicit in the rational expectations approach which means that r_{t+i} can be used as an unbiased estimate of $E_t(r_{t+i})$ (i.e. that people do not make consistent forecasting errors). However, the way that expectations are formed is not specified in equation (9.1) and early tests of the expectations theory were often based on an explicit, adaptive (backward-looking) expectations formulation.

One of the most notable contributions to adaptive expectations versions of the expectations theory was that of Keynes (1936) who outlined the normal-rate hypothesis. He argued that there was a 'normal' interest rate to which all investors expected the short rate to converge. If interest rates were above the normal rate, then there was an expectation that they would fall. In contrast, Duesenberry (1958) suggested that Keynes' argument could be turned on its head and that a rise in interest rates may generate the expectation of a further rise. De Leeuw (1965) observed that a simple adaptive scheme whereby current interest rate expectations were estimated using a weighted average of past rates could encapsulate both these hypotheses. An example of this approach was that used by Rowan and O'Brien (1970). They started with the relationship between long and short rates implied by the expectations theory which suggests that expected holding period return on a long bond is equal to that on a short bond. Assuming that the holding period is s;

$$R_t + E_t G_t^{[l]} = r_t \tag{9.2}$$

where $G_t^{[l]}$ = capital gain on an l-period bond over holding period (other terms as in (9.1)).

To estimate the expectation of capital gains on a long bond they used the weighted sum of past long rates as suggested by De Leeuw (where γ and ξ are parameters to be estimated):

$$G_t^{[l]} = \gamma \left(R_t - \sum_{i=1}^{m} \xi_i R_{t-i} \right) \tag{9.3}$$

In common with other results presented below, the results of Rowan and O'Brien for the UK differ markedly from those from the USA. For the UK they found that the distributed lag model of expectations did not fit the data well. This contrasts with Modigliani and Sutch (1969), who found that the model fitted US data quite well.

9.2.2 RATIONAL EXPECTATIONS BASED TESTS OF THE TERM STRUCTURE

Following the adoption of the efficient market paradigm in finance in the 1960s, the expectations formation process used in empirical testing of the expectations theory has, almost exclusively, been based on rational expectations. In fact, a number of market efficiency tests (e.g. Roll, 1970) have tested the hypothesis that forward rates are unforecastable using past data (i.e. that forward rates follow a martingale process). This is in direct contradiction to the adaptive expectations approach described above. In fact, Roll found that the martingale property was rejected for 1–13-week US Treasury bill data from 1949 to 1964.

As noted above, testing the efficient markets version of the expectations theory involves deleting the expectations operator from equation (9.1) and testing whether long rates provide an unbiased estimate of future short rates. Given this approach, empirical models simply become tests of the formulation of the term premium (V). If, as is widely assumed, term premia are relatively stable through time and simply vary across bond maturities, then equation (9.1) gives a complete description of the theory. If, on the other hand, term premia vary through time in a systematic way (i.e. so that they are systematically correlated with the level of r and/or R) then equation (9.1) will not hold. This second case will require an

Table 9.1   Summary of recent studies

Study	Country	Sample	Maturities tested in months (short s~ long l)	Result	Comment
Method: Simple expectations theory (constant term premium)					
Bekaert, Hodrick and Marshall (1995)	USA UK Germany	1972-91	3 ~ 6 to 60	Reject Accept Reject	Test for regime switching as an explanation of US results. Details below
Campbell and Shiller (1991)	USA	1952-87	1 to 60~2 to 120	Reject	Used zero coupon rates derived from McCulloch (1975). Details in Section 9.3
Cuthbertson and Nitzsche (1994)	Germany	1976-93	6~12	Accept	Weekly and monthly interbank rates
Dahlquist and Jonsson (1995)	Sweden	1984-92	1 to 6~2 to 12	Accept	Swedish Treasury Bills − some evidence of parameter instability
Fama (1984)	USA	1959-82	1~2 to 6	Reject	
Fama and Bliss (1987)	USA	1964-84	12~24 to 60	Reject	
Margaritis (1994)	New Zealand	1985-92	3~6 and 60	Accept	Allowed for ARCH effects in estimation (but ARCH-M not necessary)
Mankiw and Miron (1986)	USA	1890-1979	3~6	Reject	Rejected for all sub-periods except 1890-1914
Mankiw (1986)	Canada Germany UK USA	1961-84 1961-84 1961-84	3~long 3~long 3~ ∞ 3~10	Accept Accept Accept Reject	Similar results for all countries. However only for the USA was the rejection statistically significant
Mankiw and Summers (1984)	USA	1963-83	3~240	Reject	Explored the hypothesis that long rates overreact to short rates
Mills (1991)	UK	1870-1920 1919-1939 1952-1988	3~ ∞ 3~ ∞ 3~60 and 240	Reject Reject Accept	Found that the expectations hypothesis was rejected up until the Second World War and accepted after
Shiller (1979)	USA UK	1966-77 1919-58 1956-77	3~>240 12~>240 3~ ∞	Reject Reject Reject	
Shiller (1986)	USA	1953-86	3~ rollover	Accept	
Shiller, Campbell and Schoenholtz (1983)	USA	1959-73	6~360	Reject	Described in detail in Section 9.3
Tease (1986)	Australia	1980-86	3~6	Accept	
Method: Simple expectations theory + measurement error (see Section 9.3)					
Hardouvelis (1994)	Canada France Germany Italy Japan UK USA	1951-92 1969-92 1968-92 1972-92 1963-92 1962-92 1954-92	3~120 3~120 3~120 3~120 3~120 3~120 3~120	Accept Accept Accept Accept Accept Accept Reject	Used the method of Shiller, Campbell and Schoenholtz (1983) but included IV estimation to allow for measurement error. Found the simple approach (no measurement error) was accepted for France and Italy
Method: Expectations theory with time-varying term premia					
Engle, Lilien and Robins (1987)	USA	1959-84	3~6	Accept	ARCH-M estimation of the Mankiw and Summers equation. See Section 9.3 for details
Felice and Esposito (1991)	Italy	1976-1990	3~6, 6~12	Reject	Used BOT auction yields (argued that rejection due to institutional factors). Found GARCH-M estimation had little effect
Taylor (1992)	UK	1985-89	3~120 to 240	Reject	A simple and GARCH-M-based term premium: both were rejected.

explicitly time-varying term premium V_t rather than the constant premium V in equation (9.1).

Table 9.1 summarizes a representative selection of studies that have tested the rational expectation version of the expectations theory. A detailed evaluation of some of the studies shown in the table is given in Section 9.3.

Concentrating for the moment on the penultimate column — whether the expectations theory is rejected or accepted — there are two striking results. First, that there is near-unanimous rejection of the simple expectations theory in US studies. Second, results for countries other than the USA differ markedly, with most studies failing to reject (illustrated most clearly by Hardouvelis, 1994). It is the first of these — indicating the continual rejection in the USA — of a theory that is still almost universally accepted as the only plausible explanation of the term structure that led Shiller, Campbell and Schoenholtz (1983) to compare the expectations theory with Tom, from the Tom and Jerry cartoons: 'Tom the cat may be buried under a ton of boulders, blasted through a brick wall (leaving a cat-shaped hole), or flattened by a steamroller. Yet seconds later he is up again plotting his evil deeds'. But there is another similarity between the cartoon and the empirical tests to which Shiller, Campbell and Schoenholtz did not draw attention — the view that empirical evidence universally rejects the expectations theory is, like Tom and Jerry cartoons, an American export!

9.2.3 PROPERTIES OF THE TERM PREMIUM

The rejection of the simple expectation theory in US studies has led to an increased interest in the properties of the term premium. Since some form of time varying term premia must explain the observed term structure, there has been a broad and somewhat unfocused search to find a suitable explanation for why term premia actually vary. Shiller (1990) describes this search as a 'fishing expedition' since the theory of the term structure is not sufficiently developed to give us a clear indication of what form, or even sign, of term premia is acceptable (see Kessel, 1965, and Nelson, 1972, for opposite interpretations). Campbell and Shiller (1991), among others, suggest that a form of term premium causing long rates to overreact to expectations of future short rates (or alternatively to underreact to current short rates) is most likely to explain US results.

Three main theories explaining time varying term premia have been developed:

(1) *Noise or measurement error*. Mankiw (1986) suggested that there may be noise in measured long-term rates (due to fads, or measurement error). Even if this noise were serially uncorrelated and exogenous, it may lead to rejections of the expectations theory (a full description of why this is the case is given in Section 9.3). The use of instrumental variables estimation overcomes this problem.

(2) *Flow of funds.* Other things being equal, one might expect that a change in the supply of long-term assets would change the term premium (particularly if debt markets are characterized by 'preferred habitats' of investors with specific investment horizons (Modigliani and Sutch, 1966)). Although the evidence is mixed, a number of studies (e.g. Friedman, 1981, for the USA and Taylor, 1990, for the UK) have found flow of funds effects on term premia in the government bond market. However, these studies have rarely made explicit use of expectations as a determinant of the term structure and are, therefore, incomplete. For example, a change in the structure of government funding could be seen as signalling a change in future monetary policy. If this were the case, then the flow of funds results could be related to expectations not term premia. Some evidence for this interpretation is given in Robinson and Matthews (1994) who find that debt supply variables have no significant relationship with expectational errors (where expectational errors are defined as the difference between future short rates and those predicted by the yield curve).

(3) *Indicators of time-varying risk.* Measuring the riskiness of bonds in an individual portfolio presents a number of almost insuperable problems. Several studies have therefore used the volatility of holding period returns as a proxy for risk. This volatility has been measured either as a simple moving average of standard deviation (e.g. Modigliani and Shiller, 1973) or an explicit ARCH-M process (e.g. Engle, Lilien and Robins, 1987, described in more detail in Section 9.3). However, Mankiw (1986) found that, if anything, there was a negative correlation between consumption and excess returns which could mean that the term premium should be negative rather than positive as most studies have suggested (since the consumption CAPM suggests that individuals will pay a premium for an asset which has a negative covariance with their pattern of consumption). Other proxies for risk — such as business confidence measures (Nelson, 1972), or credit spreads (yield difference between low and high grade bonds, Keim and Stambaugh (1986)) — have also been used with varying degrees of success. Given the weak economic basis for these proxies, results derived from using them must be open to question.

In summary, the search for an explicit model of time-varying term premia has been hampered by the lack of a plausible economic model to support the measures used. The measurement error approach does appear plausible but has only a limited impact in estimation which seems insufficient to explain the consistent US rejection of the expectations theory.

9.2.4   EXPECTATIONAL ERRORS

Most studies have taken as axiomatic that the failure of the simple expectations theory is due to time-varying term premia. Froot (1989), however, tests the hypothesis that this failure is at least in part due to consistent expectational errors over the sample period used (i.e. that the rational expectations assumption that r_{t+i} is an unbiased estimate of $E_t(r_{t+i})$ is incorrect). To decompose the prediction error into term premia and expectational errors, Froot uses survey evidence on interest rate expectations and assumes that these are unbiased estimates of true expectations (rather than interest rate outturns). He found that over short horizons the failure of the expectations theory was due to time-varying premia but that over longer horizons the expectations theory appeared to hold, with prediction errors being due to systematic expectational errors rather than to time-varying premia (even though the *average* level of term premia was higher for long-maturity bonds). It would seem reasonable to argue that Froot's study indicates that the standard sample period used in tests of the expectations theory may be too short to purge the data of systematic errors. For example, the post-war surge in interest rates to levels never before seen inflicted large losses on long-term bond holders and may have dramatically altered investor perceptions of the interest rate process (see Figure 9.1). Fear of another surge in rates may have led to expectational errors over a long period and such errors may form a large part of any sample used to test the expectations theory. This possibility has been investigated by Bekaert, Hodrick and Marshall (1995) who examined the possibility that US rejection of the expectations theory could be due to market participants anticipating a high-inflation regime that occurs only infrequently. However, their results from using a regime — switching model suggest that this effect fails to explain the deviations from the expectations theory observed in the USA.

9.3   TESTING THE EXPECTATIONS THEORY: METHODOLOGY

Table 9.1 gives an overview of a number of studies, but those who wish to make a more rigorous assessment of the evidence or even test their own data will need to understand the potential pitfalls in conducting tests of the expectations theory and the importance of term premia. This section outlines some of the estimation problems that have led researchers to adopt different methods of testing the expectations theory. In particular, it focuses on possible solutions to five major estimation problems:

(1) How to use coupon bond data when the theory is expressed in terms of zero coupon bonds

(2) How to deal with interest rate data that do not have a fixed mean (i.e. is non-stationary)

(3) How to adjust for overlapping errors in the data caused by long-horizon expectations that are not verified until many periods into the future

(4) How to deal with possible measurement errors in the data

(5) How to relate the time-varying volatility of interest rates to the term premium.

9.3.1 DATA

Tests of the expectations theory have almost exclusively concentrated on government debt markets for three main reasons: low credit risk, high liquidity and high quality data (both in terms of sample length and number of bonds). Although futures contracts potentially offer a high-quality data source of actual forward rates with minimal credit risk (since futures are typically backed by a clearing house), such data have rarely been used in empirical studies.

Of the two main types of instrument issued to finance government debt, Treasury bills offer a far simpler opportunity to test the expectations theory than coupon bonds. As pure discount instruments, bill yields can be directly substituted into equation (9.1). Coupon paying bonds, on the other hand, must be transformed in some way before they become comparable. However, bills are usually of limited maturity and are often relatively illiquid. As Table 9.2 shows, although the USA and Italy have large and diverse bill markets, other countries tend to have relatively small bill markets that can be subject to a number of institutional

Table 9.2   Government debt instruments (1991)

Country	Instrument (z = zero coupon)	Issue maturity (in years)	% of total debt
France	BTF (z)	0.25,0.5,1	10
	BTAN	2,5	28
	OAT	7 to 30	53
Germany	U-Schätze (z)	Up to 2	4
(Federal Govt only	Schatzanweisungen (z)	Around 4	9
	Bundesobligationen	5	26
	Bundesanleihen	8 to 30	54
Italy	BOT (z)	0.25,0.5,1	32
	CCT (floating rate)	2 to 10	41
	BTP	5 to 30	16
	CTO (callable)	6 to 8	6
Japan	Treasury Bill (z)	0.25,0.5	13
	Bond	10	85
	super-longs	20	1
UK	Treasury Bill (z)	0.25,0.5	3
	gilt-edged		
	–conventional	3 to 30	70
	–index-linked	3 to 40	11
	–callable and convertible	3 to 30	14
	–irredeemable		3
USA	Treasury bill (z)	0.25,0.5,1	23
	Note	2,3,5,10	60
	Bond	30	17

influences. For example, Schnadt (1994) demonstrates that UK Treasury bills have, from time to time, been subject to a premium related to the fact that they are eligible for the Bank of England's money market operations. This makes them attractive to institutions — particularly commercial banks — which can use them to gain access to liquidity directly from the Bank of England. Since eligible securities have sometimes been in short supply, Treasury bill prices have varied in response to demand for eligible securities. Although recent money market reforms have largely removed this premium, historical data on UK Treasury bill yields cannot be taken as a reliable measure of market yields.

9.3.2 USING COUPON BONDS

In all countries, longer-maturity debt is mostly in the form of coupon bonds. As was shown in Chapter 2, these present a number of problems because a coupon bond is actually a series of cashflows not just one. As the size of the coupon varies between issues, these cash flows cannot be directly compared and must therefore be converted to a common basis (although, in the USA and France, the strips market does allow some direct comparisons of individual cashflows). One method — described in Chapter 2 — is to generate a zero coupon yield curve from a fitted discount function. However, as has been demonstrated elsewhere in this book, fitting discount functions is not straightforward and may appear to be a somewhat onerous prelude to a simple test of market expectations. Shiller, Campbell and Schoenholtz (1983) offer a relatively simple approximation which allows a direct comparison between coupon bonds. Their approach defines the yield on a long bond as a weighted sum of expected future short rates:

$$R_t = \sum_{k=0}^{i-1} W(k) E_t r_{t+k} \tag{9.4}$$

Clearly, for coupon bonds, the weights (the W's) for expected short rates in the more distant future should decline (because the discount rate for near term coupons will not be influenced by more distant expectations). The precise formulation that Shiller, Campbell and Schoenholtz produce is a weighting scheme based on a linear approximation to the non-linear relationship between long and short rates:

$$W(k) = g^k (1 - g)/(1 - g^i) \tag{9.5}$$

where

$g = 1/(1 + \bar{R})$

$\bar{R} =$ 'average' discount rate (expressed as a rate per period, e.g. for monthly data and 6% interest rates $\bar{R} = 0.005$)

This weighting scheme is based on a linearization of the true relationship between long and short rates and utilizes the assumptions that the discount rate

$\bar{R}$ is approximately constant over the life of the bond and that it is equal to the coupon on the long bond (i.e. the bond is trading at par). In practice $\bar{R}$ is usually set to the average of r over the sample. The weighting scheme means that the W's sum to 1 and that the weights decline monotonically to allow for the fact that near-term cashflows have a higher present value than longer-term ones. This weighting scheme is best understood through the closely related concept of duration (discussed in Chapter 1) where the duration of an l-period bond $D^{[l]}$ is approximately $(1 - g^l)/(1 - g)^2$. This means that equation (9.4) can be written as

$$R_t = (1/D^{[l]}) \sum_{i=0}^{l-1} (D^{[i+1]} - D^{[i]}) E_t(r_{t+i}) \tag{9.6}$$

Equation (9.7) converts the problem to first differences — i.e. changes in interest rates related to the slope of the yield curve (for reasons outlined below). If the expectations theory with a constant term premium is correct, then the following equation should hold ($R^{[l-s]}$ represents an $l - s$ maturity bond)

$$R_{t+1}^{[l-s]} - R_t = (1/(D^{[l]} - 1))((R_t - r_t) - V^{[l]}) \tag{9.7}$$

This can be tested empirically through the null hypothesis that $\beta = 1$ in the following regression equation (α allows for a constant term premium):

$$R_{t+1}^{[l-s]} - R_t = \alpha + \beta(1/(D^{[l]} - 1))(R_t - r_t) \tag{9.8}$$

This equation is directly related to the simple expectations theory of equation (9.1) since it predicts that the slope of the yield curve should predict future changes in the long rate to ensure that the holding period return on long and short bonds is equalized, after adjusting for term premia.

As noted above, this approach uses an approximation to the true term structure relation. Table 9.3, taken from Shiller, Campbell and Schoenholtz, shows that for

Table 9.3   Comparison of linearized and exact holding period yields (linearized in parentheses)

Sample	Holding period (i, j – months)	No. of observations	$\bar{R}$	Mean	σ	Correlation between exact and linearized
1977–83	24, 12	226	12.81	9.53 (9.45)	5.11 (5.12)	1.00
1977–83	360, 12	226	12.81	3.43 (3.50)	14.29 (13.41)	0.994
1953–72	240, 120	240	6.00	2.74 (2.71)	0.88 (0.87)	0.977

Holding period yield is defined as the yield from buying an i-period bond and holding it for j periods, with $\bar{R}$ as the mean level of interest rates over the period.
Source: Shiller, Campbell and Schoenholtz (1983).

short maturities the approximation error is very slight, but at longer maturities there are some significant differences.

9.3.3 STATIONARITY

Even when using estimated zero-coupon curves or bill yields, studies of the expectations theory have tended, like equations (9.9) and (9.10), to relate the slope of the yield curve to changes in yields rather than the levels relation shown in equation (9.1). For example, Campbell and Shiller (1991) estimate the following two equations — both based on changes in, rather than levels of, yields — for zero-coupon rates derived from coupon-paying bonds using McCulloch's estimation methodology:

Test 1:

$$R_{t+s}^{[l-s]} - R_t = \alpha + \beta((s/(l-s))(R_t - r_t)) \qquad (9.9)$$

Test 2:

$$\sum_{i=1}^{k-1}(1 - i/k)\Delta^s r_{t+is} = \alpha + \beta(R_t - r_t) \qquad (9.10)$$

where Δ^s = change over s.

In both cases, the expectations theory would predict that β is equal to one. One reason for the use of yield curve slopes (or spreads) rather than levels is that statistical tests commonly find interest rates and yields to be borderline non-stationary[3] and that statistical tests based on non-stationary data can be problematic. For example, Table 9.4 shows unit root tests (tests of stationarity) for 10-year yields for the G7 countries and reveals that in all cases except Germany,

Table 9.4 Unit root tests of 3-month and 10-year rates 1965–95

Country	Stationarity of 3-month rate[a]	Stationarity of 10-year rate[a]	Test of cointegration of 10-year and 3-month rates[b]	Test of unit coefficient restriction[c]
France	−2.4 (−5.3*)	−2.0 (−5.5*)	9.4	1.87
Germany	−4.0*(−4.8*)	−3.4*(−4.0*)	8.2	2.2
Japan	−2.7 (−4.8*)	−2.0 (−4.0*)	17.7†	n/a
UK	−2.6 (−5.0*)	−2.0 (−5.2*)	9.6	0.0
UK (1800–1995)	−3.7*			
USA	−2.1 (−4.0*)	−2.3 (−4.3*)	14.0	1.1

Notes
(a) ADF(12) test with test for first differences in parentheses. *Rejection of hypothesis of unit root at 95% (critical value −2.9).
(b) LR test based on maximal Eigenvalue of the Stochastic Matrix of Johansen (1988) procedure (trended case, trend in DGP, VAR length 2). †Rejection of cointegration at the 95% level (critical value 14.1).
(c) Chi-Squared test of unit restriction on cointegrating regression in Johansen procedure (critical value 3.84).

the hypothesis that the level of interest rates is non-stationary cannot be rejected. Equally, the hypothesis of non-stationarity in *changes* in interest rates can be rejected in every case. Since the statistical properties of non-stationary series are non-standard it is usually easier to convert a non-stationary series to a stationary one by differencing it.

Although the hypothesis of non-stationarity in interest rates would seem to be questionable in terms of economic theory (it can imply, *inter alia*, that interest rates can go to infinity), most tests indicate that interest rates are on the borderline between stationarity and non-stationarity. Unfortunately, these unit root tests have low power and so it is easy to draw the wrong inference, particularly when the tests are borderline. Researchers are therefore left with a difficult choice between modelling levels and differences. If interest rates are stationary then modelling first differences reduces the power of any hypothesis tests. However, if interest rates are non-stationary then modelling the levels means that normal statistical inference cannot be undertaken. In practice, most researchers have assumed that interest rates are non-stationary and have therefore concentrated on changes in interest rates.

Interestingly, Table 9.4 shows that when using a longer data period (1800 to 1995), the hypothesis of stationarity of UK short-term interest rates is accepted. This result is consistent with a visual inspection of the data (Figure 9.1) which covers an even longer sample (1694–1995). Figure 9.1 shows that interest rates tended to be very stable and apparently mean reverting over most of the period but since the Second World War have been more erratic and possibly trending upward. The long sample evidence supports the idea that interest rates are indeed stationary but may appear to be non-stationary over the relatively short post-war sample used in most studies.

If interest rates are non-stationary over conventional sample periods, this offers a further, relatively weak, test of the expectations theory. This occurs because, for the expectations theory to hold, long rates and short rates should cointegrate with a unit coefficient. Cointegration means that although two series are individually non-stationary (or, more precisely, integrated of order 1), there is some linear combination of them that is stationary. In the case of long and short rates, equation 9.1 shows that the long rate is in fact a linear function of expected short rates so that they should cointegrate unless expectational errors or the term premium are non-stationary. This means that if the expectations theory holds, then a regression of long rates on short rates should cointegrate (i.e. generate stationary residuals) with a coefficient of unity. The final column of Table 9.4 show the results of this test. The test is weak since it only requires that expectational errors and the term premium are stationary (i.e. it is consistent with stationary, time-varying term premia). Despite this, it appears that Japanese long and short rates do not cointegrate and that US rates are borderline. In a more detailed study, Evans and Lewis (1994) find that US Treasury bill yields of

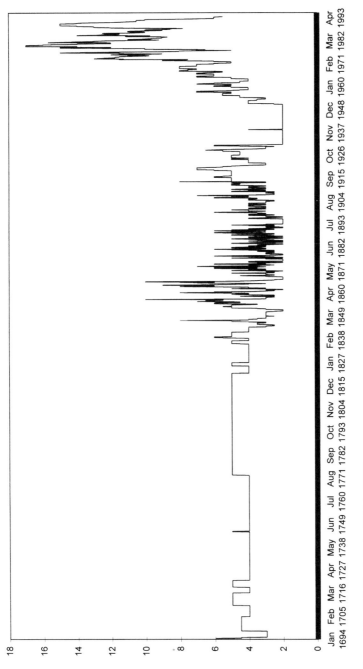

Figure 9.1   UK Bank Rate 1694 to 1995

various maturities do not cointegrate, which implies that not even a time-varying but stationary term premium could be used to explain US results.

9.3.4   OVERLAPPING ERRORS

A further estimation problem arises from the fact that expectational errors are likely to be serially correlated. Although in many cases the estimation of expectations equations (such as (9.8)) can be conducted using OLS, certain formulations of the test may induce serial correlation (correlation through time in the residuals of the regression). If the difference in maturity between R and r is longer than the frequency of the data, the residuals of estimated equations such as (9.9) and (9.10) may be subject to a moving-average error process. For example, if R has a twelve-month maturity and r has a three-month maturity, R will implicitly contain forecasts of future r's three, six, and nine months ahead. If we are using quarterly data, it is very likely that in three months' time when we next observe R that any error made in forecasting r more than three months ahead will remain; and that it will persist until we actually observe the full set of r's implicit in R. Effectively, if the difference in maturity of the two yields being tested is longer than the data frequency, then each observation of the long rate is not independent (since forecast errors are correlated) and the amount of information in each observation is relatively small.

One solution to this problem is simply to lengthen the data frequency to the length of the maturity difference but this throws away some useful information. However, using all the available data means that simple OLS estimators cannot be used as they generate standard errors that are biased downward (since they do not allow for the fact that the incremental information in each observation is smaller if there are overlapping errors). Fortunately, there are a number of robust estimators — called generalized methods of moments estimators (GMM) — which, in large samples, give the correct standard errors in the presence of overlapping errors. Examples of these estimators are given in White (1980), Newey and West (1987) and Hansen and Hodrick (1980). GMM estimators also offer the advantage of being robust to heteroscedasticity (discussed below). However, it should be noted that the small sample properties of these GMM estimators have been subject to question (see, for example, Gotizman and Jorion, 1994), particularly when the length of the moving-average error process is long.

9.3.5   MEASUREMENT ERRORS

As Mankiw (1986) points out, if there is some measurement error in R (the l-period long rate) then estimates of β, as in equations such as (9.8), will be biased downward. Whatever the source of the error, if there is a white noise error component (ε_t) in the measured long rate (such that the measured long rate

$R_t = R_t^* + \varepsilon_t$ where R_t^* is the true, unobserved, long rate) then

$$R_{t+1} - R_t = R_{t+1}^* - R_t^* + (\varepsilon_{t+1} - \varepsilon_t) \qquad (9.11)$$

and

$$R_t - r_t = R_t^* - r_t + \varepsilon_t \qquad (9.12)$$

This introduces a bias into the estimated β which is related to the variance of ε and the covariance of R_t and r_t. In the Shiller, Campbell and Schoenholtz set-up the bias is equal to

$$(D^{[l]} - 1)\, \text{cov}((\varepsilon_{t+1} - \varepsilon_t)\varepsilon_t)/\, \text{var}(R_t - r_t) = -(D^{[l]} - 1)(\sigma_\varepsilon^2/\sigma_{R-r}^2) \qquad (9.13)$$

By calculating the extent of measurement error required to explain his results, Mankiw argued that the required error was too big to be plausible (up to 60 bp). However, he viewed this error purely as an econometric measurement error while Hardouvelis (1994) suggests that other forms of error such as market mistakes or fads may be reasonably classed under this form of measurement error and therefore an error of 60 bp might indeed be acceptable. In any event, this problem is easily overcome by using instrumental variables estimation where lags of the spread can be used as instruments. However, if the instruments are poor, then the expectations theory may be accepted purely because of larger standard errors.

9.3.6   HETEROSCEDASTICITY

In addition to potential problems with overlapping errors, many studies have drawn attention to the presence of time-varying volatility (heteroscedasticity) in bond yield data. This can be seen in Figure 9.2 which shows daily holding period returns for an index of UK gilts calculated by *JP Morgan*. The figure shows how holding-period returns appear to be more volatile in some periods (like 1994) than in others.

Although, as noted above, a number of estimators are robust to heteroscedasticity (in large samples), some studies have used the heteroscedasticity of bond yields as a potential determinant of time-varying term premia. In many cases, this has involved the explicit estimation of an ARCH (autoregressive conditional heteroscedastic) process as part of the testing process. These models allow for time-varying volatility by allowing the variance to follow an autoregressive process (i.e. assuming that current variance is a function of past variance). Engle, Lilien and Robins (1987) estimated an ARCH-M model to assess the impact of time-varying volatility on the term premium. They assumed that all conditional volatility (the expected volatility conditional on current information) of long bonds is undiversifiable (cannot be removed by holding a diversified portfolio of assets other than bonds) and so feeds directly through to the term premium. They then proposed that the term premium on a long bond can be modelled in terms

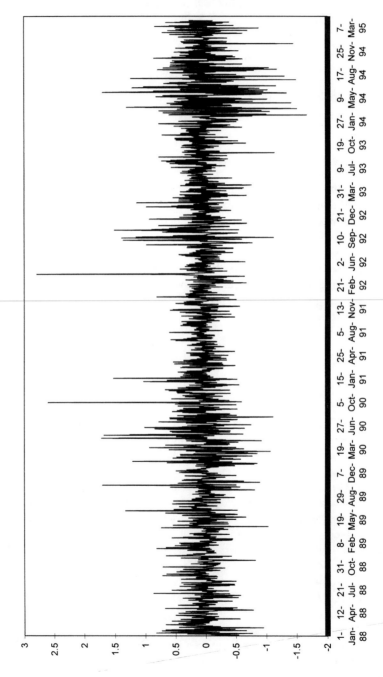

Figure 9.2 Daily holding period returns on UK gilts

of an ARCH process. They examined the case of the excess holding yield on a six-month bill (R) relative to a three-month bill (r) where the excess holding yield (Y_t) is

$$Y_t = ((1 + R_t)^2/(1 + r_t)) - (1 + r_t) \qquad (9.14)$$

This excess yield — which is an estimate of the term premium — is then related to its' own conditional volatility through an ARCH process, where Ω_t is past information available at t (note that the choice of maximum value of i is arbitrary):

$$Y_t = \beta + \delta h_t + \varepsilon_t \qquad \varepsilon_t/\Omega_t \sim N(0, h_t^2)$$

$$h_t^2 = \gamma + \alpha \sum_{i=1}^{4} w_i \varepsilon_{t-i}^2 \qquad w_i = (5 - i)/10 \qquad (9.15)$$

Using this model of the term premium, they assessed the results of Mankiw and Summers (1984), who had found that the yield spread was a significant determinant of the excess holding period yield, indicating a time-varying term premium (see above). Engle, Lilien and Robins found that when they included the conditional variance into the Mankiw and Summers regression, the coefficient on the yield spread fell dramatically and although it was still significant at the 5% level by both the Wald and Likelihood Ratio tests, it was not significant at the 1% level (or the 5% level using the LM test). As a result, they argue that this conditional variance model can explain the rejection of the expectations theory in the US. This model has however been less successful for other countries; for example, Taylor (1992) estimated a GARCH[4] version of the above model for the UK but found no role for time-varying volatility.

9.4   TESTING THE EXPECTATIONS THEORY FOR THE UK

This section applies some of the techniques described above to a dataset of zero coupon yields for the UK. The data were derived by fitting a Svensson forward curve (as described in Chapter 2, with the Mastronikola, 1991, tax adjustment as described in Chapter 5) to end-month UK government bond prices between 1982 and 1995.

Table 9.5 shows the results of testing if $\beta = 1$ in Campbell and Shiller's spread test (test 2, equation (9.11) above) over a range of maturities. It also shows the difference between simple OLS standard errors and robust standard errors calculated using the Newey and West (1987) procedure.

As Table 9.5 shows, there are very few rejections of the hypothesis that $\beta = 1$ so that the simple version of the expectations theory with a constant term premium is largely accepted by these data. Of the rejections shown, those for long maturity spreads (i.e. $R = 8$ and $r = 0.5$, $R = 8$ and $r = 1$) show the problems associated with very long moving-average error processes (caused by overlapping errors).

Table 9.5 Regression of the yield spread $(R_t - R_t)$ on future change in short rates $\sum_{i=1}^{k-1}(1 - i/k)\Delta^s r_{t+is}$

Maturity of R	Maturity of r (the short rate) in years				
	0.5	1	2	3	4
1	0.61*				
	(0.11,0.13)				
2	0.73	0.63			
	(0.12,0.18)	(0.16,0.31)			
3	0.93	0.79			
	(0.14,0.13)	(0.17,0.18)			
4	1.07	0.99	1.02		
	(0.13,0.27)	(0.16,0.25)	(0.21,0.27)		
6	0.81	0.98	1.07	0.96	
	(0.10,0.28)	(0.12,0.41)	(0.16,0.51)	(0.22,0.53)	
8	0.76*	0.41*	0.88		0.89
	(0.09,0.09)	(0.13,0.16)	(0.13,0.33)		(0.20,0.75)

Standard errors in parentheses, first OLS, second Newey and West. *The hypothesis of a unit coefficient on the regression can be rejected at the 95% level (i.e. the expectations theory as formulated in equation (9.1) can be rejected).

Despite a very significant problem of serial correlation, the robust standard errors are very similar to the simple OLS errors. This confirms that robust estimators do not adjust for serial correlation correctly if the moving average error process is long in relation to the available sample.

Table 9.6 shows the results of the same test undertaken using instrumental variables to allow for possible measurement errors (as described above). Robust standard errors are shown in parentheses.

A comparison of Tables 9.5 and 9.6 indicates that IV estimation does not change the results significantly, suggesting that the problem of measurement

Table 9.6 IV estimation of yield spread regression (three lags of yield spread used as instruments)

R (the long rate)	Maturity of r (the short rate) in years				
	0.5	1	2	3	4
1	0.60				
	(0.22)				
2	0.84	0.56			
	(0.22)	(0.34)			
3	0.98	0.84			
	(0.15)	(0.18)			
4	1.04	0.96	1.07		
	(0.20)	(0.21)	(0.34)		
6	0.89	1.01	1.06	1.07	
	(0.28)	(0.20)	(0.44)	(0.51)	
8	0.68*	0.46*	1.05		1.45
	(0.06)	(0.07)	(0.17)		(0.73)

Table 9.7   Yield spread estimates for data frequency equal to $R - r$

$R = 1, r = 0.5$ (23 observations)	$R = 2, r = 1$ (10 observations)
0.60 (0.34)	0.55 (0.71)

Standard errors in parentheses.

error is small in this dataset. The main difference between the two methods is the increase in standard errors caused by IV estimation which means that the unit coefficient hypothesis cannot be rejected for the $R = 1, r = 0.5$ spread.

Table 9.7 shows the results of yield spread tests using sample frequencies equal to the $R - r$ maturity of the spread being tested (i.e. semi-annual data for the 1-year/half-year spread and annual data for the 2-year/1-year spread). This removes the problem of overlapping errors but substantially decreases the efficiency of estimation. This is shown in the large standard errors which mean that the hypothesis of a unit coefficient cannot be rejected for the 1-year/half-year spread as it was using a monthly data frequency.

Finally, to illustrate the difference between UK and US results, Table 9.8 compares the results presented above with those derived by Campbell and Shiller (1991) using the same methodology. Inevitably, there are a number of differences between the two studies, the most important being the difference in sample period (1952 to 1987 in the Campbell and Shiller study rather than 1982 to 1995). Zero-coupon rates are derived using the McCulloch rather than the Svensson yield curve (both yield curve estimation techniques are described in Chapter 2). However, the difference in estimated parameters is quite dramatic and since Campbell and Shiller find qualitatively similar results in subsamples, this suggests that the difference is genuine and not just attributable to the different methods used in the two studies.

Table 9.8   Comparison of UK and US results for yield spread regression

R	0.5		1		2	
	USA	UK	USA	UK	USA	UK
1	0.04*	0.61*				
	(0.33)	(0.13)				
2	0.18*	0.73	−0.02*	0.63		
	(0.32)	(0.18)	(0.37)	(0.31)		
3	0.53*	0.93	0.26	0.79		
	(0.23)	(0.13)	(0.41)	(0.18)		
4	0.94	1.07	0.72	0.99	1.35	1.02
	(0.088)	(0.27)	(0.33)	(0.25)	(0.17)	(0.27)

Robust standard errors in parentheses. * Rejection of unit coefficient.

9.5   CONCLUSION

This chapter has reviewed the empirical evidence on the expectations theory of the yield curve. In practice, this means testing whether term premia are constant or time varying. A constant term premium would be consistent with the simple yield curve models described in Chapter 8 and would make it relatively easy to derive underlying market expectations from observed bond prices (since changes in yields would only be caused by changes in market expectations). A significant time-varying term premium, on the other hand, would be problematic and make yield curve interpretation extremely difficult unless movements in the term premium could be disentangled from changes in expectations.

The evidence in this chapter produces the surprising conclusion that for most countries the expectations theory with a constant term premium cannot be rejected (although this need not mean that the term premium must be exactly constant, merely that its movements are small enough to be ignored). The only exception to this is the largest and most sophisticated bond market in the world, the USA.

In the USA, it appears that the yield curve overreacts to expected future short rates: that when the yield curve is upward sloping, it is too upward sloping and future short rates do not come out as high as the yield curve predicts (and, conversely, when the curve is downward sloping, it is too downward sloping). This appears to give market participants an easy trading rule to follow in order to make excess profits, although it is possible that these excess profits are simply fair compensation for risk. Such easy trading rules, however, do not appear to exist in other markets.

NOTES

1.   Note that equation (9.1) is only a (very close) approximation to the expectations theory which is actually in terms of forward rates.
2.   The duration of an i-period bond is defined as

$$D_i = (gc_i + 2g^2c_i + \cdots + ig^ic_i + ig^i)/(gc_i + g^2c_i + \cdots + g^ic_i + g^i).$$

If c (the coupon) is equal to $\bar{R}$ then duration collapses to the formula above.
3.   A non-stationary series is one that does not have a tendency to revert back to a mean.
4.   GARCH includes a lagged h_t term in the conditional variance equation.

REFERENCES

Bekaert, G., Hodrick, R. and Marshall D. (1995) 'Peso Problem' explanations for term structure anomalies, mimeo, Stanford University.

Campbell, J. and Shiller, R. (1991) Yield spreads and interest rate movements: A bird's eye view, *Review of Economic Studies*, **58**, 495–514.

Cuthbertson, K. and Nitzsche, D. (1994) Are German money market rates well behaved? mimeo, City University Business School.

Dahlquist, M. and Jonsson, G. (1995) The information in Swedish short-maturity forward rates, *European Economic Review*, **39**, 1115–31.

De Leeuw, F. (1965) A model of financial behaviour, in *The Brooking Quarterly Econometric Model of the United States*, edited by Duesenberry, J., Fromm, G., Klein, L. and Kuh, E., Rand McNally, Chicago.

Duesenberry, J. (1958) *Business Cycles and Economic Growth*, McGraw-Hill, New York.

Engle, R., Lilien, D. and Robins, R. (1987) Estimating time-varying premia in the term structure: the ARCH-M model, *Econometrica*, **55**, 251–77.

Evans, M. and Lewis, K. (1994) Do stationary risk premia explain it all? *Journal of Monetary Economics*, **33**, 285–318.

Fama, E. (1984) The information in the term structure, *Journal of Financial Economics*, **13**, 509–28.

Fama, E. and Bliss, R. (1987) The information in long-maturity forward rates, *American Economic Review* **77**, 680–92.

Felice, G. and Esposito, M. (1991) The expectations theory of interest rates: an application to the Italian T-bills market, Banca Commerciale Italiana Discussion Paper R91–2.

Friedman, B. (1981) Debt management policy, interest rates and economic activity, NBER Working Paper.

Froot, K. (1989) New hope for the expectations hypothesis of the term structure, *Journal of Finance*, **45**, 283–305.

Gotizman, W. and Jorion, P. (1994) Testing the predictive power of dividend yields, *Journal of Finance*, **50**, 663–79.

Hansen, L. and Hodrick, R. (1980) Forward exchange rates as optimal predictors of future spot rates, *Journal of Political Economy*, **88**, 829–53.

Hardouvelis, G. (1994) The term structure spread and future changes in long and short rates in the G7 countries, *Journal of Monetary Economics*, **33**, 255–83.

Johansen, S. (1988) Statistical analysis of cointegrating vectors, *Journal of Economic Dynamics and Control*, **12**, 231–54.

Keim, D and Stambaugh, R (1986) Predicting returns in the stock and bond markets, *Journal of Financial Economics*, **17**, 357–90.

Kessel, R. (1965) *The Cyclical Behaviour of the Term Structure of Interest Rates*, NBER, New York.

Keynes, J. (1936) *The General Theory of Employment, Interest and Money*, Macmillan, London.

Mankiw, N. (1986) The term structure of interest rates revisited, *Brookings Papers on Economic Activity*, **1**, 61–96.

Mankiw, N. and Miron, J. (1986) The changing behaviour of the term structure of interest rates, *Quarterly Journal of Economics*, **101**, 211–42.

Mankiw, N. and Summers, L. (1984) Do long-term interest rates overreact to short-term rates? *Brookings Papers on Economic Activity*, **1**, 223–42.

Margaritis, J. (1994) Time-varying risk premia in the term structure of interest rates in New Zealand, *Applied Financial Economics*, **4**(2), 111–20.

Mills, T. (1991) The term structure of UK interest rates: tests of the expectations hypothesis, *Applied Economics*, **23**, 599–606.

Modigliani, F. and Shiller, R. (1973) Inflation, rational expectations and the term structure of interest rates, *Economica*, **40**, 12–43.

Modigliani, F. and Sutch, R. (1969) The term structure of interest rates: a re-examination of the evidence, *Journal of Money Credit and Banking*, 112–20.

Nelson, C. (1972) Estimation of term premiums from average yield differentials in the term structure of interest rates, *Econometrica*, **40**, 277–87.

Newey, W. and West, K. (1987) A simple, positive definite heteroscedasticity and autocorrelation consistent covariance matrix, *Econometrica*, **55**, 703–8.

Robinson, P. and Matthews, R. (1994) Government funding and expectational errors, mimeo, Bank of England.

Roll, R. (1970) *The Behaviour of Interest Rates: An application of the efficient market model to the U.S.*, Basic Books, New York.

Rowan, D. and O'Brien, R. (1970) Expectations, the interest rate structure and debt policy, in *The Econometric Study of the United Kingdom*, edited by Hilton, K. and Heathfield, D., Kelley, London.

Schnadt, N. (1994) The excess liquidity premium on sterling eligible bills, mimeo, LSE Financial Markets Group.

Shiller, R. (1979) The volatility of long-term interest rates and expectations models of the term structure, *Journal of Political Economy*, **87**, 1190–1219.

Shiller, R. (1986) Comments and discussion, *Brookings Papers on Economic Activity*, **1**, 100–107.

Shiller, R. (1990) The term structure of interest rates, in *Handbook of Monetary Economics*, edited by Friedman, B. and Hahn, F., North Holland.

Shiller, R., Campbell, J. and Schoenholtz, K. (1983) Forward rates and future policy: interpreting the term structure of interest rates, *Brookings Papers on Economic Activity*, **1**, 173–217.

Taylor, M. (1992) Modelling the yield curve, *Economic Journal*, **102**, 524–37.

Tease, W. (1986) The expectations theory of the term structure and short-term interest rates in Australia, Reserve Bank of Australia Discussion Paper 8607.

White, H. (1980) A heteroscedasticity-consistent covariance matrix estimator and a direct test for heteroscedasticity, *Econometrica*, **48**, 817–38.

INDEX

Index compiled by Geoffrey Jones